EXISTENTIAL METAPSYCHIATRY

EXISTENTIAL METAPSYCHIATRY

Thomas Hora

A Crossroad Book
The Seabury Press • New York

1977

The Seabury Press
815 Second Avenue
New York, N.Y. 10017

Printed in the United States of America

Library of Congress Cataloging In Publication Data

Hora, Thomas.
    Existential Metapsychiatry.

    "A Crossroad book."
    Bibliography: p.
    1. Psychotherapy. 2. Existential psychology.
I. Title.
RC480.5.H65   616.8'91   76–54217
ISBN 0–8164–0337–6

To Madeleine, my beloved
companion on the path.

Again he said unto me,
Prophesy upon these bones,
and say unto them, O ye dry bones,
hear the word of the Lord.

—Ezekiel 37:4

CONTENTS

notism—Positive thinking and right thinking—Anxiety and malice—The
dangers of "little knowledge"—"The good which I would I do not: but the
evil which I would not, that I do."

A new method of case presentation based on two intelligent questions—A
departure from traditional ways of thinking—Mental health and existential
context—Boundaries of contexts—Infinite context—Freedom and context
—Freedom fighters and freedom realizers—A question of age—What is the
"abundant life"?—Enlightenment versus religious conversion—What is
what *is?*

What is depression? What is the difference between official diagnostic categories and existential determination of modes of being-in-the-world? Heidegger's view of mourning—The two essential elements underlying all
depressions—Drug addiction—Mental attachments—Dynamic interplay
between depressed patient and therapist—"Only attachment can bring freedom from attachment"—Quality of therapeutic presence.

The existentially valid concept of marriage—Joint participation versus marital relationship—The role of psychological thinking in marriage—The
good of God—Escape from tribulation—The wrong kind of happiness in
marriage—The dangers of being admired—The universal meaning underlying all problems—The only "I am"—The broadest possible context in
which to view existence.

What is the divine mind?—What is cosmic intelligence?—Man as conception—Creative intelligence—Creativity in artists—Dynamism of creative
ideas—Inspired thought versus calculative thinking—The serpent as symbol of calculative thinking—The serpent throughout the Bible—Dominion
over the serpent in the Old Testament and the New Testament—The one
evil, the universal enemy—Self-confirmatory calculative ideation.

What is rebellion?—Feeling or thinking?—The "good life"—The tragedy
of miseducatedness—Misdirected modes of being-in-the-world—The existentially valid mode of being-in-the-world—The pearl of great price—Developing the motivation for change—Suffering and wisdom—The process
of reeducation.

American male prototype—The horizontal perspective—Consequential
and inconsequential people—The meaning of sexual problems—The mean-

ing of certain visual problems—The therapeutic task—The therapist's qual-
ifications—The spiritual dimension—Miseducation and reeducation.

Session No. 1

BASIC CONCEPTS

This seminar is dedicated to the sincere seekers after the truth who are willing to forego intellectual conformity in exchange for freedom and authenticity.

In Ecclesiastes it is written: "That which hath been is now; and that which is to be hath already been" (Ecclesiastes 3:15).

At the New York Institute of Metapsychiatry we existentialists believe that metapsychiatry is the wave of the future. It is the knowledge which is to be but has already been.

Metapsychiatry* is a scientific discipline based on a metaphysical concept of man. Man is here understood to be a spiritual being, capable of reflecting the consciousness of cosmic Love-Intelligence. Love-Intelligence is the harmonizing principle of the universe.

Metapsychiatry has its philosophical and epistemological roots in theistic existentialism. In order to understand the practical import of metapsychiatry, a great deal of attention must be paid to a clear statement about the particular brand of existentialism and existential psychotherapy upon which it is based.

Let us, therefore, begin by clarifying our concepts and defining our terms. What then is existentialism? Existentialism is a philosophical inquiry into the nature of human existence and the context in which it manifests itself. Existential philosophy asks: What is man? What is life and what are the laws which govern it? What is its meaning and purpose? What is real, what is unreal? What is truth, health, evil, disease, death? How are these elements of existence cognized?

*The term was first introduced in the United States by Prof. Stanley Dean of Miami, Florida. However, he is not responsible for any part of the content of this book.

The term existential is used to connote whatever deals with the above issues. Existential psychotherapy is an endeavor to help individuals and groups to attain greater conscious harmony with the fundamental order of existence.

What is the derivation of the word existence? Existence is etymologically rooted in the word *ek-sistere,* or *ek-stare.* The word ecstasis is one which is frequently assumed to refer to some intense emotional experience. However, that is not really correct. Ecstasis, or *ek-stasis,* refers to a peculiar ability of man to stand apart and be an observer of his own experiences and thought processes. We say man has the capacity of self-transcendence. No other creature, as far as we know, seems to have this ability. There is a mental disturbance where this human capacity is temporarily lost. It is called depersonalization and derealization. These terms are not quite correct, because what is really happening in such situations is a loss of awareness of one's own identity and reality under the impact of severe anxiety. The faculty of transcendence gives man a sense of orientation and assurance about himself. "I am that I am." I know that I am.

It is said that in order to solve any problem, one has to be able to look at it from the outside. If we look at a problem from within, we cannot solve it. Man, being a complex phenomenon, must be able to look at himself from a transcendent perspective in order to understand himself correctly. This is an essential principle of existential psychotherapy. We said just now that man is a phenomenon. What is a phenomenon? The word phenomenon is derived from the Greek *phainein, phainomenon,* which means light or appearance. How could that be? Isn't man real? Well, man is not what he seems to be. Jesus said: "Judge not according to the appearance, but judge righteous judgment" (John 7:24). This seems to imply that we need to look beyond what seems to be and discern what really is behind the mask, so to speak.

We mentioned that phenomenon also means light. Thus we can see that appearances shed light on things which are not immediately perceptible. These things we call meanings. What are meanings? Meanings are mental equivalents of phenomena. Which means that every appearance is a thought having taken shape either as word, action, activity, mannerism, gesture, behavior, or symptom. Now if man himself is a phenomenon, then he must be an idea, a very complex idea in visible form. The question, of course, offers itself immediately: whose idea is man? But let us now postpone dealing with this question until we have learned more about the principles of metapsychiatry.

The faculty of discerning the meaning behind phenomena is called phenomenological perception. This is a very important tool in existential psychotherapy. It requires the therapist to refrain from preconceived explanations, cliché interpretations, and irresponsible speculations. He must learn the open-minded receptive listening, *allowing* the meaning to reveal itself to his unbiased consciousness. It is crucial to understand the difference between interpretation and phenomenological elucidation.

In existential psychotherapy there is no interpretation. Either we can perceive the meaning of what is going on, or we fail. There are no predigested explanations. Everything is very specific to the individual and to the moment in which it occurs. For instance, if we see someone scratching his nose while we are talking with him, he is not scratching his nose because, say, his mother used to pamper him as a child. The scratching indicates that some thoughts are passing through his mind at this moment and in this situation. There is a fundamental uniqueness to the existential psychotherapeutic way of understanding an individual. It is moment by moment.

Ordinarily we see people in the context of their relationships to other people, or in the context of their backgrounds, or other contexts. Interpersonal relationships are secondary in the existential view of man. The primary issue is his mode of being-in-the-world. What does that complicated hyphenated phrase mean? It sounds very mysterious. In order to understand the mode of being-in-the-world, we come to another word which is important, namely, value. What is value? Value is that which we value. Whatever man values will determine his mode of being-in-the-world. "As he thinketh in his heart, so is he" (Proverbs 23:7). Why is there reference to the heart in this quotation? It points to that which we cherish. Whatever we cherish will determine our mode of being-in-the-world. Unenlightened people are naturally inclined to cherish pleasure from childhood on. All children have a spontaneous value, namely, pleasure.

It is very easy to cherish the so-called pleasure principle. We all like to have pleasure. In existential psychotherapy we distinguish two kinds of values: existentially valid values and existentially invalid values. Existentially valid values bear good fruit, they are health-promoting; existentially invalid values bear bad fruit, they are illness-producing. Discord and disease are disintegrative; existentially valid values are integrative.

Question: What does it take to develop the faculty of phenomenological perceptiveness?

Dr. Hora: What is required here is a complete openness of mind. We have to learn to approach phenomena without preconceived ideas. The German philosopher Husserl has coined the word *epoché* which means putting our preconceived ideas and notions on a shelf momentarily, so that whatever reveals itself can be perceived in its purity. After we have worked with someone for a while, his particular mode of being-in-the-world becomes clear to us to such an extent that it will facilitate our ability to discern the meanings of his phenomena. But this will be in the context of his particular mode of being-in-the-world rather than our preconceived systems of thought in which we may have been trained to view things.

This may seem difficult at first glance but it is not really so. It is continually spontaneous, never artificial, and forever inspiring to both therapist and patient. There is never a dull moment here, which does not mean that it is exciting. It is not exciting, it is inspiring. What is the difference between excitement and inspiration? Excitement is an experience and is essentially disintegrative in quality, even though it is so popular that most people seek it. Essentially, excitement is an existentially invalid value, it is pleasurable but disintegrative, and it is experiential. Whereas inspiration is integrative and therefore existentially valid, and it is not an experience. What is it? In juxtaposition to experience we call it realization. What is realization? When something becomes real to us, that is a realization. In general usage these two concepts are not distinguished, they are often used interchangeably. But for the purpose of clarity it is helpful to learn to distinguish between realization and experience. We may experience many experiences without having realized anything. Once we realize something it is ours forever. Jesus said: "That which is born of the flesh is flesh; and that which is born of the Spirit is spirit" (John 3: 6). Experience is of the flesh, realization is spiritual.

Inspiration is unique to the human condition, animals can get excited but only man can be inspired.

Question: What about orgasm?

Dr. Hora: At times we are victimized by slipshod semantics and popular misconceptions. We have come to believe, for instance, that orgasm, in and of itself, has integrative value. Orgasm in itself is an experience, it has no integrative value whatsoever. Just as scratching one's nose will not make one healthy, titillating oneself genitally has nothing to do with becoming healthier. Which does not imply that abstinence in and of itself is good. What is of integrative value is love. Unfortunately, love is getting more and more lost in lust. Men and women are neither for pleasure nor for excitement nor for orgasm; they are manifestations of Love-Intelligence. Love is inspiring; it is inspired and it is health promoting. Sex is exciting, it is experiential and, without love, it is disintegrative, notwithstanding the intensity of the orgasm.

Love cannot be made and love cannot be done; sexual gymnastics can be done. Good questions to ask are: "How can we express love?" "How can one be loving?" "How do we work on being loving?" We are not generating love within ourselves. We cannot produce love, there is no technique but there is a method. Who knows the secret method of becoming loving? The way to become loving is through prayer. Prayer is the method whereby we become loving.

Question: What is prayer?

Dr. Hora: Prayer is the method whereby we become connected with the source of love, intelligence, vitality, assurance, peace, joy, gratitude. These are existentially integrative values. What happens in this kind of prayer? In prayer we come to cherish existentially integrative values. We become transformed because our mode of being-in-the-world is determined by the values we cherish. In existential psychotherapy we endeavor to help people to replace their disintegrative values with existentially valid values. Patients come to cherish, appreciate and desire to be filled with these values; in turn, these values transform their modes of being-in-the-world. This may take some time because we are usually attached to our false values.

Often much confrontation of value systems is taking place, but gradually the right values come to be appreciated. Sometimes it is necessary to go into great detail in clarifying these desirable values. For instance, it is amazing how much confusion there is in the world about love.

Question: Could you give a definition of love?

Dr. Hora: Love, of course, is of primary value from the standpoint of harmony with existence. Let us try to define this mysterious thing called love. Most people who attempt to define love reveal an interpersonal context in their preconceptions about life and love. They believe that it takes two to love, but does it? Can't one be loving when alone? It is generally believed that love must have an object, but we say, not necessarily. *The object of love is love.* The important thing is to be loving. What does it mean to be loving? *Love is a desire to express goodness, unconditionally.* The desire to express the good makes man Christlike. Man becomes a channel through whom the love of God flows into the world. Such a man is called a beneficial presence. His mode of being-in-the-world is that of a beneficial presence; mind you, not a beneficial person but a beneficial presence. What is the difference? A beneficial person tends to become self-righteous and manipulative. It is important to understand the difference between a beneficial person and a beneficial presence in the world.

It is indeed a great thing for us to know how to pray effectively, rather than to waste our time in futile supplications. It is important to know that we cannot pray for what should be or shouldn't be. When we pray effectively we cultivate a deep appreciation for the values we have mentioned, and these values wash our consciousness clean of all polluting values. We are continually exposed to pollutants. We are exposed to suggestions which flood our consciousness with invalid ideas and false values. Prayer helps us to purify our consciousness. The more we are exposed to mental pollution, the more frequently and fervently we must practice this self-administered method of salutary brainwashing. For that's what meditation is, cleaning our consciousness and filling ourselves with wholesome values. If our consciousness is filled with these values, our mode of being-in-the-world manifests it as a harmonious, beneficial, wholesome presence. All things work together for good to those who love being loving.

Man is a manifestation of inspired wisdom. The source of intelligence is not within him. We are spiritual beings and our intelligence, our love, and our vitality have a transcendent derivation.

Let us ask the question: How is it possible that there are so many different schools of psychotherapy? This is possible because there are various definitions of man. The question: "what is man?" is the most puzzling question anyone can ask. Whatever the preconceived idea about man is will determine the entire system of ideas which will evolve from it. If we assume that man is an animal, we will develop a sort of behavioristic system of therapy where man will be conditioned to behave in certain desirable ways. If we assume that man is a biological organism, we will utilize all sorts of biological, biochemical, and physiological means of helping him. If we assume that man is a psychological being, molded by his early environment, then we shall evolve methods of helping him by trying to get him to correct certain childhood experiences. If we assume that man is a computer, then we will try to program him and deprogram him. There are many ways we can speculate about what we are. Now the question is: How will it ever be decided what man really is? There are many ways of claiming what man is and every one of them seems helpful to some extent. So there is a mystery here. Theistic existentialism accepts the biblical definition of man, namely, that man is the image and likeness of God, that he is spiritual and therefore can achieve the optimum realization of his potentialities, the optimum fulfillment through cultivating his spiritual consciousness. And indeed, this has proven to be a supremely helpful way.

Jesus said: "I am the way, the truth, and the life" (John 14:6), and: "I am the light of the world: he that followeth me shall not walk in darkness, but shall have the light of life" (John 8:12).

Session No. 2

EXISTENTIAL VALIDATION

At times we are confronted with these questions: How widespread is this school of thought and who is behind it? Such questions reveal a certain insecurity and doubt, whether or not one has the ability to discern what is valid and what is not valid. Indeed, this is not an easy thing to do. In most areas of life we are accustomed to go with the crowd. If a sufficient number of people believe in something, and the people look nice and distinguished enough, wear the right clothes, move in the right circles, maybe what they are believing in or professing is the truth. And we accept it. We are inclined to believe what they believe. This gives us a certain sense of security, but of course this is a mistake. We cannot go by who is behind a certain movement, or how widespread a movement is, whether it is an "in" thing or not. There must be a way to know whether a proposition is valid or not so that we may avoid being swayed by one fad or another.

I am sure that in the course of our education and life experiences we all have gone through various phases of being caught up in certain enthusiasm for this school or that school, this movement or that movement, always being impressed by the people who are behind it or by the number of people attracted to it. There must be a better way, otherwise we would be condemned to a lifetime of continuous running hither and yon, picking up this fad and that fad, becoming partisans rather than having a sense of assurance that we are in touch with a truth that is valid and that will not be disproven next year. How can we do this? How can we find a way of being secure? There is a principle we can rely on, it is called *existential validation*. It is not social or statistical, it is not philosophical or academic; it is existential validation. What do we mean by that?

Existential validation means considering the following questions: In what way does a certain idea contribute to the improvement of the quality of our lives? Does it heal us? Does it liberate us? Does it bring harmony into our lives? Does it contribute to a sense of peace, assurance? Does it fill us with a sense of gratitude? Does it inspire us with wisdom and love? Does it make it possible for us to find the answers we need to the problems of daily living? If what we are learning has this effect, then it must be existentially valid. Jesus put it very simply, he said: "By their fruits ye shall know them" (Matthew 7: 20). Further, he said: "When you come to know the truth, it will make you free."

So there are criteria which help us to validate whatever we are learning. We do not have to take anybody's word for it, we do not have to believe what we hear, we do not have to agree with anything that is being said, we do not have to accept anything. All that is needed is to consider the proposition and observe its effects, primarily on our own lives. An important point to consider is that if we were having here a course in engineering or salesmanship or business administration or law or politics or carpentry, we could gather information and this information could be useful in an operational sense; it would help us to know how to do something. And that's practical. But the field of psychotherapy is entirely different, here technical considerations do not apply.

It is impossible to help anyone unless we ourselves have been helped by the very truth which we are attempting to convey. It is a mistake to think that one can learn how to do psychotherapy. It is preposterous to assume that a patient, a friend, or a loved one can become an object of our technical intervention. In surgery it is possible, but in psychotherapy it is not possible. It is not possible to benefit anyone if we treat him as an object.

What is man? Man is a spiritual being. What do we mean by that? When we speak of man as a spiritual being, we are not talking of religion, we are trying to go beyond religion. We are trying to clarify the peculiarity of human consciousness which is capable of becoming aware of invisible factors in life. What are these invisible factors in life which only man is capable of cognizing? Only man is capable of being consciously aware of love, meaning, truth, life, beauty, goodness, freedom, joy, harmony. Only man is capable of being aware of ideas. This makes man a unique manifestation among all life forms. It is this uniqueness that man is endowed with which makes him an individual spiritual consciousness. Therefore, as far as we know, man is radically different from anything else that exists on the planet Earth. It is this difference which is the foundation of the existential viewpoint of man.

Man is viewed as an individual spiritual consciousness. Indeed, when this is clearly realized, this particular quality of human consciousness lifts man out of the possibility of being an object. He is neither an object nor a subject. He is a phenomenon and a manifestation of the divine. It is through the spiritual radiancy of human consciousness that we become aware of the divine. *"L'homme clairière de l'Existence."** Loosely translated, this means: "Man is an image and likeness of God." The existence of man reveals the existence of God. Without man God could not be known. St. Paul writes in one of his more obscure passages: "For the invisible things of him from the creation of the world are clearly seen, being understood by the things that are made, even his eternal power and Godhead" (Romans 1:20). What does this mean?

Comment: It sounds as if it means that the world reveals God.

Dr. Hora: The purpose of man is to reveal the existence of God. Metapsychiatry is not founded by personalities, famous people, philosophers, psychiatrists; it is not founded on statistical data; it is founded on a pure endeavor to discern what is valid and what is not valid existentially.

There is another aspect of metapsychiatry which is epistemological. What does that mean? Epistemology explores the nature of knowing. Much difficulty arises in our lives from thinking that we know something when we don't really know it. There seem to be different levels of knowing. Most of the time we are satisfied with knowledge which only has the power to inform. But knowledge that is information has no therapeutic value. We must concern ourselves

*French translation of Heidegger's *Lichtung des Daseins.*

with providing patients with knowledge that has the power to transform. For this we need to understand what we mean by existential issues. Existential issues are cherished ideas which affect an individual's mode of being-in-the-world.

We are concerned with understanding, with discerning ideas of existential significance to the patient. For instance, we heard about a young man for whom effeminacy was an idea which colored his entire life experience. Suppose we were simply to label this individual a homosexual. Would it help him or us? It would not. It is all right for filling out forms, but when it comes to helping the patient, we confront him with the idea of effeminacy and help him to understand what it is, what its meaning is, in what way it is invalid for his existence, and we try to help him know something that might free him from his mental fixation on an existentially invalid idea.

It is always the ideas we cherish or hate or fear that underlie our problems. How is it possible that something we cherish, something we hate, or something we fear could each have the same effect? Whatever we cherish or hate or fear is very important to us, and whatever is important to us will determine our mode of being-in-the-world. This can be conscious or unconscious. It is often wrapped in a thick fog of rationalizations. It really makes no difference whether we cherish, fear, or hate something, the common denominator is a powerful emotional charge. In psychoanalysis it is called cathexis.

Question: Could you please explain what you mean by conscious and unconscious?

Dr. Hora: Conscious is that which we are aware of, unconscious is that which we are not aware of. Quite often we do not like to be aware of certain things and then they become unconscious. For instance, if we hate something, we may not want to know it and we say it is repressed or suppressed or avoided.

We are always keeping in mind that we want to help the patient to gain such knowledge which will heal him, will have the power to transform him, and we must avoid communicating knowledge that would remain only information. Information tends to become a tool of resistance. We must not hand out unnecessary information. We have to try to keep in mind that whatever we say must contribute to the kind of knowledge that would result in transformation.

Question: How does one distinguish between knowledge that is information and knowledge that is transformation?

Dr. Hora: The knowledge that will carry within itself the power to transform must be eminently relevant to the patient's mode of being-in-the-world. The more experienced a therapist is, the more relevant his responses become. He does not waste a word, he does not say a single word that is purely intellectualization. Unless we can say something specifically relevant to the patient's need, it is better to say nothing.

In order to be more relevant, the therapist must be able to discern in a specific way the patient's need. And here we come to the issue of phenomenological perception. Phenomenological perception is the discerning of those cherished ideas which disrupt the patient's life. This is called discerning the meaning of phenomena. In proportion that we become proficient in discerning the meaning of phenomena, in that proportion our responses can be specific and to the point and have transforming power.

Session No. 3

COMMITMENT

Question: There is an impression that the metapsychiatric view somehow negates all other schools of thought. You probably don't quite feel that way. People seem to think that anything that preceded, like scientific psychology, is not valid anymore. Could you say something about that?

Dr. Hora: Whatever is of value in any other school of thought is certainly worth preserving. What we are talking about here has not sprung up out of thin air but is an evolution of everything else that preceded. We all reach a point where we may say, I have seen this and I have known that, but now I understand something on a different level and therefore I can go beyond what I have known previously. We are evolving continually. It is a good idea to look at life in a dynamic evolutionary sense, not only in terms of society and the race but individually as well. There is nothing more pathetic than someone who has learned a certain technique right after college and gets stuck with it. He may go on year in and year out applying the same platitudes, having closed his mind to everything else and not advancing any more. What has become of him? He has become a hack. His life and his work have become routinized and dull.

But if we are willing to be perennial students, then our life is a daily challenge, a continuously unfolding process of new realizations. We will never get stale or repetitious, boring or bored. Every day will be a new adventure. Every session with a patient will be a new discovery. It is the willingness to grow that makes life beautiful and work challenging. It is as with art. An artist will never stop growing even if he has worked in his particular medium for thirty years. Every time he approaches his work, it is a discovery and a new growth experience. What is the difference between an artist and an artisan? An artisan is someone who has acquired a certain skill, which may be good or bad, and he is stuck with it, making the same things over and over again. This has its usefulness but he is not an artist, he is an artisan.

Comment: An artisan produces and an artist creates.

Dr. Hora: In our field, too, there are artists and there are artisans. There are certain creative people who are forever exploring new frontiers, who are involved in their work existentially rather than just professionally. What does it mean to be involved in our work existentially rather than just professionally? What is a professional?

Comment: A professional is someone who professes a body of knowledge.

Dr. Hora: Right. What does it mean to profess? It means to talk about something. What does it mean to be involved in our work existentially?

Comment: To live it.

Dr. Hora: That's right. It is a way of life with us. And whatever constitutes a way of life has within itself the dynamism of progress. We are all naturally desirous of more and more perfect fulfillment in this life, just as a tree wants to grow ever higher and higher toward heaven. If we are involved in our work existentially, it is a part of our fulfillment, and in the process of trying to help our patients we are continuously learning about ourselves and about reality and about truth. So, without our becoming fanatical about it, this kind of commitment makes life beautiful, interesting, and challenging.

There is, however, a danger sometimes that if we become involved with something very seriously, we may become fanatics. For instance, if we are involved with a political ideology, or with a religious belief, or with a psychotherapeutic system, it can deteriorate into an emotional involvement. If we are involved with something emotionally, then there is a danger of fanaticism. In true existential commitment there is no fanaticism. How is it possible to be committed to something with one's entire being and yet not become fanatical about it? Fanaticism is a pathological condition, existential commitment is

a supremely healthy condition. What in psychiatry is called pathological religiosity is synonymous with fanaticism. How can we tell
whether someone is religious or fanatical? There is a specific differential diagnostic criterion which enables us to immediately tell the
difference. We call it self-confirmatory ideation. A fanatical individual will exploit whatever he is committed to, be it political ideology,
religious belief, or anything else, for purposes of self-glorification.

In juxtaposition to this, existential commitment is focused on a
search for the knowledge of the truth which heals and liberates. The
Bible speaks of existential commitment the following way: "Commit
thy works unto the Lord, and thy thoughts shall be established"
(Proverbs 16:3). The fanatic is committed to his ego, the existentially
committed individual has committed himself to the quest for truth.
One is personal, the other is transpersonal. When we are committed
to a search after the truth in such a way that we will follow wherever
it will lead us, we will be continually growing and learning. There
will never be a time when we will say: Well, now I know everything.

Question: What about peace? Isn't peace the cessation of movement?

Dr. Hora: That would be a static concept of peace. Peace is not
stagnation; peace is dynamic, dynamic harmony and assurance.
What is static peace? It is death. If we have that kind of peace, we
are dead.

Question: What about structure?

Dr. Hora: There is dynamic structure. The work of Buckminster
Fuller illustrates this point beautifully in his theory of synergetic
structures. Existential structure is dynamic. Nothing stands still. In
the universe everything is in constant motion.

The existential psychotherapist desires to develop his faculty of
attentiveness to the maximum degree, where he is able to discern the
patient's need and the meaning of phenomena as they reveal themselves, so that his responses can be optimally relevant. Previously we
were talking about knowledge which is information and knowledge
which is transformation. In order for the transforming knowledge to
be presented to a patient in a particular situation, the responses of
the therapist must be optimally relevant. We cannot afford to tell a
patient about the Oedipus complex or some other predigested idea.

If we do that, we are only giving information about something that we have read or heard about in a lecture, or telling him what we were planning to tell him. This is information, and it is grist to the mill of resistance. Paying attention is a form of love; the more capable we are of paying attention, the more loving we are, and the more loving we are, the more attentive we are to the patient's needs as they reveal themselves in the course of our intercommunication.

Seeking to find fault with a patient and to diagnose him is not love, neither is it attentiveness. It is scrutinizing. It is interesting to contemplate the following three expressions in our language: curiosity, inquisitiveness, and interest. Only the interested individual is loving. The curious one is selfish, the inquisitive one is a trespasser. What is the derivation of the word interest? *Inter-esse* literally means to be between, to be involved. What are we involved with? Are we involved with our patients? That would be interpersonal, wouldn't it? That would not be very helpful. When a therapist becomes involved with his patient, what happens? There is transference and there is countertransference. If we are not involved with our patients and we are interested in them, what are we involved with?

Comment: The solution of their problems.

Dr. Hora: We are involved in understanding the meaning of their problems and finding a creative, effective way of communicating some aspect of the truth to them in such a way that a healing might occur. So it is nonpersonal, transpersonal.

When we say we are loving, what do we mean? Sometimes when a therapist is loving toward his patient, and his outlook on life is an interpersonal one, there develops a love affair which is a formidable type of resistance. When we speak of love, we do not speak of personal love. What kind of love are we talking about?

Comment: The concern for the well-being of the patient.

Dr. Hora: Love desires to be beneficial. If a therapist were to express personal goodness, what would happen? The patient would fall in love with the therapist, and that is not desirable. Or the patient would become so indebted to the therapist that he would lose his freedom. Whenever the personal element enters into the therapeutic situation, it becomes complicated. It is, therefore, quite important to gain a transpersonal idea of love.

The love of being loving is the desire to manifest or reflect the goodness of God unconditionally and nonpersonally. If we can learn to love in this manner, there will be no complications of a transferential or countertransferential nature.

Everyone of us needs to learn to love the way God loves, after all, we are manifestations of Love-Intelligence, which is God. Man is the image and likeness of God; *"L'homme clairière de l'Existence."* We are all capable of manifesting spiritual love. Spiritual love is nonpersonal, unconditional benevolence. We can give it some thought, we can contemplate it, we can meditate on it, we can pray over it, we can behold it, and we can become it. And that is certainly a challenge —to become what we really are. Oddly enough, it was Nietzsche who said: "We must become what we already are." In proportion that we approximate the truth of our own being, in that proportion we shall be able to effectively benefit the people who seek our assistance.

Session No. 4

THE PRAYER
OF BEHOLDING

Question: Would you please speak more about prayer?

Dr. Hora: The ability to pray is uniquely human. Man is the only being who prays. Interestingly enough everyone prays, perhaps all the time, without realizing it. There is a saying that there are no atheists in foxholes. Regardless of whether we consider ourselves to be agnostics or atheists or something else, we all have something we cherish and trust in, cling to or lean on. Whatever we cherish, trust in or cling to is really our God. Everyone has at least one god, some have more. It is almost impossible to be human without prayer. Man is an eminently prayerful being. The question is not whether we are praying but what we are praying to and how? Prayer and transcendence seem to be the two most significant aspects of being human.

Transcendence is the unique ability of man to reflect upon himself, to be aware of what he is thinking. Another ability is prayer. Prayer may be mental, verbal, behavioral, formal or informal, conscious or unconscious, always relating to something cherished or feared. The Bible says: "The fear of the Lord is the beginning of wisdom" (Proverbs 9:10). This is a peculiar-sounding quotation. Does God recommend that we live in fear? It could be better understood if we altered it somewhat and said: Reverence for God, the cherishing of God, is the beginning of wisdom. If we do not cherish God, we are liable to cherish something else. And if we cherish something else, this may not be existentially valid. People sometimes cling to a rabbit's foot, or to another person, or to knocking on wood. There are innumerable things we can pray to. There are also pathological forms of prayer; for instance: obsessive ruminations, mannerisms, compulsions.

Question: What is behavioral prayer?

Dr. Hora: Ritualisms, mannerisms, and various physical activities. Ritualistic prayers often are forms of superstitious prayer. These may involve an element of magic thinking, performance of certain gestures like bowing three times or touching the head to the floor.

In this context fear and anxiety are manifestations of a belief in a God capable of evil. If our concept of God includes the possibility of evil, then we are caught up in a system of prayer which is connected with fear lest we do it wrong or fail to please our God. Propitiating and fearing always have to do with the belief in evil of some sort. So the beginning of wisdom is to worship the right God. Freud is known to have said that religion is a private neurosis, and although it often is it need not be so. The question arises: What concept of God and what form of prayer would be most compatible with healthy living? How could we come to worship something that is existentially valid? Let us see whether it is possible to know and to pray to a God who, instead of victimizing us, would rather sustain us.

Now, in considering prayer, we have reached the point where we realize the importance of love as an eminently integrative value. In order to be healthy we must always orient ourselves in the direction of being optimally and maximally loving. Dr. Blanton wrote a successful book entitled *Love or Perish* (New York: Fawcett/World, 1971). Just as it is not possible for us to live without prayer, it is really not possible to remain healthy without love. Love, of course, has many variations and interpretations; therefore, not only do we have to appreciate love but we must also subject our love to careful scrutiny. Is it really love or is it one of its many distortions? Prayer is a way of increasing our ability to love.

Previously we have defined health as a certain mode of being-in-the-world—a beneficial presence in the world. Our aim then is to cultivate a consciousness which is capable of loving in order to be a beneficial presence in the world. When we attain this state of being, we are engaged in existential worshiping. That is a form of prayer which is beyond words and thoughts. It is the actualization of existentially valid values.

Question: What do we mean by spiritual values? What are spiritual values?

Dr. Hora: Man is a spiritual being and he becomes a beneficial presence in the world by virtue of cherishing and manifesting and consciously expressing spiritual values. Among these are love, honesty, humility, joy, generosity, peace, assurance, freedom, harmony, health.

Question: Of what help is it to a therapist to have positive values and an idealized concept of man in his thought when he is with a patient? Isn't it going to repress the pathology and make things worse?

Dr. Hora: Let us try to clarify two things. We are not talking about positive values but about existential values; they happen to be positive, but not all positive values are existentially valid. Similarly, spiritual values underlie all religions but not all religions are spiritual. Once I heard someone tell a charming story. A little boy was watching a sculptor at work. For weeks this sculptor kept chipping away at a big block of marble. After a few weeks, he had created a beautiful marble lion. The little boy was amazed and said: "Mister, how did you know there was a lion in that rock?" Can you see the relevancy of this story to holding the right concept of man in consciousness?

This also points up the difference between the traditional way of meeting a patient and what is called "existential encounter." The word "encounter" has become popular but it has been trivialized. It was originally introduced by existential philosophers to emphasize a fundamental qualitative difference in meeting our fellow man or, if we happen to be therapists, our patients. The traditional way of meeting our friends and patients is to assess their weak points. Binswanger, the famous Swiss existential psychiatrist, called it *Beim schwachen Punkte fassen* (to exploit their weaknesses). This means to seek out the weak spot in people to gain sort of a handle on them. One of the social handicaps of our profession is that people are afraid we will find fault with them. We have a kind of evaluative approach to people and unwittingly we seek to find something wrong with them. In an encounter we should be like that sculptor we mentioned, not looking to find out what is wrong with people but looking to see the Christ in them, the model of the perfect man. This may not be easy, however. Pathology tends to obtrude itself on consciousness and often fascinates us. (Evil is fascinating.) Evil has the tendency to attract attention and keep it riveted on itself. Evil thrives on attention. Perhaps this is one of the reasons why psychology is so popular. It is exciting to find out what is wrong with us. It is much more difficult to see the lion in the rock. For that, one has to be an artist, a creative individual, a creative mind, and a lover of beauty and harmony and truth. One has to be spiritually oriented and look for the perfect man.

Question: What is the perfect man?

Dr. Hora: The perfect man is the image and likeness of God. What does that mean? It does not mean that he has big muscles, is ten feet tall, has blond hair and blue eyes. No, the perfect man is one who reflects spiritual qualities. He is honest, forthright, loving, joyous, peaceful, assured, fearless. It is our ignorance that keeps us from becoming what we really are. The lion was in that rock for thousands of years and no one saw it except that sculptor. When a sculptor wants to make a sculpture, he has to see the object of his creation long before anyone else. He looks at a piece of rock and he already sees there the thing which will eventually emerge from it; only that way can he produce a work of art. We too have to see the good instead of being fascinated by pathology. The artist would look to see something spiritually valuable, such as beauty, harmony, balance; or, in case of an abstract sculptor like Brancusi, he may look for the harmony of form. Some so-called modern artists are seeing ugliness, evil, injustice, misery, and squalor. What are we to make of that?

Whatever the therapist is interested in, overtly or covertly, has a powerful influence on the patient. It is well known that Freudian patients tend to have Freudian dreams and Jungian patients Jungian dreams. This has been described in the literature as "doctrinal compliance." (Ehrenwald. *See* p. 235.)

Whatever parents cherish in their secret thoughts, their children too will cherish; and whatever gods the therapist worships, overtly or covertly, consciously or unconsciously, the patients will pick up and embrace or rebel against—which is all the same because it means they are involved with it. "Stand fast therefore in the liberty wherewith Christ hath made us free, and be not entangled again with the yoke of bondage" (Galatians 5:1). It is vitally important for the therapist to be really devoted to something wholesome, something existentially valid. If one becomes imbued with a value system which is existentially valid, it acts not like a hammer and chisel but like a blowtorch; it will just melt away all pathology and what emerges is the real man who was there all the time.

An interesting and important differential diagnostic point must be considered here because we know that mental hospitals frequently have inmates who appear to be religious and even spiritually minded, claiming to have had mystical experiences. How do we differentiate pathological religiosity from true spiritual-mindedness? True spiritual-mindedness is wholesome, but the counterfeits are mental diseases. To discern what is pathological and what is healthy, there is one important criterion. All pathology has the character and quality of *self-confirmation*. What is self-confirmation? In traditional psychoanalysis it is called self-referential thinking. In pathology, every concept, whether religious, spiritual, or political, is exploited for the purpose of self-promotion. Healthy individuals can transcend egotistic tendencies and seek fulfillment in something more constructive.

Self-confirmatory thinking can take on paranoid forms when the individual believes himself to be persecuted or the center of the universe. So, in pathological religiosity the patient seems to be talking about Jesus Christ, God, the Virgin Mary, or whatever, but the real issue in all his verbalizations and behavior is the self. This way it is easy to make the differential diagnosis. Self-confirmatory ideation means that thought is constantly reverting to itself. A beneficial presence in the world is a channel through whom the good of God expresses itself. He is not a person, he is a presence. When self-confirmatory elements disappear, health takes over. The central focus is on the good rather than on the self. The Zen Master says: "In the realm of the Real there is neither self nor other, there is only that which really is." The good of God *is*. That is an essential quality of being healthy. Man becomes good-centered rather than self-centered or other-oriented. Healthy man is neither egotistical nor altruistic but good-oriented. Good is that which is existentially valid. It is health-promoting, integrative, harmony-producing, healing.

To return to the subject of art. There seem to be artists who are fascinated by evil and they utilize their skills to portray squalor, ugliness, garbage—literally garbage. Recently there was a story in the papers of an artist who was gathering Henry Kissinger's garbage for the purpose of making a collage portrait of him. There are also gifted psychologists who make a great work of art of describing psychopathology and studying everything that is wrong in the world. While this has its merits, let us not be drowned in it. It only helps us to know what to get rid of. Healthy man appreciates the good, the beautiful, and the true because that is what really *is*.

Perhaps we could point out another phenomenon, namely, that man has a tendency to be influenced by group pressures and social trends. From time to time we see various fads arising: there are fads in the field of psychotherapy, in the world of art, in politics, and in all aspects of life. In art there are fads like dadaism and abstract expressionism. At certain periods of time certain types of trash are admired because they are promoted by self-styled authorities. These become the "in" things. But if we know what is valid from an existential standpoint, we do not get confused. We can say with St. Paul: "None of these things move me" (Acts 20:24).

Question: What is beauty? Is beauty concrete or abstract?

Dr. Hora: Before the sculptor brought out his beautiful lion, it was an abstract idea in his consciousness. When he brought it out, it became a concrete representation of this abstract idea. We are tempted to say that beauty can be both abstract and concrete. But, in fact, it is neither abstract nor concrete, it is real. Beauty itself is real. When we say something is abstract, we say it is mental; when we say something is concrete, we say it is material. The abstract is intangible, the concrete is tangible, but beauty is real.

What is real? How could we define the real? Real is that which is immutable. You remember the Zen Master saying: "In the realm of the Real there is neither self nor other, there is only that which really is." The understanding of what is real has great value. It makes it possible for us to practice the highest form of prayer, which is called *beholding*. Beholding is really the prayer described by Jesus when he said: "God is a Spirit: and they that worship him must worship him in spirit and in truth" (John 4:24). When we come to understand what is real, we can attain communion with reality and that is the prayer of beholding. Beholding is beyond words and beyond thoughts. It is pure consciousness of reality. And just a split second of beholding can have great integrative value. The supreme attainment is the ability to pray the prayer of beholding. In Zen meditation it is called *kensho*. In all religions there are individuals who have attained this capacity to penetrate into the realm of reality which is beyond words and beyond thoughts.

It may come as a surprise to some, but we do not really live in reality. By this is meant that we cannot experience reality, we only experience our thoughts about reality. Did you ever consider how it is possible that so many people all over the world pray in the context of various religious systems with so little to show for it? The fact is that we do not really know how to pray. But we can aspire for it and endeavor to grow in understanding. We can become so vitally interested in the nature of reality that eventually we can improve our ability to pray. It is just a matter of evolving spiritually. We can reach a point, for at least short periods of time, when we can be beyond words and thoughts in a state of complete openness. The Zen Master puts it this way: "God speaks to us in the space between two thoughts."

Let us consider once again the sculptor who saw the lion in the rock, and let us ask ourselves: How did he do that? What sensory organ was he using when he was beholding the lion in the rock? It could be called the inner eye, creative intelligence, or spiritual awareness. We can call it by many names, but it is something beyond sensory perception and beyond imagination. We have faculties we haven't dreamed of yet.

A little boy was asked, "Did you pray tonight before going to bed?" He said, "No." "Why not?" he was asked. "Because I don't need nothing." Most of us believe that prayer is asking for something, and that is also a mistake. It is not really possible to pray for what should be, we can only pray to see what already is. In the light of what was said, we can define prayer as *an endeavor to behold what is real.* It is an endeavor to connect with reality. What does this have to do with psychotherapy? If we have reverence for truth and we appreciate spiritual values, then our life becomes a prayer. Life is then lived in the consciousness of what is true, beautiful, and good.

Question: What are the signs of integration? How can we tell whether we are praying right and whether we are praying to the right God?

Dr. Hora: In order really to know whether our prayers are effective, we have to understand first the difference between experiencing something and realizing something. Experiences are subjective, they are unreliable. We can easily deceive ourselves that we feel something. When we are praying for something, we may feel good about it and have the illusion that we prayed well, and yet nothing happened, nothing has been achieved. In Proverbs there is a line which says: "He that trusteth in his own heart is a fool" (Proverbs 28:26). In other words, our subjective feelings and experiences are not reliable criteria. Realization is very much akin to experiencing but it takes place on a higher level of awareness. Experiences are sensory, emotional, or intellectual. Realizations are spiritual. They occur not in the neurovegetative system but in consciousness. It is a transcendent mode of knowing. Now when we pray we want to connect with reality, to somehow behold the truth of what really is beyond words, thoughts, and time, beyond feelings and experiences. "They that worship Him must worship Him in spirit and in truth."

Therefore, what we are looking for is cognitive evidence that we have succeeded in getting in touch with reality rather than just with statements about reality. For instance, if we were to say: "God is good," it would not be the truth, it would only be a statement about the truth. In order to pray effectively we have to get in touch with the truth, so we have to find a way of coming into contact with that truth which is beyond a statement about the truth. Every time we succeed something good happens to us, we reach a point which I have named for didactic purposes, the "PAGL" point. The PAGL point means that we are at the point of realizing Peace, Assurance, Gratitude and Love (PAGL). When that realization dawns upon us, we can stop. We have here a criterion which indicates that we have succeeded. PAGL is evidence that we have come successfully in contact with transcendent reality. This is the supreme point of integration. It is easy to lose that point, to slip out of it, but we can get back into it. This may be called "ceaseless prayer." As we practice living in reality, the struggle to maintain contact becomes somewhat easier and more meaningful. Our lives begin to be more wholesome and harmonious.

At first it may not be easy to differentiate between experiencing something and realizing something. But if we give it some thought, try to remember it and practice it, we will find that there indeed is a higher modality of awareness we are capable of, which is beyond experiencing. When we are in harmony with existence, we are in harmony with our fellow man as well, but it does not necessarily follow the other way around. One can get along with people beautifully and still be in disharmony with existence. We know of politicians and psychopaths who are masters of human relation techniques, and yet they are completely disjointed as far as reality is concerned. So the primary task in life would seem to be harmony with the fundamental order of existence. Lao-tzu said: "The enlightened man does not contend, therefore no man contends with him," and so he lives in harmony not only with nature around him but also with his fellow man.

Question: If man is integrated, what happens to his hostility, anger, and aggressiveness—things which according to Freud are natural to man? What happens to the disruptiveness of the natural person?

Dr. Hora: The answer is that man is not a natural person. Man is a spiritual being and once he understands what that means, many things change in his life. The concept of natural man implies that man is a biological organism living in the context of his environment, not unlike animals do. Earlier we have discussed the various presuppositions about man. Existentialism, at least the type of existentialism we are talking about here, is based on the presupposition that the biblical definition of man as a spiritual image and likeness of God is existentially valid. Starting from that premise, we arrive at all the insights and more which we have touched upon until now.

CASE PRESENTATION

A thirty-nine-year-old housewife, mother of three children. Neat, colorful, and attractive in appearance, but anxious. Her hands shake and she sighs a lot. Complains of dizzy spells, tensions, greatly burdened by guilt and anger. One of her children is mentally retarded. There are also marital problems.

Commentary on Case Presentation

When we are sitting with someone in a room there is a certain quality of presence which can be phenomenologically discerned. The way an individual participates in a situation reveals a great deal about his mode of being-in-the-world. This makes it superfluous to inquire into the background of the individual. In traditional psychoanalysis we were trained to look for what is wrong with the patient, and how this wrong came about. In the back of our minds there is always the question, "Why is the patient the way he is?" Now in existential psychotherapy we are not interested in "why." The "why" question becomes completely useless. We are focusing our attention on meaning.

As mentioned before, meanings are mental equivalents of phenomena. Cause-and-effect thinking has already been discarded in advanced forms of scientific thinking, as for instance in Heisenberg's theory of indeterminacy for which he received the Nobel prize in physics. In metapsychiatry we have come to recognize that cause-and-effect thinking does not apply and is an indication of narrow-mindedness. Let us just imagine what would have happened if Newton had asked: "Why did the apple fall from the tree?" He could have come up with several answers. For instance, he could have said: "The apple fell from the tree because it was too heavy for its stem to support it." Or he could have said: "Perhaps the wind was blowing, or something shook the ground around the apple tree." He would have found an explanation. But explanations are not synonymous with realizations. He who seeks reasons only finds excuses. But Newton was interested in the deeper issues which lie behind the phenomena. So he asked: "What does the falling apple reveal about the laws governing nature?"

The word "problem" is of interest here. It exemplifies the surprising wisdom and insight hidden in language. For instance, the linguistic analysis of this word reveals that problems are emblematic. What do we mean by that? Emblem is synonymous with symbol. Problem,

pro-emblema, means symbolic. Our problems have symbolic meaning. They indicate involvement with symbols rather than reality. The
right understanding of problems will reveal in every instance a certain misapprehension of existential reality in terms of its symbol. For
instance, a woman was suffering from recurring inflammation of her
fingers around the nail bed. If we examined this problem from a
cause-and-effect standpoint, we would probably surmise that her
manicurist had used unsanitary scissors and implements. However,
if we examine the situation from an emblematic standpoint, we see
that the problem itself is a form of symbolic communication. We
discover that this lady has a tendency to be manipulative. And
indeed, her history reveals that her manipulativeness has inflamed
strife, hatred, discord, and fear among the members of her family.
She tends to "stick her fingers" into other peoples' affairs to exercise
control over them.

The word "manipulativeness" is also revealing, for it is derived
from the Latin word *manus,* which means hand. To be manipulative
means to handle. Manipulativeness is a mental form of handling
people and situations in such a way as to make them conform to our
wishes and preconceived notions. Whenever we are confronted with
a problem, it can be most helpful if we are willing to refrain from
the standard cause-and-effect reasoning and turn our attention to the
message which the problem is trying to convey to us. It is important
to start out with the question: What is the meaning of what seems
to be? And then proceed to the next question: What is what really
is?

We could say that all of life is a school which is designed to teach
us the answers to these two questions.

In an endeavor to understand his patient, the therapist rises above
cause-and-effect reasoning and seeks to understand the meaning of
the presenting problem. For instance, when a mother reports having
problems with her child, who seems to repeatedly provoke reactions
of rage and exasperation in her, it is helpful to consider one of the
lesser known principles of metapsychiatry, namely, that nothing
comes into experience uninvited. When a child behaves in a certain
way, we do not ask why the child does this, or what we should do
to stop him, or how we should handle him. We ask: What is the
meaning of this problem?

In the context of the patient's mode of being-in-the-world it reveals itself spontaneously to us that the child, without realizing it, is reminding the mother that she is culpable and unworthy as a mother and as a human being. Having discovered the meaning of this complex phenomenon of mother and child, we see that there is nothing that needs to be done, that the child does not have to be punished, that the mother does not have to feel guilty. All that is needed is for the mother to improve her thoughts about herself. That will take care of the child's behavior. This patient has a need to fulfill herself as a good, wholesome individual. That's all she has to be interested in and the behavior of her entire family will change. If we ask wrong questions, we get wrong answers and we wind up floundering. It is the quality of the patient's thoughts that determines the circumstances of her experience. Our therapeutic task is to lift her out of her habitual ways of perceiving herself and encourage her to realize that she is fully entitled to be a wholesome, free individual who is a beneficial presence in the world because she is a spiritual being.

Getting out of the rut of cause-and-effect thinking may be initially somewhat difficult, but after we have seen that it opens up a broader horizon on life we learn to appreciate it. Essentially we have only one problem, we are miseducated. To think in terms of cause and effect is also a condition of miseducation.

We always focus our attention on meanings. We can do it either by inviting the patient to participate in it or, if it reveals itself to us spontaneously, we can just directly acquaint the patient with it. Often we can go even beyond this and offer the patient the solution to the problem. The solution to every problem is always in consciousness. There is nothing outside that has not been inside. There is an apocryphal quotation by Jesus in the Gospel of St. Thomas which says: "The Kingdom of God will come when the inside will be outside, and outside will be inside, and the two shall be one, neither inside nor outside." When we understand that nothing comes into experience uninvited, then we shall understand that what is happening on the outside is just an externalization of certain thought processes which are taking place on the inside. The therapeutic task consists always of helping to improve the quality of consciousness. In the final analysis, man is an individualized consciousness. "As he thinketh in his heart, so is he" (Proverbs 23:7). There is a dynamism of spirit in all of us which seeks fulfillment to be the best we can possibly be. But most of the time we do not know what it is and in which direction it lies. Here Jesus' words give us direction: "I am the way, the truth, and the life" (John 14:6). Psychiatry and psychoanalysis have not yet succeeded in finding a proper definition of health and a concept of the healthy man.

It is interesting that when we meet our friends and loved ones, we have the tendency to ask: "What's wrong with you?" "What's wrong?" Our bodies are always telling us what's wrong, and when we look in the mirror, we ask: "What's wrong?" "What's wrong today?" Wouldn't it be much better to ask: "What is right today?" "What is right with me today?" It is counterproductive to ask what's wrong, it reinforces our fascination with evil and pathology.

Question: How come we are so fascinated with evil? Where does that come from?

Dr. Hora: A better question would be, what is the meaning of our fascination with evil? Evil is more accessible to sensory perception than the good. The good is spiritual and is not as easily seen. We have eyes and see not because we use our eyes and our perceptive faculties to focus on that which is easy to see.

"Having eyes, see ye not? and having ears, hear ye not?" (Mark 8:18). "Natural man receiveth not the things of the Spirit of God: for they are foolishness unto him: neither can he know them, because they are spiritually discerned" (I Corinthians 2:14).

Session No. 5

THE TRANSPERSONAL

Question: What is meant by the transpersonal perspective?

Dr. Hora: It is important to understand transpersonal perspective because it changes our entire outlook on life. It can be illustrated with two hands. The interpersonal perspective on life can be illustrated by interlocking the fingers of both hands. It is an interaction of one individual with another on all levels, sensual, emotional, intellectual. The hands approach, proceed, interlock and end up in a stalemate. If we don't like the stalemate, we back off. As we back off, there is friction; then there is movement back and forth, always accompanied by friction until we get tired of stalemates and frictions. Then we break and turn our backs on one another. This is the interpersonal perspective which is commonly practiced. Most psychotherapies are based on the assumption that the essential issue of life is interpersonal relationship. As a matter of fact, the aim of psychotherapy in many instances is to help us somehow to make this a viable situation, to learn how to get along with people, how to have a good relationship in marriage and friendship, or with colleagues, or in life in general.

How do we make the interpersonal perspective workable? Unfortunately, it is not workable, as many have already discovered. Wherever there is a relationship it is always both good and bad. Any marriage, based on the assumption that marriage is a relationship between a man and a woman, will be both good and bad. It starts out good and becomes worse and worse until there is a stalemate, then there are frictions and other stalemates, more friction and finally a break, a turning away from one another and trying to make it work someplace else. There are people who get married and divorced many times. This is a painful way of life. The interpersonal perspective on life is one of the basic sources of conflict in family life as well as in group dynamics.

People want to live together harmoniously but they don't know how. There is a saying: "Familiarity breeds contempt." It is not familiarity, it is just a cognitive deficiency. What do we mean by that? It is the misperception of reality which underlies most of our difficulties. Jesus warned against judging by appearances. When we judge by appearances we see life in the context of interpersonal relationships, group interactions, and international affairs. One of the most characteristic aspects of this kind of perspective is that thought remains horizontal. We think horizontally when we see life in the context of interpersonal relationships. "As thou seest, so thou beest."

Earlier we were talking about the limiting aspects of cause-and-effect thinking. Again there is the problem that the mental horizon is narrowed by certain habits of thought. Today we can say the same thing about horizontal thinking. Horizontal thinking restricts the ability to perceive reality in its full dimension. Cause-and-effect thinking makes man narrow-minded; interpersonal thinking makes him shallow-minded.

The transpersonal perspective may be illustrated by the hands coming together parallel, pointing upwards, reaching a prayerful position. This gesture symbolizes the vertical position, it is not interlocking and therefore there is freedom of movement without friction. Such a marriage is not a relationship, it is a *joint participation* in existence with complete freedom to be closer or further away at any moment without friction—"with no strings attached." The orientation is vertical at all times. In juxtaposition to the interpersonal perspective on life, the transpersonal perspective is not a relationship, it is a participation.

We can see how easy it is to bring harmony into a marriage, or any other situation, if we can help people see life in a broader perspective. When people come to us with marital problems we do not have to straighten out their marital conflicts, all that is needed is to reveal to them that they are not in a marital relationship. There is really no such thing. The whole idea of relationships is based on an inadequate perception of reality. They need to see that they are jointly participating in existence as two individuals who love to be loving. Again, the idea of love needs to be broadened.

More often than not we are victims of a misconception about love. We have learned that in order to love, there must be an object. So we came to think in terms of object-love and were turning one another into objects, which is a subtle way of dehumanizing one another under the guise of love.

If we broaden our perspective on love, we see that we do not have to love one another, we just have to love being loving. And that takes care of everything. If we love being loving, we will have a natural desire to reflect the goodness of God in all situations. When we understand life in its spiritual dimension, it is an entirely different reality we live in.

Another point worth making is that when we see reality in its spiritual dimension, we are not so much concerned about experiences, we are concerned with reality, with what is real, what is beautiful, what is good, what is valid, what is harmonious, what is joyful, what is peaceful, what is assured. Our main desire is to be grateful all the time and to be joyous and free. Our value system becomes elevated, and spiritual values constitute our basic longings. In this way we transcend ourselves too. We rise higher in consciousness rather than just being preoccupied with experiences.

Let us ask: Where does an experience take place? If it is an intellectual experience, it is in the brain; if it is an emotional experience, it takes place in the neurovegetative system or the so-called splanchnic system. If it is a sensory experience, it takes place in the sense organs. These are three different kinds of experiences and they are all taking place in the organism. When we are oriented toward experiencing, we see ourselves as a biological organism. Experiences, just like interpersonal relationships, are both good and bad. Interestingly enough, they have a downward tendency; they always go from good to bad, from pleasure to pain.

So it is with everything if our mental horizon is flat and narrow because we are not living in reality. In order to be healthy and whole and integrated we have to be cognitively integrated with reality.

What does that mean? We have to develop a capacity to perceive reality in its full-dimensional scale. A narrow-minded man cannot see reality, a shallow-minded man cannot see reality, an experientially oriented man cannot see reality in its full dimension. Jesus used to say to people: "For this people's heart is waxed gross, and their ears are dull of hearing, and their eyes they have closed; lest at any time they should see with their eyes, and hear with their ears, and should understand with their heart, and should be converted, and I should heal them" (Matthew 13:15). Healing seems to have something to do with cognitive unfoldment.

Question: What is conversion? What does it mean to be converted?

Dr. Hora: There are three types of conversions:

1. Emotional conversion, when someone gets to like certain religious sentiments.

2. Ideological (intellectual) conversion, which is essentially conceptual, when someone accepts a certain system of beliefs which certain people are espousing. Someone can become converted to communism, conservatism, or anything conceptual. These forms of conversion have no existential relevancy.

3. Real conversion is cognitive, when someone wakes up to a realization that there is more to life than he previously believed and was able to see.

This real conversion is not religious, it is cognitive. It reveals a dimension of reality commonly called spiritual. St. Paul said: "While we look not at things which are seen, but at the things which are not seen: for the things which are seen are temporal; but the things which are not seen are eternal" (II Corinthians 4:18). It is interesting to consider that St. Paul was blinded at the moment of his conversion, which points up the cognitive, perceptual element in the change which took place in him. It was a cognitive conversion.

CASE PRESENTATION

A thirty-year-old white male, well educated, former Catholic priest. His problems are: occupational failures, sexual dysfunctions, obsessive ruminations, hemorrhoids, managerial ambitions, prejudice against minorities—blacks, Jews, subordinates—blasphemous ideas in church, hate of policemen, rape fantasies against his wife.

Commentary on Case Presentation

It is useful to remember that when patients are coming for help, they have overt rationalizations, conscious and unconscious reasons and expectations. It is good to clarify these things in the course of working with them, because if they are not clarified, the secret expectations can go on as an undercurrent, and communication is not completely open. This can give rise to misunderstanding.

There are two things we are looking for in existential psychotherapy: First, to clarify what the patient's expectations are. We try to get them to verbalize their overt expectations, and then we try to discern phenomenologically their covert desires. We have to confront them with this as soon as possible in an acceptable way and with certain tact. The second thing we seek is to know this individual's mode of being-in-the-world? Does it reveal itself? It can reveal itself in the context of the therapeutic encounter, and it can reveal itself in the context of the patient's history.

How would we characterize this patient's mode of being-in-the-world? In order to understand his mode of being-in-the-world, it would be helpful to clarify the difference between dominion and domination. The Bible says that God gave man "dominion over the fish of the sea, and over the fowl of the air, and over the cattle, and over all the earth, and over every creeping thing that creepeth upon the earth" (Genesis 1:26). Now what is the difference between dominion and domination? It is significant to note that the Bible does not say that man has dominion over his fellow man, he has dominion only over certain lower life forms. He also has dominion over his own thoughts. If the difference between dominion and domination is understood, then we see that this individual is a victim of a misperception of man's functioning in life. Man is endowed with a potential for higher intelligence than other life forms. He has a responsibility to care for them and exercise a beneficial dominion or influence over them, but he has no right to exercise dominion over his fellow man, not to mention domination. Domination is the imposition of one's own will upon others.

Now here we have an individual who is a victim of miseducation, just as we all tend to be. We have been educated to misperceive reality and misunderstand the Bible. We have been told that an

educated man "uses his head" in order to have control over his life
and every situation in which he may find himself. And the smarter
he is, the greater control he can exercise over his affairs and over his
fellow man. It is, therefore, very desirable to get a good education
and become intellectually proficient in all spects of life, including
religion, so that we may become masters of our affairs and captains
of our ships and may exercise executive or leadership qualities. The
assumption is that the cultivation of the intellect through education
can facilitate this kind of successful "managing" of life. So we see
that this individual is a victim of miseducation and of misperception
of what life is all about.

Essentially, the problem is called intellectualism. Intellectualism
is an error which has all sorts of implications for a man's mode of
being-in-the-world; it is domineering, competitive, sadistic, masochistic, intolerant, bigoted, and it is religiously hypocritical. And yet
this man is not to blame for anything, he is just a victim of miseducation. It is important that we exculpate him. We are told he is coming
for treatment to have someone relieve his guilt and his sense of
responsibility for failure. When we explain to him that he is a victim
of miseducation and misperception of life, he will find great relief,
which will make it possible for him to reconsider his total mode of
being-in-the-world.

We have heard that this patient suffers of obsessive thoughts and
sexual fantasies. Let us consider now what are obsessive thoughts
and what are sexual fantasies? The moment we understand this
patient's mode of being-in-the-world, all details reveal themselves in
a meaningful way. We heard something about toilet training and anal
fixation connected with obsessive thinking and hemorrhoids. Then
we heard about the dilemma of sexual fantasies in connection with
Catholic dogma of guilt and sin. If we consider these phenomena
separately and apart from the total picture of the patient's mode of
being-in-the-world, then we have nothing to go by but the classical
developmental theories of Freudian psychology. If we accept these
things on the basis of what somebody said about somebody else, then
we are guilty of inauthentic cliché thinking. Every symptom must be
understood in its proper context.

We have come to see that this patient's mode of being-in-the-world was under the influence of a belief in the importance of exercising managerial domination over every aspect of life. Therefore, it is understandable that in this case obsessive-compulsive ruminations were actually mental rehearsals of planned domineering activities. Analogously, the reported sexual fantasies and their acting out were not really sexual but exercises in managerial assertions of personal dominance over others.

Question: How is this therapy actually done?

Dr. Hora: When we gain a clear understanding of a patient's mode of being-in-the-world, everything falls into its place. The "how" is not a problem if we understand the "what." There is no technique in existential psychotherapy. It is a way of seeing, a way of perceiving, understanding, shedding light, and leading the patient toward a more harmonious life. It is important to know that everyone is innocent. Man is the victim of miseducation and of universally deficient cognitive ability. Once we understand this, we will not be judgmental. There is no one to blame except ignorance. Ignorance is not a person.

Session No. 6

OPERATIONALISM

Question: Could you talk more about phenomenology?
Dr. Hora: In phenomenology there is a term called "bracketing." It means putting aside preconceived notions. There is a story about an American professor who went to Japan to study Zen. He was introduced to a Zen Master, and this Zen Master invited him to tea. They were sitting at a table and the Zen Master was pouring tea. He kept pouring even after the cup was full and the tea was spilling over. The professor was saying, "You are spilling the tea!" And the Zen Master said, "This is your first lesson in Zen. To study Zen, the mind must be empty of preconceptions or else there is no room for anything to come in."

There are many things that seem very logical, natural, rational, and realistic, and yet they are not necessarily true. First we bracket them, then we throw them out. Whatever prevents us from seeing beyond what we are used to, we must not let it stand in the way. For instance, we are led to believe that it is important to remember everything from our past so that we might improve the present and prevent it from influencing the future. A lot of energy is being expended in helping people to remember in great detail their past, what happened, why it happened, and who is to blame for it.

There is a story about a man who was in analysis for about a year or two. His main problem was nail-biting. One day he met a friend who asked him: "How do you like your analysis?" He said, "It's great, I am telling you, everybody should have it. It is wonderful!" "Well, have you stopped biting your nails already?" asked the friend.

The man said, "No, but now I know why I do it." A French psychiatrist once said: *"On ne guérit pas en souvenant, mais on se souvient en guérissant."* In other words, "We don't get well because we remember, but we remember as we get well."

Now in existential psychotherapy we do not probe the past, we allow it to reveal itself in the course of gaining a better understanding of what is. There are certain questions which become superfluous in existential psychotherapy. The question "Why?" becomes completely superfluous. We don't ask the question "How?" because therapy is not an operational process. We don't ask the question "Who is to blame?" or "What should I do?" Mainly we ask two questions:
  1. What is the meaning of what seems to be?
  2. What is what really *is?*

The therapeutic process is not a relationship but a situation in which we jointly participate. It is an encounter situation where many aspects of the patient's mode of being-in-the-world reveal themselves. All that is needed is the open-minded receptivity which is devoid of preconceived ideas about what should be and what should not be. By the way, this is also a very important principle. Ordinarily, life is not really lived, it is conducted along routine, preconceived lines based on thoughts about what should be or what should not be. Ordinary life is pretension. If we made a practice of observing our thought processes, we would find that most frequently our thoughts have a tendency to revolve around what should be or should not be. We all have many preconceived ideas and it is very helpful to purify our consciousnesses, whether in the context of our therapeutic concerns, or in our private lives. We will find that if our consciousness is released from these preconceptions, we are much more able to perceive what really is.

Psychotherapy could be described as an endeavor to discern the good beneath the pathology. What is pathology made of? It is made of misperceptions. For instance, last week we had a case presentation here of an individual who misperceived the difference between dominion and domination. To exercise dominion is healthy, but to twist it around into dominance is a sickness. Now we can help a patient understand how he misperceives something and clarify to him what is existentially valid. Thereby he discovers that he really has healthy intentions which have become distorted through misinterpretations and misperceptions. So we could say that pathology consists of misconceptions of what is good, what is true, what is existentially valid. Earlier we said that existential psychotherapy is not interpretative but hermeneutic, elucidating, clarifying, helping people to see more clearly the existential issues. The interpersonal perspective intends to help people to get along with other people. Anybody can learn that, but it is not synonymous with being healthy. The existential approach aims to help people come into harmony with the fundamental order of existence.

What is the fundamental order of being? To understand it better, we must become aware that there are several obstacles to coming into harmony with it. And one of them is operationalism. What is operationalism? It is a concern with how to do things even before we have found out what is what is. There is a certain bent of mind which is always concerned with how to do things. This interferes with focusing attention on that which really is. It is necessary to place the "how to" concerns into secondary place so that we may be more fully aware of what is.

What is the nature of the fundamental order of being? It is perfect harmony, peace, assurance, gratitude, joy, love, freedom. The fundamental order of existence is spiritual and man is a spiritual being. Spiritual values are inherently health-promoting. The more we get immersed in spiritual values the healthier we become. But a warning must be sounded. We must make sure we do not confuse spiritual values with religious values. The Bible is not a religious book but a record of the evolution of human consciousness. Some people have the impression that religious and spiritual values are one and the same thing. Religious practices often amount to collective formalized endeavors to influence God; spiritual values make man available to God; they make it possible for us to be influenced by God. If we could influence God, we would be greater than God. Furthermore, most religions are based on the assumption that man belongs to the Adamic race, that he is the miscreation of an inept God. He created the race of Adam, which is inherently sinful, disobedient. But God created man perfect and good. This man was portrayed by Jesus Christ. "For as in Adam all die, even so in Christ shall all be made alive" (I Corinthians 15:22). Jesus presented the true idea of man, a spiritual model of man.

If we consider the fact that in Genesis there are two accounts of creation, and if we ask the question: What could be the meaning of this clearly contradictory record? we are led to the realization that the first account records what really is (the Christ idea), and the second account is a description of what seems to be (Adam, the material appearance, phenomenal man). Traditional religions have accepted the phenomenal world as a reality and become materialistic. Therefore, we have to differentiate between religion and spirituality. This may explain the popularity of oriental religions in the United States and shed some light on the widespread dissatisfaction with traditional religions. People are looking for something more meaningful and relevant but, of course, they are not finding it in oriental religions either, because these are also susceptible to trivialization. Human perceptivity is unequipped to see beyond what meets the eye and, therefore, there is the tendency to trivialize and materialize everything in life—religion, psychotherapy, concepts of health. It would take us too far to get into greater detail on these issues. Suffice it to say for now that it is by being immersed in spiritual values and endeavoring to actualize them existentially that we become healthy and enlightened.

CASE PRESENTATION

A twenty-nine-year-old male school teacher, youthful and muscular in appearance, seeks treatment after his marriage of two and a half years duration ended in separation at his wife's request. He is very successful as a teacher, but cannot find happiness in his social relationships.

Commentary on Case Presentation

We must guard against the temptation to speculate. We have to base our remarks on whatever information is available and not go beyond it. We have now spent thirty minutes speculating about this patient's relationships with other people as if, by figuring this out, we could help him to improve. We have fallen into the trap of reasoning within the context of the same assumptions the patient has. The patient presents a certain way of life—it is a shallow perspective on existence —and we are sucked into an endeavor which is not unlike trying to straighten out a snake or, as the Chinese sage puts it, "putting legs on a snake." No matter how many times we straighten out a snake, it will coil up again; there is no such thing as a straight snake. And there is no such thing as a lasting good relationship. In trying to help this patient to improve his relationships, we remain cognitively on the same level as he is. And the very problem is that the patient's perspective on life is a shallow one. So if we now ask the question, what is this patient's mode of being-in-the-world, the answer is— shallow thinking. His life is a series of endeavors to manage a viable system of relationships. This is just as impossible as it is to have a straight snake.

It makes no difference whatsoever whether someone is active or passive; most people are passive-aggressive anyway. Nobody is just passive, unless he is in a state of apathy temporarily. The important issue is: How does he perceive life? And this particular gentleman is highly influenced by contemporary psychological thinking. But he has also good qualities and talents which come to the foreground when he does not engage in managing relationships. He can function according to his inherent talents in teaching. He can be a brilliant teacher, because in teaching he is not in an interpersonal relationship, he transcends the situation. While he is a teacher, he can release his intelligence, love, and usefulness, and these qualities freely express themselves. Here again, if we understand the "what," the "how" offers itself naturally. The man needs to be helped to see life in a full-dimensional way. The essence of life is not interpersonal relationships but being a beneficial presence in the world, expressing all the inherent potentialities for good, for usefulness, entirely apart from preconceptions about what other people are thinking about what he is thinking.

There are five gates of hell, they are as follows: sensualism, emotionalism, intellectualism, materialism, and personalism. This gentleman is a victim of personalism. Personalism is thinking about what others are thinking about what we are thinking. In psychology it is called interpersonal relationships, and we will never help our patients by trying to improve their technique in relating to other people unless they have come to us to learn how to become politicians. But that would not be therapy; it would be schooling in psychopathology. In order to be healed, we must be concerned with spiritual values. We must start by pointing out to this individual the tremendous distance between his functioning as a teacher and his social and marital life, pointing out that he is really a gifted, intelligent image and likeness of God. But we can help him to see that the social life takes care of itself once one has succeeded in realizing one's true potential as an individual manifestation of Love-Intelligence. When Jesus said, "Be ye therefore perfect, even as your Father which is in heaven is perfect" (Matthew 5:48), he did not speak about nice relationships with people; he meant: express your God-given qualities and talents, become a beneficial presence in the world and everything else will be harmonious. When we devote ourselves to the task of expressing our inherent spiritual qualities, our social life is no problem, our marriage is harmonious, and our background is of no consequence.

Eventually, the patient will wake up to perceive broader issues in life than just seeking happiness in discotheques. He will wake up to the realization that it is not possible to find happiness in interpersonal relationships. Happiness must be brought into social situations. It is our happiness that makes our social life and marriage harmonious. We cannot get happiness out of our social life.

Question: Are you then saying that we shouldn't socialize and should become like hermits and loners?

Dr. Hora: We must be careful here not to fall into the error of dualistic thinking. What is dualistic thinking? Dualistic thinking is still another form of shallow thinking which says: "If it is not white, it is black."

The healthy alternative to relationships is participation. When a good teacher is teaching a class, he is involving the class, not in an interpersonal relationship with himself but in participation in the subject matter being taught. And that is a good teacher. What we have in teaching is a joint participation in a subject matter of shared interest. In marriage there is a joint participation in building a beautiful, harmonious life. And so the alternative to thinking in terms of interpersonal relationships is not schizoid withdrawal, it is participation in existence as a beneficial presence in the world. In interpersonal relationships there is no possibility of being healthy; they are inherently manipulative and horizontal. There is more to reality than the horizontal dimension.

Session No. 7

COMPASSION

Human beings are very complex and could be likened to a multifaceted crystal. Depending on what facet we look at, things will seem to make sense according to the particular way we are looking at them. There was a time when it was believed that the Earth was flat. Things seemed much simpler then, the sun seemed to rise in the east, set in the west, and move over the horizon. The Earth was believed to be the center of the universe, and all this could be plainly seen by anyone. It was all very simple, acceptable and comfortable, except that eventually there came along individuals who challenged these self-evident "truths." These individuals disturbed the status quo and they generated anxiety and upheaval. They were in danger of being burned at the stake. Every time someone comes along and points out that what has been taken for granted, and what seemed rational, logical, and comfortable, actually does not correspond to the truth, it disturbs us. What we would like to do is to kill the truth so as to preserve the status quo. It is troublesome to revise our thinking habits and be confronted with the fact that what seemed to be true, is not.

In the practice of psychotherapy we are similarly exposed to challenges, to new insights, and new ways of looking at man. If it was disturbing to the world to realize that the sun did not revolve around the Earth, and that the Earth was not the center of the universe, it is even more disturbing to realize that man is not what we assumed him to be and what he appears to be.

When we feel comfortable with a certain set of ideas, there develops an inertia of mind, and this inertia is reluctant to hear or to consider anything new. This was always going on in science, philosophy, religion, as well as in psychotherapy. This inertia, however, can be overcome. What is needed is an overriding love of the truth. Someone might ask: What is so great about truth that we should be willing to give it such great importance? The great value of truth, whether scientific or philosophical, is that it liberates; whereas error in any form, whether in science or religion, is progressively imprisoning, limiting.

It is common knowledge that phobias are very difficult to treat. Lately, it has been fashionable to treat them through behavioral methods. People are not being helped to understand anything, they are just being trained to overcome their fears through conditioning methods and without insights. The hope is that after they have overcome their symptoms, they may come to understand something. There is a way to be liberated from phobias through understanding the truth. I would like to tell of a case which was quickly healed. A young lady about sixteen years old, whose great hobby was horseback riding, suffered from a dreadful fear of fire. She was not in treatment but her mother was. On one occasion the mother mentioned that the child was afraid of fire. She was then asked what thoughts she entertains most often in connection with her daughter. She said, "I see her all the time involved with horses, that's all she is interested in, she is a real horsey girl." She was then told the following: "Well, isn't your child a spiritual being? Isn't she really a spiritual child of God? Could you behold the qualities of intelligence, love, grace, assurance, gratitude, and wholesomeness in her? Wouldn't it be better to think of her in terms of spiritual qualities rather than in terms of her passion for horses?" She agreed. That night, when they were setting the table for dinner, the child turned to her and said: "Mother, would it be all right if I lit the candles tonight?" And to her mother's great surprise, she took a box of matches and lit the candles without the slightest fear.

Now what happened here? Horses are known to be afraid of fire. When the mother began to see the child from a spiritual standpoint, the horsey qualities disappeared from her thoughts and the truth took over. Whenever the truth is known, it sets us free.

Always fundamental to healing is the patient's conscious and unconscious concept of his self-identity. This is crucial. "As man thinketh in his heart, so is he" (Proverbs 23:7). It is important to have an existentially valid concept of self-identity. Parents especially must be very careful how they are thinking about their children.

I know two young people, college graduates, one male the other female. Both have a strange way of suffering in life. They tend to make a mess of their situations and then mock themselves for having made a mess. They get fired from jobs, they bungle a project, and then they speak about it in a self-mocking way. They also have a tendency to mock others. Now what is the problem? It is very simple. They have grown up and accepted a deprecating concept of their self-identities. Perhaps they were exposed to some teasing and mocking from meaningful individuals in their childhood and have accepted it unthinkingly. Now they are trying to make a go of life with that kind of self-concept. In order to help these people, it is necessary to liberate them from their existentially invalid concepts of themselves and of others, and help them to realize that they are God's perfect spiritual children, worthy of all "acceptation."

CASE PRESENTATION

Patient is a thirty-six-year-old woman, a part-time editorial assistant. Her appearance is presentable, she is friendly and communicative. She complains of assorted fears (mugging, rape, burglary) and difficulties in social and family life. These became aggravated after her previous psychiatrist died suddenly at the age of thirty.

Commentary on Case Presentation

When we present a case, it is helpful to put aside temporarily our thoughts about the dynamics of the case. Let us just present purely the facts as they appear to us. Then let us wait and see what understanding unfolds. Otherwise, if the presentation is interspersed with the presenter's own interpretations, we get confused and we don't know where the patient ends and where the therapist's opinions begin.

What we have received here is a picture of a disturbed young lady, beset by many fears, and whose mother is not very helpful to her.

It may be desirable here to make a few remarks about countertransference. Countertransference is usually a liability in therapy, unless it is used to advantage. In what way can it be used to advantage in therapy? When we understand the meaning of our reaction we will suddenly understand the patient's mode of being-in-the-world. It is good to allow ourselves to become fully aware of the temptations which a patient's mode of being-in-the-world arouses within us. How would we describe the feelings, emotions, and reactions that this particular patient is arousing in us? When we are hostile we are not really hostile, we feel threatened; and when a patient seems to be hostile he is not really hostile, he is just afraid. If we see him as hostile, we condemn him, and then we cannot help him. It is absolutely impossible to help anyone if we condemn him in any way. So it is very helpful to avoid thinking about patients in terms of judgments; what we are aiming at is understanding. We want to understand the patient's mode of being-in-the-world, which means we want to understand how he perceives the world.

How does this patient perceive herself in the world? What are the thought processes which enter into her misperceptions about life? When we are aiming at understanding the patient's outlook on life, we don't get misled by superficial appearances which would tempt us to pass judgment. The moment we judge a patient he is beyond reach as far as we are concerned. The greatest therapeutic tool we have is compassion. If we cannot have compassion for a patient, we are not qualified to help him, which does not mean that we are unqualified. We may get into a situation where someone is so provoking and disturbing to us that we cannot have compassion for him; but this is temporary and we can always heal ourselves by withdrawing into prayer and meditation. We can ask our supervisor to help us develop the right thoughts about the patient, and by the time the next session comes around we are already healed of our countertransference reaction. It is of the utmost importance to meet all our patients with a clear awareness of compassion, because that is the foundation upon which a new self-concept can be built. What a patient needs from us is a new concept of self-identity based on his spiritual qualities rather than on his pathology. Patients come to us with their pathology and we meet them with our compassion and reveal to them their spiritual perfection. And it is this corrective emotional experience which is conducive to healing. But it is more than just a corrective emotional experience, we help patients to see the truth about themselves.

If we can appreciate a patient's spiritual qualities without reservations and in spite of all the pathology, then it is like pulling a pearl necklace out from a pile of garbage. The garbage disappears and what we have is the beautiful, the good, and the true. Everyone is essentially a perfect spiritual being. To bring this into consciousness is our job.

We are not asking our patients to believe anything or to accept anything. What happens in the therapeutic situation is a confrontation of two concepts: what the patient's concept is of himself, and what the therapist's concept is of the patient. And if the therapist's concept of the patient is a genuinely loving one, if he can clearly see the good in him, then the patient will perceive it. The issue in therapy is not to undo the patient's past, to persuade him, or to get him to believe or accept anything; it is witnessing to the truth up to the point where the patient begins to see it. "Whereas I was blind, now I see" (John 9:25).

We have to work on ourselves through prayer and meditation, and continually improve our understanding of our spiritual perfection. Otherwise what we are is "blind leaders of the blind" (Matthew 15:14).

Let us make one thing clear, namely, that we have absolutely no right to open the eyes of anyone unless explicitly requested to. But in proportion that our own eyes are free of the beam, we will spontaneously be beneficial presences in any situation. If we understand the Chinese saying: "The way to do, is to be," then we are not going to influence people, not even our patients. We are going to be influential. Influencing is trespassing, it is really a sin; to be influential is God's demand upon us. We do not aim to influence people, but we aim to be influential through the quality of our presence. It is what we know of the truth that determines the quality of our being, and the truth we know is present in our consciousness, is active there and colors the quality of our being. This in turn, communicates itself explicitly and implicitly to all those who are with us, whether it is a therapeutic or a social situation.

We have now arrived at an understanding of this patient's mode of being-in-the-world as characterized by a self-concept which proclaims: "I am a nuisance, I am a liability, and you better watch out because I am going to give you trouble and disgrace you if you aren't smart enough to keep away from me." In other words, the patient projects a mode of being-in-the-world that is not only destructive to herself but is also threatening to others by inducing a false sense of responsibility in people.

What is a false sense of responsibility? The patient implies: "You should do something on my behalf, but you are not competent to do it." Such a patient can drive the therapist up the wall. This patient is also throwing double binds. What is a double bind? "If you help me, you are no good; if you don't help me, you are no good." Such a patient can generate anxiety only in people who think of themselves as doers, whether in a professional or social setting. But if we know that we are not doers but manifestations of the light, then we cannot become panicky or frustrated or resentful. None of these things are affecting us; a countertransference reaction is not provoked, and we don't make irrational statements. So what we do with such patients is that we constantly endeavor to improve our compassion, and prayerfully seek to discern some spiritual qualities which are in evidence. For instance, there is evidence of intelligence in this patient. We are told that she is good at doing medical abstracts in her job. There is also capability and competency in this patient. The patient discovers that she is a perfect spiritual child of God and that everything else is of no importance. We are not what other people think us to be, we are really what God is thinking about us. The Bible says: "I know the thoughts that I think toward you, saith the Lord, thoughts of peace, and not of evil, to give you an expected end" (Jeremiah 29:11). What is the expected end that we are looking forward to? It is healing, liberation, *restitutio ad integrum,* that's what we are looking to. And that's how we become what we have always been.

When we speak of compassion and love, it could be easily misunderstood as weakness. There is nothing weak or jellylike about compassion and love. One can be very firm and find great strength in love. Love is not just softness, it may be gentle but it has the power of light. How does light destroy darkness? Gently but very effectively. And that is what love, compassion, understanding, receptivity does. The power of light which overcomes darkness, no matter what form darkness may assume.

Session No. 8

BELIEVING
AND DISBELIEVING

Question: What is interaction? What is nonverbal interaction?

Dr. Hora: In psychoanalysis there is a principle held that it does not matter what one thinks as long as one is not doing it. Is this really valid? For instance, according to this principle, entertaining lecherous thoughts would not be a problem. Jesus placed great emphasis on the importance of thoughts. He said that if one is only thinking of committing adultery, one has already committed it. This is a principle which goes counter to the psychoanalytic idea. What is this judgment we are liable to if we allow ourselves to entertain thoughts of lust, anger, hatred, prejudice, evil of any kind, or any other unloving thoughts? Jesus often said, "Take no thought . . ." His principles were right thinking. The way he saw life was that everything starts with a thought, that there is no action without thought, that there is no communication without underlying thoughts.

Thoughts can be conscious or unconscious, but that is not really the issue. The issue is: Are they loving thoughts or are they unloving thoughts? In psychiatry there is a fear of placing too much importance on thoughts, because of the belief that this could lead to magic thinking, that is, ascribing magic powers to thoughts and thus one could conceivably become psychotic. Or one could become an obsessional thinker.

So two things have been going on simultaneously in psychiatry. One was the underemphasis of the importance of thoughts, the other the overemphasis of it. We could say that psychiatrists were underemphasizing the importance of thoughts, and that patients tended to overemphasize it. Jesus had the right position from the standpoint of intelligent living. He said there is no power but love; love is the only power there is; therefore, if you want to be healthy, if you want to be a beneficial presence in the world, you must learn to discipline your thoughts in such a way that they may be prevalently loving thoughts. Should we happen to fall into a situation where we are flooded with unloving thoughts, we can quickly reject them and replace them with loving thoughts, and there will be no ill effect. But if we don't do this, if we do not live a disciplined mental life, we can become victims of our own unloving thoughts.

Jesus said something very relevant. He said: "A man's foes shall be they of his own household" (Matthew 10:36). What did he mean by that in the light of what we were just talking about? What could that mean? Our unloving thoughts will be most noticeable in our immediate surroundings; those closest to us are most aware of and most affected by our unloving thoughts. Sometimes we can function much better in the world than in our own homes. Sometimes it is easier to be kind to strangers than to our own family. But it behooves all of us to learn the discipline of mind whereby we reject unloving thoughts and constantly endeavor to maintain a loving outlook in any situation. That is how we become beneficial presences in the world.

Certainly we do not want to fall into the pathological error where we overestimate the power of our own thinking, either in the direction of its beneficence or in the direction of its evil-producing quality. How do we then reconcile the overemphasizing and de-emphasizing of the importance of thoughts? That is a dilemma. Suppose someone is cursing us and is saying all sorts of horrible things to us directly or secretly. What can happen? We may reject it and yet we may be somehow affected. Cursing has been in vogue from time immemorial. Does evil thinking have power? Only if one believes in it. The problem is not so much the curse but the belief in the power of the curse, the fear of evil.

We are used to thinking in terms of verbal and nonverbal interaction and communication through attitudes, gestures, and behavior. But there is more. It is helpful to consider the possibility that an event does not have to be external in any way, it can take place purely in consciousness and it can have a salutary effect on ourselves, on a loved one, or on someone who is seeking help. I am reminded here of someone who wrote me a letter telling about his bleeding ulcer of the stomach. Two days later I received another letter saying: "The moment I sent the letter to you, the bleeding stopped and my ulcer healed." Even before I received the first letter, he was healed of his stomach ulcer. Something happened in his consciousness in the course of writing the letter. It was an event in consciousness. This is the mystery of consciousness. In psychoanalysis this would probably be called a transference cure. If it were a transference cure, it would not last, there would be a relapse the moment the transference wore off or turned sour—and we know that transference can easily turn sour. It is believed in psychoanalysis that transference cures are not to be taken seriously, they tend to be temporary. In this case the healing remained permanent; therefore, something more must have taken place than just transference. There must be some other factor working here which made a beneficial shift in consciousness lasting. What could it be? Clearly, there is a third party which must be taken into consideration. In a transference relationship, whether it is beneficial or harmful, there is only self and other, patient and therapist. You may recall that we called it the horizontal mode, indicative of shallowness of thought. But in real life there is much more, there is also the dimension of the spirit, the transcendent, the third party called GOD. That third party is present.

So what happens when a favorable shift in consciousness takes place in a therapy which is not interpersonal but transpersonal? Then this favorable shift is not a transference shift in thinking, but the power of divine love entering into consciousness and neutralizing all fearful, unloving, pathogenic thoughts. In what way is divine love, spiritual love, different from interpersonal sympathies or positive transferential thoughts? It is about as different as a line is from a sphere. What is the difference between a line and a sphere? Dimensionality. Therefore, the consequences of such an event in consciousness are qualitatively different.

It is helpful to learn to think in terms of qualities of consciousness rather than interpersonal communication through gestures, attitudes, behavior, which are communicated only visually. There is a greater depth to life than what is visible on the surface. The whole process of therapy can move from the surface of interpersonal interaction into the issues of dimensions of consciousness. Man is an individualized manifestation of cosmic consciousness; therefore, it is the quality of his consciousness that determines his state of health. And whenever we are engaged in helping people to improve their lives, it is best to become concerned with their consciousness rather than just with their behavior or activity, or their relationships with other people.

Ideally, if we are well advanced in the work of existential psychotherapy, there is no occasion for transference to develop. Is this possible? Is it possible to have an intensive psychotherapeutic process going on without transference to develop? When we are able to conduct our work in such a way that transference does not develop, all energy flows into a value system which is not solely our own, for it is a transcendent value system. The patient is then oriented toward something greater than we are. Then the therapy is not characterized by a line but by a sphere. There is no transference, there is only a constant process of clarification of dark areas of thought. Such therapy is hermeneutic.

Question: Doesn't evil have power? Don't we have to take it into consideration? Didn't Jesus believe in the evil one?

Dr. Hora: The *belief* in evil is the problem. Love is like light and evil is like darkness, and light abolishes darkness. But one of the great tragedies of mankind is that there is a belief in the power of evil. For instance, as long as we believe ourselves to be susceptible to accidents, we are susceptible to accidents. But when love fills consciousness, it helps us to dispel the belief in the power of evil. The nature of evil is essentially hypnotic. The more people believe in some danger, the more real it appears and the more powerful it seems to be. Hypnotists find it easier to hypnotize people in groups. The power of the hypnotist is no particular power, a hypnotist has no power. Hypnotic phenomena appear from the belief of the subjects. What is contagious is the belief. The more people participate in a belief, the stronger it appears to be. This explains mass hysteria, collective panic, violence, fashions, looting, pornography, and all the various things that come and go. A free society such as ours is exposed to many fads which sweep the country from time to time.

From time immemorial evil has claimed to have power. But today we understand that the power is not in the evil, the power of evil lies in the tendency to believe in the evil. When this tendency is recognized, the wind is removed from the sail of evil and it collapses, it has no power.

Question: How do we account for the tendency of man to believe in evil? How about children who are victims of evil, do they believe in evil?

Dr. Hora: Children are extensions of parental consciousness. Whatever the parents believe, consciously or unconsciously, the children believe as well. We know that there are such things as collective beliefs. Fads are phenomena of collective beliefs. At times it is difficult not to be swept along by collective beliefs. If we ask the question: How can we explain the existence of such proclivity in man? then we will have to say that man has quite a number of proclivities which are derived from his inability to cognize what really is. "Natural man receiveth not the things of the Spirit of God: for they are foolishness unto him: neither can he know them, because they are spiritually discerned" (I Corinthians 2:14).

Question: Do you mean to say that if we disbelieve in evil, nothing can happen to us?

Dr. Hora: To believe or to disbelieve is the same. Let us not fall again into this dualistic trap. The alternative to believing in evil is not disbelieving in it.

Question: If believing and disbelieving is the same, what else is there left?

Dr. Hora: Let us try something very simple. Suppose someone believes that two and two is five; then he is in trouble as far as his arithmetic is concerned. But suppose he disbelieved that two and two is five, would that help him? Disbelieving is not the solution to the problem of believing. What is the solution? The solution is always to know the truth. "Ye shall know the truth and the truth shall make you free," free from the dualism and the thralldom of believing and disbelieving.

Is there a way of improving our mode of being-in-the-world to such an extent that the possibilities of evil befalling us would be minimized? When we learn right thinking and asking the right questions, there is hope of understanding and there is hope of growing into a more harmonious mode of being-in-the-world.

There is a tendency to make the following mistakes:

1. Dualistic thinking.
2. Cause-and-effect thinking.
3. Seeking to blame.
4. Horizontal thinking.
5. Shallow thinking.
6. Narrow thinking.
7. Calculative thinking.

None of these things are helpful. What do we mean when we ask about meaning? Suppose something unpleasant happens to us. Suppose, for example, a man falls down and breaks a leg. Let us also suppose that he has someone who can help him to understand. It would be helpful to him to recollect the thoughts passing through his mind just prior to the accident. Invariably, we will find that he had been fearful, resentful, or jealous, that he had some sort of unloving thoughts in his consciousness. Now are we saying that he should blame himself? That would not be fair and it would be most unkind and unloving to say this to him. But what could we say? We could say that thoughts in general have a tendency to externalize themselves in experiences.

We do not do our own thinking either. Who does our thinking? Thoughts *obtain*. That's an interesting word. Thoughts obtain in consciousness. If we are looking in one direction, we obtain different thoughts than if we are looking in another direction. In other words, stimuli reach our awareness and generate certain thoughts that we can either retain or lose. The thoughts we extend hospitality to will have a tendency to externalize themselves in behavior, action, symptom, or experience. A Chinese sage said: "We cannot prevent birds flying over our heads, but we need not let them nest in our hair." All sorts of thoughts are constantly obtaining in consciousness, but we have the power to select which ones we shall entertain or reject.

Question: What is the difference between rejecting certain thoughts and repressing them?

If we are repressing thoughts, we are extending hospitality to them but putting them in a closet. Whatever is in consciousness has a tendency to externalize itself in behavior, action, speech, symptoms, or experiences. Therefore it behooves us to be very careful of our guests and be very selective about the thoughts we entertain.

It is the truth entertained in consciousness that is the healer and not the therapist. Every little glimpse of the truth helps the patient to become healthier and relieve whatever problems he is preoccupied with. We only clarify the problem in order to make the truth more poignantly clear. For instance, a man allows himself to entertain thoughts of burdensomeness, self-pity, or resentment—perhaps fantasies of being a victim. Then what he needs is to realize that this kind of thinking is dangerous. He needs to be vigilant, sober, and alert and to replace such thoughts with something more existentially valid, like forgiveness, love, kindness, generosity, hope, prayer. We must not allow ourselves to dwell on such thoughts as resentment, hatred, or self-pity. That is why prayer is so important. Prayer is a method whereby we can tune in on existentially valid ideas. We are safest when our consciousness is filled with love.

Question: How do we know that love is the only power?

Dr. Hora: We must specify that spiritual, nonpersonal love is the only power. God is love, and beside him there is no other power. What do we mean by nonpersonal or transpersonal love? It is love that gives itself. We do not personally give love, we become instruments of this love. We do not produce love, we allow love to express itself through us. How do we do that? That is prayer in action. How do we reach that point where this can happen? By being interested in it. We can say: To be enlightened is easy, it's just difficult to be interested in it. The word "interest" consists of the word *inter-esse,* which means to be between, that is, to be involved. To be interested in something means to be mentally involved with it.

Session No. 9

LOVE-INTELLIGENCE

Question: How do you discern meanings?

Dr. Hora: We have defined meaning as the mental equivalent of a phenomenon. When we sit with a patient, the patient presents to us certain problems, and if we know the right questions to ask, the meaning will then reveal itself to us. The emphasis must be on *revealing* itself to us. Sometimes inexperienced therapists who have not yet been liberated from the operational and calculative way of thinking and seeing life, have a tendency to try to figure it out. Meaning cannot be figured out, the meaning of phenomena reveals itself to us. If we take a Ping-Pong ball, submerge it in water and let go of it, it will invariably pop up to the surface. It is similar with meaning. If we let go of trying to figure out the meaning, it will spontaneously reveal itself to us.

Question: How do you do this therapy?

Dr. Hora: As we said previously, neither the therapist nor the patient can do it. Love-Intelligence does the therapy. Who is this person called Love-Intelligence? How can we be sure that it is really so? It is an axiom of traditional psycotherapy that there must be a good relationship between therapist and patient in order for progress to occur. This is but a distant shadow of the power which we call Love-Intelligence, which is present and actually does the work. How does Love-Intelligence do the work?

Question: Would you explain to us what Love-Intelligence means?

Dr. Hora: Love-Intelligence is the basic attribute of God, the most fundamental aspect of divine reality. It becomes manifest every time

we let it. *God helps those who let Him!* When we do not understand
the nature of Love-Intelligence, its omnipotence, its omnipresence
and omniscience, we are not aware of it and we slip into the operational mode of working. It is an invisible power, like buoyancy. Has
anyone ever seen buoyancy? No one can see buoyancy—but we can
certainly lean on it, can't we?

Let us take swimming as an analogy. What would be the right
question to ask about swimming? Some people have a hard time
learning to swim because they are inclined to ask, how do you do it?
If we are going to ask the wrong question, we are going to have a
hard time learning anything. People who have difficulty in learning
to swim, probably have in the back of their minds the wrong questions. How do you do it? What would be the right question? What
is swimming? Swimming is floating. The essence of swimming is
floating. Once we understand that, doesn't it make it easier to learn
to swim?

Now the question arises, is floating passive? Is it correct to say that
we surrender ourselves to the water when we float? If we were to
surrender ourselves to the water, we would drown. What is required
in order to float? What kind of activity is required in floating? Attention. Floating is an activity occurring in consciousness. Floating is
not passive, floating is not surrendering to the water, floating is not
relaxing. It is the quality of consciousness which is alert, attentive,
and responsive to that *invisible power* present in the water which is
called buoyancy. If we judge by appearances, floating may seem
passive.

But we must not judge by appearances, we need to understand
what is really involved. It is a quality of attention. How would we
describe the quality of attention which is required for successful
floating? The primary requirement is to love floating. We have to love
it and we have to be responsive. In other words, the essential quality
of consciousness which is required for floating is *loving responsiveness
to the invisible power upon which we are endeavoring to lean.*

What will make it possible to float? Understanding of buoyancy.
We have to move from faith to realization. And the same applies to
life when it comes to God, or Love-Intelligence. First we doubt, then
we believe, then we get faith, and then we move from faith to realiza-

tion. And when we have realized, we've got it. This power called Love-Intelligence provides us continually with what is needed to understand the meaning of phenomena, it gives us the intelligence to clarify them, and it inspires us with right solutions to whatever seems to be the problem.

So we see that psychotherapy is not being *done* by anybody; it is allowed to occur. It is not passive; neither is it active. It is reverent, loving responsiveness to that which *is* from moment to moment.

It is interesting to consider the fact that some people swim with great effort, while others swim effortlessly for hours on end without getting tired; they don't even get winded. And the same goes for life and for psychotherapy. The difference lies in the quality of awareness. If we believe that we have to do our own swimming, it will then be a very strenuous, exhausting exercise and we will be poor swimmers. But if we understand that there is a sustaining power present, then it becomes easier and easier. Similarly, if we believe that we have to get somebody well in psychotherapy, that we have to cure him, that we have to personally change him, we will have a very strenuous job and we will get exhausted and frustrated.

This reminds me of a story about two psychiatrists who worked in a professional building. At the end of the day they would ride down together in the elevator. One was an elderly gentleman, very dapper and neat looking, the other was a young man and he was exhausted and tired looking. One day the younger man said, "I don't know how you do it. All day long you were working, seeing one patient after another, and yet you are not showing any tiredness at all. I am exhausted from listening to all those patients. Tell me how do you do it?" The older man replied, "Who listens?" Of course this is not what we are trying to do. There is a way of working actively, effectively, and effortlessly by letting Love-Intelligence do the work. In the Bible there is a mysterious saying which goes like this: "My Father worketh hitherto, and I work" (John 5:17). In terms of what we were talking about, it means: Love-Intelligence is doing the work and I am continually conscious of it; therein lies my participation in the work. This principle applies universally. We can learn to do any kind of work—even physical labor—intelligently, with love, and with minimal effort.

The question is sometimes asked: Are you always successful, or do you have to send some patients to someone else? Well, a therapist is never successful, but Love-Intelligence is always successful, and to the extent that we allow Love-Intelligence to do the work, we shall see beneficial results taking place. But it is not for us to determine what should happen, or how it should happen, or when it should happen.

CASE PRESENTATION

Patient is a white male, twenty-eight years old, a novice in a religious order. He is neat, weak, and diffident, much younger in appearance than his years, with a slightly mincing walk. Presented himself as a "sweet little boy."

He is referred by the novice master because of his difficulty in relating to others in the community.

The problems are his lack of a sense of identity, a tendency to live in fantasy, feminine identification, and hostility.

Commentary on Case Presentation

This case stimulates us to ask a number of questions: What is this young man's mode of being-in-the-world? What is effeminacy and what is virility from an existential standpoint?

The categories of passivity and activity are not helpful here. From an existential standpoint only dead people are passive. What is effeminacy? It is an idea about happiness. Some people believe that they could be happier in a feminine role, others believe they could be happier in a masculine role; it is just an idea. Certain ideas are more socially acceptable than other ideas. If a man gets the idea that he could be happier in a feminine way and sees that this idea is socially unattractive, he will try to find a rationale with which to justify such an unacceptable idea. He may often blame someone for it. This patient says, "My father gave me a doll for Christmas and therefore I am effeminate." It sounds plausible—but so what? Once he finds a cause, he has an excuse. He has not really understood anything, he has only provided himself with an explanation. He who seeks reasons only finds excuses. Effeminacy does not have a cause, it only has a meaning.

The meaning of effeminacy in this case seems to be a desire to be free to enjoy life according to one's own fancy, and somehow to reconcile it with circumstances. So the problem is that we are faced here with a particular way of trying to find happiness in life. This young man is in triple jeopardy because his way of seeking happiness is not compatible with social restrictions and religious taboos; neither is it existentially valid.

Question: Wouldn't you say that it would be therapeutically desirable for him to become virile?

Dr. Hora: Certainly not. Happiness cannot be found in either masculinity nor femininity, not even in bisexuality or polymorphous perversity. There are five misdirected ways in which people try to find happiness. We have already discussed them. They are called the five gates of hell: 1. sensualism, 2. emotionalism, 3. intellectualism, 4. materialism, 5. personalism. Which particular gate of hell is the dwelling place of our patient? Sensualism. There will inevitably come a time when this young man will become very dissatisfied with life, and then he will be ready to exchange his misdirected mode of seeking happiness for something that is existentially valid. What is an existentially valid way to seek happiness? It is helpful if a therapist understands this. Do we have some authoritative information available to us? The Bible puts it very plainly: "This is life eternal, that they might know thee the only true God, and Jesus Christ, whom thou hast sent" (John 17:3). Now in what way does this relate to happiness? What's so happy about knowing God? Ordinarily we think that the knowledge of God makes us religious; it seems to belong in the domain of religion. But here we are talking about exchanging the pleasures and the excitement of sensualism, effeminacy, and homosexuality for knowing God.

Question: Since this patient lives in a monastery, is he not seeking God?

Dr. Hora: Not everyone who enters a monastery is seeking to find God, and not everyone who enters psychotherapy is looking for help. Again, we must not judge by appearances. However, it would be very helpful to understand how in the world getting to know God would give us more happiness than, for instance, sex.

We must understand the difference between pleasure and happiness. What is the difference between pleasure and happiness? Pleasure is an illusory experience inseparable from pain; there is no pleasure without pain. Happiness is spiritual and is an aspect of being in conscious harmony with the fundamental order of existence. Where there is happiness, pleasure is an incidental by-product of no great significance. The less significance we ascribe to pleasure, the less pain there will be in our lives. Contrariwise, the more emphasis we place on pleasure, the more shall we suffer pain, sickness, and strife. It is not a sin or a crime to have pleasure, but it is only valid if it is a by-product of happiness. Sex is only valid if it is an incidental aspect of love, otherwise it is just masturbation. What is masturbation? It is a quest for sensual pleasure invariably followed by an unpleasant aftertaste. For a man involved in seeking happiness through sensualism, it may take a while to reach a point of willingness to consider the possibility of something better. When this patient will become ready to receive this message, he will lose interest in the thrills of effeminacy and homosexuality, and he will understand them to be just childishness.

In the meanwhile, however, he could be helped by seeing that he cannot blame anyone else for his particular choice of pleasure seeking. Blaming is irrelevant and not helpful. If we are pursuing existentially invalid aims in life, we are constantly running into trouble, and we go from one crisis to another. Of course, a crisis is always an opportunity. When a patient is in a crisis, this is the opportunity to help him. As long as a patient is comfortable, not much is happening, except getting ready for the moment when something will be seriously considered.

The word "responsibility" is loaded with implications of blame. First of all, the patient is not to blame, neither is his father. Remember the story from the Bible where the disciples asked Jesus who was to blame that a child was born blind? We must be very careful not to blame. The culprit is always ignorance. If the patient understands that he personally is not to blame, he can more easily understand that no one else is to blame. And when there is no one to blame, we come face to face with the specter of ignorance. Ignorance is embarrassing; people would rather blame someone, or blame themselves, or feel guilty. As long as that is allowed to go on, there is no possibility of change. If someone is to blame, there is an excuse; and if we have an excuse, there is stagnation. It is remarkable how unwilling we are to admit to ignorance. We do not like to know that we don't know.

Session No. 10

NIHILATION

The word "responsibility" has to be applied carefully. Responsibility is not synonymous with blame. This must be made clear to the patient, and it must be particularly clear to ourselves. Responsibility means the ability to respond. Man has the ability to respond to the good, the true, the beautiful, and the valid. This is a God-given ability, that is, response-ability. Blame is an entirely different matter. In common usage the words blame and responsibility are often used interchangeably, and much confusion comes from this.

Choice is not necessarily connected with responsibility, one can choose out of ignorance. One can be ignorant of the fact that one has the ability to respond, so that one can be in double darkness. It is the task of the therapist to shed light wherever there is darkness. He can do it by leaning on Love-Intelligence, because Love-Intelligence is constantly present and revealing itself to him as an understanding of the meaning of phenomena.

We cannot separate psychotherapy from life because it is a segment of life, an aspect of life. We are not technicians of psychotherapy, we are therapeutically beneficial presences in the world. Our beneficence is spontaneous and continuous, and not limited to our professional life. Everything in the life of a therapist has to be wholesome, otherwise he is just pretending.

What is pretentiousness? One of the most unhappy traits in the profession is pretentiousness. What is pretension? Pretending to be something which one is not. Pretending to be healthier, more virile, more feminine; pretending to know, pretending to love. What does the word "pretending" mean? Putting something in front. Putting up a front. Pretending makes life difficult. Much of social anxiety has to do with unconsciously endeavoring to pretend to be something which we are not yet. We have an idea of how we should be and then we proceed to pretend to be that.

There was a time when there was much dispute about whether the therapist should sit behind the desk or beside the desk, whether the couch should be in this corner or that. All sorts of technical considerations and artificialities were being considered and this, of course, was pure operationalism. Operationalism is the belief that one can do the being. "I am what I do . . ."

In a therapeutic situation, just as in a class, there are three ways we can avoid learning something. One is if we agree, the other is if we disagree. The third is if we are daydreaming. It is important to bring this to the patient's attention as soon as possible. We can make it clear to him that the only way to benefit from a session, or a lecture, is if we are interested in understanding something.

Right from the beginning we can make it clear to the patient what is required of him in order to benefit and to come to know. The patient is thereby forewarned. Another pitfall which needs to be clarified to patients is the difference between knowing that is information and knowing that is transformation. For instance, there are patients who ask permission to write things down. Some patients even ask permission to record the session. It stands to reason that if a patient writes down what is said, he is collecting information, and that does not help. That is why one cannot be healed by reading a book, one cannot be transformed with the help of information. The very purpose of writing something down is to help us forget. If we have it on paper, we don't have to have it in our hearts. Therapy is transformation. The quality of knowledge is radically different. Information remains intellectual knowledge, transformation is existential knowledge. It alters one's perceptions and motivations and improves one's mode of being-in-the-world.

The third type of individual, one who daydreams, gets very little out of a lecture or therapeutic session because he is interested in neither transformation nor information but in feeling good. His mode of being-in-the-world is self-indulgent. There are three forms of self-indulgence: sensual, emotional, and intellectual. Once a patient came in late and said, "I almost didn't make it today." The therapist answered, "Now that you have made it, are you going to be here?" It is important to get the patient to realize that he is not really paying attention. And then we make it a temporary objective of our work to help the patient develop his focusing abilities and pay attention. Usually, when patients realize that the therapist pays attention to them, they will become interested.

It is important, however, that we have no special interests of our own besides understanding the patient. Sometimes a therapist may be mentally involved with his own project, such as: "How am I going to present this case at the next case conference?" Or, "How could I produce a good result here?" When we have our own project, the patient has his own project. But when we are wholeheartedly focusing on one single thing, namely, to understand him, to understand his mode of being-in-the-world, he will pay attention. The quality of attention in the therapist can improve the quality of attention in the patient.

When we are discussing a patient, it is important to keep in mind one issue at a time. For instance, we began talking about the difficulty of maintaining a meaningful communication with the patient. Pretty soon we have slipped into discussing his dynamics. That's a different issue. Dynamics is one issue, communication another. The two may be related but not necessarily.

We mentioned that there are three ways of not benefiting from either therapy or from a lecture, namely, by agreeing, by disagreeing, or by being "not there." What is the requirement on the part of the therapist for good communication to come into being? What is it about some therapists that they have no problems in communication? There are some individuals who can go into a mental hospital and sit down with a patient who hasn't spoken for years to anybody, and pretty soon the patient will start talking, whereas others may have tried for years to speak to this patient and he would get worse every time he was approached. What is this mysterious quality? Is it magic? No, it is motivation. The therapist must have the right motivation. In order for communication to take place in a meaningful and therapeutically beneficial way, there are certain requirements. One of the first requirements is that the therapist must be free from his desire to therapeutize. This is not easy. The desire to therapeutize may mean to the patient that he is being intruded upon and manipulated. The quality of presence in every one of us is different and it is determined by our value system and by our motivation.

One of the most frequent motivations of a psychotherapist is to therapeutize. This is inevitable, especially among those therapists who have an operational approach to life. If the therapist's mode of being-in-the-world is an operational one, his patients will manifest a great deal of resistance. Nobody likes to be therapeutized. So what then is it that can facilitate communication? There has to be a quality of *letting-be.* Many people misunderstand the principle of letting-be as leaving alone. There is a very subtle but radical difference between letting be and leaving alone. Letting-be is a reverent form of spiritual love, leaving alone is neglect. Letting be is rather difficult to learn.

Let me just quickly comment on the word "acceptance." Who are we to accept or not accept anyone? The moment we think this way, we have immediately set up a certain kind of structure wherein we are superior to the patient. The category of acceptance is better left out, we are not acceptors nor rejectors, we are there to understand whatever reveals itself from moment to moment, and we are available to comment on it in case someone is interested. If not, we will sit there in quiet receptivity to that which *is* from moment to moment. It is total unobtrusiveness in the spirit of love. We are available to the patient. We sit with him in that spirit of availability and help to clarify whatever he may desire to know or to understand.

Previously we were talking about influencing. Influencing is a great curse in life—in friendship, family life, business, and profession —and it is absolutely poisonous in therapy. Certainly we have no right to try to influence our patients in any direction whatsoever; however, we can be influential by the quality of our presence and by our availability to clarify what we have understood and what is asked of us. When we sit with a patient in that spirit, there is usually no difficulty in communication. Pretty soon the patient begins to ask questions, and more and more questions arise. Whenever something is asked, we are there to comment on it to our best understanding.

If we happen to understand *what* is, the question *"how?"* does not arise. Therapy is a hermeneutic process of clarifying whatever needs clarification. And it is the clarity of understanding of certain issues that has the power to heal the patient. The healing power is not in the therapist, it is in the correctness of his clarifications. It is the truth that heals, not the man who bears witness to the truth. "The finger pointing to the moon is not the moon," say the Zen Masters. So this way we don't do anything, the patient doesn't do anything; therapy isn't being *done*, it is spontaneously unfolding as a progressive process of clarification, dawning.

Question: If you are not a person, what are you?

Dr. Hora: Does anyone know the story of Yen-Hui? Yen-Hui was a legendary figure in ancient China. He was a disciple of a famous Taoist sage by the name of Chuang-tzu. This Yen-Hui was also a prominent figure at the Imperial Court and was to become an adviser to the emperor. This emperor happened to have a great predilection for chopping off the heads of his advisors if they made a mistake. It was, therefore, a dangerous job. Yen-Hui was afraid of this job and came to his teacher for advice. He said to his teacher, "I don't think I am sufficiently enlightened to be safe in this exalted position." Chuang-tzu said to him, "In that case, you must retire and practice mind-fasting." Yen-Hui asked, "What is mind-fasting?" Chuang-tzu gave him the following instruction: "When you want to hear with your ears, don't listen with your ears; when you want to see with your eyes, don't look with your eyes; when you want to understand with your mind, don't think with your mind. Listen, see, and understand with the spirit." Yen-Hui retired and spent three years practicing this discipline. After three years he returned to his teacher and said, "Master, I think I am ready." Chuang-tzu said, "Well, prove it." And so Yen-Hui said, "Before I practiced mind-fasting I was sure I am Yen-Hui; but now, after I have practiced mind-fasting, I have come to realize that there never was a Yen-Hui." His teacher said, "You are ready."

Now what did he mean by this? If he never was Yen-Hui, then what was he? And if Yen-Hui never was, what are we? Yen-Hui discovered that he was not a person with an ego of his own, a mind of his own, opinions of his own, that he was an individual divine consciousness, a manifestation of Love-Intelligence. He became a beneficial presence in the world who does not lean on personal opinions but on inspired wisdom. Such a man lives in safety. The Bible describes such a man in similar circumstances. His name was Daniel.

CASE PRESENTATION

A thirty-four-year-old married woman neat, clean, simply dressed, mother of five children, seeks treatment for boredom, loneliness, disinterest in her children and husband. She sleeps a great deal and drinks in order to sleep longer. She neglects her work and cannot keep a job. Nevertheless, she is able to go out of the house and meet people. She joined the Welcome Wagon and went to a meeting of the National Organization of Women (NOW). She said, "It is a joke, all of them want to run away." After one session in therapy, she paid off the therapist and announced that she would not see her again.

Commentary on Case Presentation

This patient presents us with an interesting differential diagnostic challenge. What is her mode of being-in-the-world? Is she schizoid? Is she a detached schizophrenic? Is she depressed? She is none of these. A schizoid patient would never join the Welcome Wagon. A detached schizoid patient would probably never go to a NOW meeting. A depressed patient would not be able to communicate as well as this patient does. Then what could be the meaning of her strange behavior? What did she do to her therapist? She annihilated her in the first session. Having one session and proclaiming that she will not return, is a form of nihilation. It reveals the meaning of her life-style. The patient has a nihilating mode of being-in-the-world, which means that she seeks to negate or destroy the positive values of life. This appears to be a serious condition.

The danger here is the possibility of suicide. By commiting suicide, we can annihilate the world. Suicide is the ultimate form of self-confirmation. This also presents a difficult therapeutic problem. Such a mode of being-in-the-world can be progressive. Whatever anyone wants, this patient will want him not to have it. Suppose the therapist would reveal a certain eagerness to help, then this patient would want to deprive him of the pleasure of successfully helping her.

Whatever anybody would cherish, this patient would want to destroy. The therapist must not reveal any kind of personal desire in such a situation. If we don't want anything, there is nothing to annihilate. On this basis, something could get started with such a patient. If there is nothing to annihilate, then it is possible to communicate.

Sometimes, when we become very bitter about life, it disturbs us if someone has anything he cherishes. If a child is unhappy and another child has a toy, then the unhappy child wants to destroy the toy. If a therapist is happy being a therapist, then such a patient will want to render him into a nontherapist. One way to render a therapist into a nontherapist is by not coming back.

It was mentioned that the patient lacked enthusiasm. It is indeed enthusiasm which this patient needs most of all, and if we want to help her get it, we need to know what enthusiasm is. Sometimes enthusiasm is confused with ambition. What is the difference between enthusiasm and ambition? Ambition is a desire to make it in life on one's own steam, a desire to achieve certain objectives through personal effort. But enthusiasm is something entirely different. What does the word mean? *En-theos* means to be with God. Enthusiasm means that we are consciously aware that God is with us. If we have an awareness that all things work together for good for those who love God, we have enthusiasm. And this is exactly what this patient desperately needs. A sense of being loved, supported, guided, protected, and provided with infinite energy by a transcendent power. When we have that awareness, we have enthusiasm and we are healthy.

Now the question is, suppose the patient would return to her therapist—and it can happen—how would the therapist help her become enthusiastic? Above all, the patient would need to come to know that she is loved, that her life has meaning and purpose, that everyone has unlimited possibilities for good, regardless of whether one is male or female, married or unmarried, living alone or in a family. None of these things alter the fact that man has unlimited potentialities when reflecting the infinitude of Love-Intelligence.

Question: Do you mean the therapist should show affection to the patient?

Dr. Hora: We need to understand the difference between love and affection. What is the meaning of the word "affect"? Affect is emotion. Affection is the expression of positive emotions. On the human level we are mostly expressing feelings and emotions; we are affectionate toward one another under favorable circumstances. But love is much more. We must not confuse the two. We are affectionate toward those who make us feel good. Our affections dry up quickly if someone doesn't make us feel good. A patient once said, "I feel very bad if I don't feel good." Affections are always labile, precarious. How did we define love previously? We have spoken of love as a desire to reflect the good of God. Love is always derived from God. It is not something we produce, it is something that *is.* We can help a patient become aware of the fact that this love really is available to all, it fills the universe, it is the medium in which we live and move and have our being. Whenever we take the trouble to mentally affirm its presence and endeavor to become conscious of it, our outlook on life becomes immediately transformed, elevated. Our problems diminish. We may become so proficient in doing this that we may be enthusiastic most of the time. And this is how this patient could be helped to become enthusiastic, even permanently healed.

Question: What is the difference between nihilation and nihilism?

Dr. Hora: Nihilism is a philosophy which claims that nothing is real. If there is nothing, there is nothing to annihilate. A nihilating individual says: "There are many things which other people cherish and I want to annihilate them." There was a Zen Master by the name of Hui-neng who made the following startling statement: "From the beginning nothing is." What did he mean by that? This utterance, made several thousand years before Christ, was later elaborated by Heidegger and Sartre. These philosophers are speaking about nothing in the sense of "no thing." From the beginning "no thing" is, which means that creation is spiritual. Heidegger expressed it the following way: "Nothingness by contrast to all that seems to be, is the veil of being." Sartre's main work is entitled *Being and Nothingness.* Neither Hui-neng nor Heidegger nor Sartre are nihilists, they are explorers of ultimate reality; they recognized the importance of what really *is* in contrast to what seems to be.

Love really *is,* even though it doesn't seem to be; and many things which seem to be, really are not, they are only phenomena, which means appearances. The world is called the phenomenal world. That which really is cannot be annihilated. The basic premise that defines reality is immutability, indestructibility.

Question: Would you say the prognosis for this patient is very poor?

Dr. Hora: Yes, unless this patient can find a therapist who knows how to pray. It is not written in the textbooks of psychiatry and psychoanalysis that therapists should pray for their patients; nevertheless, this can be very helpful. And the more we learn how to pray for our patients, the more they will prosper. And this particular patient is in desperate need of someone to pray for her.

Question: How would you go about praying for a patient?

Dr. Hora: Would you like to join me in prayer for this patient? It simply consists of considering the fact that God never created a nihilating person. We deny the reality of this kind of a child of God, and affirm the fact that this patient is a spiritual being. Even though she may not know anything about God, the love of God is available to her and is with her and is protecting her. We endeavor to *behold* this patient as embraced by the love of God. And the more clearly we can do this beholding, the more likely it will be that this patient will respond in a favorable way. We don't know how, we don't know when, but experience tells us that it is always helpful.

Session No. 11

COMPETITION

If we know how to pray, we have a great advantage in life, both as therapists and as individuals. Prayer is the most important thing we can possibly learn. I suppose not many psychotherapists would admit publicly to praying. What is it about prayer that is so embarrassing to people? Prayer is embarrassing, just as God is embarrassing, because it has been discredited and misunderstood. When we speak about prayer and mention the word God, people immediately jump to the conclusion that we are either religious fanatics, evangelists, or silly superstitious people, and not worthy even to listen to. Most therapists, even if they are prayerful in their private lives, would not dare to let anyone know about it, nor mention it to their patients.

The Bible says: "The stone which the builders rejected is become the head of the corner" (Mark 12:10). Sophisticated people reject the idea of prayer, reject the idea of God, and reject the idea of religion. Everything that has to do with spiritual reality is labeled as supernatural or superstitious folly. What is the stone which is the head of the corner? The cornerstone is the most important stone in a building, an archway, or whatever structure is being built of stones; it is the support of all the other stones. The right understanding of God and of prayer can become the cornerstone upon which our entire lives and work are founded, stabilized, established, and can give us a great sense of assurance and effectiveness.

How can prayer be such a solid foundation if millions of people all over the world are going to churches, reading the Bible, and praying, and still the world seems in a mess. Prayer doesn't seem to work. However, let us look at it this way: if fifty million people would believe that two and two is five, it still wouldn't make it so. But if one would know that two and two is four, it would make all the difference. Similarly, if millions of people pray and go to church and believe in God and yet have so little to show for it, it does not mean that there is no God, that prayer is nonsense, or that we have to reject the stone (principle) which is the foundation of health, sanity, freedom, peace, assurance, intelligence and love.

All that is needed is a better understanding of what prayer is and of what God is. If fifty million people say mathematics is no good because it never works out right, this does not mean that we have to reject mathematics, that mathematics is not a useful discipline. All that is needed is a better understanding of the principles of mathematics. So it is with prayer. Once we come to understand the principles which underlie effective prayer, then the "stone" that has been rejected will become "the head of the corner." Our lives will be based on prayer, which I like to call *existential worshiping*.

What is existential worshiping? Existential worshiping is spoken of in the Bible as "ceaseless prayer." It is a prayerful mode of being-in-the-world, which is an endeavor to continuously see everyone and everything in the context of divine reality. Everything we look at, think about, and see, whether we are aware of it or not, we are seeing and evaluating in a certain context. There is the Freudian context, the Jungian context, the Adlerian, the Sullivanian context. According to how we were conditioned, we see everything and interpret everything within a certain context. Nothing can be seen in and of itself apart from a context. For instance, if there were no background, nothing could be noticed in the foreground, nothing can be seen just by itself. It is the background that makes it possible to see the foreground. Whatever we see, we see in a certain context. Some contexts are existentially more valid than are others.

Existentialism looks at patients not in the context of their relationships to other people, nor in the context of their personal history or family background, but in the context of their relationship to the fundamental order of existence.

The aim of existential psychotherapy is to help people come

into greater harmony with the fundamental order of existence. Prayer is an endeavor to behold an individual, a situation, and oneself in the context of existence or divine reality. In the context of reality everything is in order, everyone is healthy and good and intelligent and loving. So in proportion as we learn to pray for our patients, for our loved ones, for ourselves, we develop the ability to behold them in the context of perfect spiritual reality, and whenever we do that, something good happens. Pathology has a tendency to disappear. How is it possible for pathology to disappear? Isn't it just wishful thinking that we are engaged in? Or magic thinking?

Let us ask the question: What is pathology? Pathology is a phenomenon. Pathology is externalization of certain existentially invalid thoughts. It can happen as either disturbances of thinking, of speech, of behavior, or of somatizations, that is, physical symptoms. That which is an appearance includes the possibility of disappearance. How does the disappearance of an appearance come about? What happens in the therapeutic situation is that the therapist's valid outlook on reality jolts the patient's viewpoint to a realization that there are other ways of seeing life than what he has been accustomed to. In other words, the therapist lives in a different world than the patient and, hopefully, the therapist's world is more valid existentially. In a therapeutic encounter there is a collision of two worlds.

Patients usually enter into the therapeutic situation with an intensive involvement in the interpersonal context of life. Most pathologies arise from disturbed interpersonal thinking. This stems from interpreting life as a process of interpersonal relationships. So the patient is a patient as long as he sees life in the context of interpersonal relationships. When these interpersonal relationships are pleasant, then he feels good; when they become disturbed, he feels bad. The context of interpersonal relationships involves horizontal thinking—self and other.

It is interesting to consider the naïvete which underlies the assumption that if pathology and suffering stem from disturbed interpersonal relationships, then therapy must aim at improving these interpersonal relationships. It is as if someone would say, if the water coming out of the faucet is not good for drinking, let us fix the faucet. In medicine this is called: *"Post hoc ergo propter hoc."* This fallacy contains two erroneous modes of thinking, namely, cause-and-effect thinking and dualistic thinking. These are poignant signs of narrow-mindedness.

The therapist's outlook on life is, we hope, not a one-dimensional but a full-dimensional one. Namely, he sees his life in the context of existence and there is a different perception of reality. Out of that different perception of reality the patient is given a chance to discover that life is not necessarily the way he thought it to be. As the patient becomes interested in seeing life in a different context, pathology begins to fade.

We started out talking today about prayer. I must warn against misunderstanding prayer as a technique of psychotherapy whereby we endeavor to influence the patient to give up his own context and accept our context. That's not what prayer is. When we pray we are always praying to purify our own consciousness. Now that sounds very selfish, doesn't it? What do we mean? We are praying that we may see clearly. Prayer helps us to remain conscious of the only existentially valid context, namely, the context of divine reality. It is easy to become distracted by life, by television, by newspapers, and by patients. It sometimes happens that instead of the patient becoming favorably affected by the therapist, the therapist becomes unfavorably affected by the patient. The traditional way to deal with this is to ask for a supervisory session in order to clear up the countertransference. But we do not have to do that if we live the life of ceaseless prayer. Because with the help of prayer we can maintain a spiritual perspective on life and it is this spiritual perspective, this quality of consciousness, which then has its therapeutic impact on the patient.

It is interesting, and seemingly magical, that the therapist's consciousness can have a beneficial effect on the patient even after the patient has left. If we behold a patient in the context of divine reality, we are healed of our diagnostic preoccupations—and perchance of our condemnation of the patient, which is implied in every diagnosis. Whenever we make a diagnosis, we cannot help but condemn. We sit in judgment, and that in itself is very harmful. With the help of prayer, we can quickly cleanse our consciousness. As long as we think of a patient as a diagnostic category, he cannot be healed. This is the tragedy of hospitalization. When someone is hospitalized, he becomes, of necessity, a diagnostic category. He is not seen as a spiritual manifestation of Love-Intelligence, but as a diagnostic category. And he becomes a prisoner of a label. It is very hard for a patient to be healed in a hospital. In our work we can greatly benefit our patients if we quickly dismiss our diagnosis from thought and prayerfully endeavor to see them as spiritual manifestations of the good of God.

When we are learning to play the piano, we are learning the technique of piano playing. But after we have learned to play the piano, we are not "playing the piano" anymore, we are making music. We transcend whatever we have learned, whether it is piano or psychodynamics or linguistics. Otherwise we are not healing, we are only diagnosing and studying pathology.

Everything we have said up till now boils down to refraining from asking the wrong questions and knowing how to ask the right questions.

Question: What is the difference between discerning and figuring out a meaning?

Dr. Hora: The meaning reveals itself to us when we are confronting the situation in an open-minded, nonjudgmental, unprejudiced way. If we try to figure something out, we will pin something on someone on the basis of some preconceived ideas, and it will always be a mistake. So what is required is an open-minded, reverent, loving perception of that which reveals itself within the encounter situation. And that which reveals itself is not what really *is,* it is the meaning of what seems to be. For instance our previously mentioned patient revealed herself to be an annihilating individual. This is what seems to be, but it is not what really is. What really is is a spiritual child of God, a manifestation of Love-Intelligence.

When we speak about the meaning revealing itself to us, we are referring to phenomenological perception, which means the open-minded, unprejudiced, nonjudgmental discernment of the meaning of phenomena. A phenomenon is a thought manifesting itself as a perception. When we sit with a patient various phenomena will manifest themselves, and if we confront these phenomena with an open mind in an unprejudiced nonjudgmental way, we will be able to perceive their meaning. For instance, when the "annihilating" patient said: "I want to make out a check for you because I won't be coming back," that was a phenomenon the meaning of which was, "I want to annihilate you as a therapist." Now usually we get hurt if someone tries to annihilate us. But, of course, a therapist or an enlightened individual cannot afford such sensitivities. People have a right to "annihilate" us as many times as they want to, but we cannot take it personally.

All that was necessary in this case was to be gracious and friendly and let her be. After she leaves we may find ourselves somewhat disturbed or even worried because, mind you, this patient is in danger of suicide. If we find ourselves either worried about her or personally hurt by her rejection, then we must quickly turn to prayer and heal ourselves both of worry and hurt feelings, perhaps even of condemnation. None of these things must be allowed to fester in our consciousness. We must quickly, with the help of prayer, become loving and compassionate in thought about the patient. We liberate ourselves from the effects of the patient's pathology. And our freedom has a therapeutic effect on the patient, even if she never comes back. Interestingly enough, a patient may return if we have successfully prayed for ourselves.

The healing quality in the therapist is also called the Christ consciousness. This consciousness has a drawing effect on all those who are in need of healing. We do not have to motivate patients for therapy. There is a well-known mistaken idea in the field that we have to motivate a patient to come back and accept therapy. What do we really mean by motivating a patient? Motivating is influencing. We have no right to influence anybody. It is the Christ consciousness which has the power to influence and to heal. We don't really do anything. Prayer helps us to maintain the Christ consciousness and that is the power that heals. It communicates itself as love, as freedom, and as everything that is needed. We say that psychotherapy cannot be done. It is a process in which we participate in a certain manner. Prayer is the cornerstone, the foundation upon which our effectiveness depends.

CASE PRESENTATION

A twenty-four-year-old, white, athletic looking, well-dressed male student, part-time lifeguard, seeks treatment. He appears quiet and somewhat shy in manner, but behaves in an abusive way with the receptionist when she asks him to sign his name. Though his outward appearance is reserved, his behavior is often brusque and hostile. He says he is upset because his fiancée changed her mind about marrying him. He complains about depressions, a sense of isolation, and occasional suicidal thoughts.

Commentary on Case Presentation

What is this patient's mode of being-in-the-world? Essentially, this patient's mode of being-in-the-world appears to be a competitive one. If he cannot be on top, he cannot live with himself. If his girl friend, whom he wants to marry, says no, he feels that he is a loser; if she says yes, he is still a loser because she makes more money than he does. He is constantly measuring himself against others and would like to be above them. He wants to be above his girl friend and above the therapist. When the therapist explains to him that she is not here to judge but to enlighten, this does not comfort him, it makes him feel inferior. "Here is this woman. She wants to enlighten me!" This is not acceptable. In the competitive mode of being-in-the-world the very fact of having to seek help is in itself interpreted as a defeat. In the competitive mode of being-in-the-world every experience is sort of a put-down. The patient sees life in terms of being superior or inferior. He does not quite succeed in making it to the superior level. The basic assumption is that if he could be superior, then perhaps he could be happy. But if he could succeed in being superior to his girl friend, he would lose interest in her. If she says no, he feels rejected; if she says yes, he is not enthusiastic either. This is one of the more common forms of misdirected modes of being-in-the-world —seeing life in terms of who is on top.

Let us now resist the temptation to ask: "Why is he this way? Who is to blame for him being this way? And what should we do about it? And how should we do it?" We have to forget about these questions, transcend them, and then ask: "What is the meaning of what seems to be?" This is a misperception of life in terms of one-upmanship. Now we know his mode of being-in-the-world. And so we come to the second question, "What is what really *is*?" What really is is that the patient is a unique individual manifestation of Love-Intelligence, totally independent from comparisons to other people. In the entire universe there isn't anybody who could be compared to him because we are all unique manifestations of the same God-principle. We can never measure ourselves against another individual because there is no one just like us. The patient needs to understand himself in terms of his unique value as an individual. We could ask him: "Look here, which number is more important in mathematics, six or seven?" (*Comment:* This patient would probably say seven because it is higher.) Six is as important as seven, and there is no way of measuring one against the other. Every individual has his unique importance in the total scheme of things.

Question: But don't we have to be realistic and consider the job situation of this patient?

Dr. Hora: Let us consider the difference between being realistic and being real. There is modern furniture, for instance, and there is modernistic furniture. The realistic is the counterfeit of the real, it means "like real." Modernistic means "like modern." Detroit came up with an advertisment which went like this: "This is the low-priced car most like high-priced cars."

We can move from being realistic to being real. Realistic is not real, it is a pretense of being real; it is not life, it is a counterfeit of life. If we try to live realistically, life is a continuous process of tribulations, one problem after another, and there is no way of reaching harmony, peace, and assurance. So let us not settle for being realistic, let us endeavor to reach reality.

Question: Must we believe in God?

Dr. Hora: In our discussions we never spoke of believing in God as a desirable goal in therapy. What we were trying to do was to get acquainted with divine reality, with what really is, to get to *know* reality. Nobody advocated here a belief in reality. Belief has no therapeutic value, but right knowing has. Believing in buoyancy will not help us to swim, but being acquainted with buoyancy will make it possible for us to float and to swim. "Acquaint now thyself with him, and be at peace" (Job 22:21).

Question: Dr. Hora, before you leave, would you please teach us again how to pray for our patient?

Dr. Hora: All right. We start out by denying what seems to be. In all of God's kingdom there is absolutely no competition. In divine reality all of God's manifestations live and move and have their being in perfect harmony. We behold the patient in the context of divine reality and come to know him as he really is.

Session No. 12

LAWS AND PRINCIPLES

Life, the universe, and existence are not haphazard, chaotic, or governed by chance. Life, the universe, and reality are ultimately meaningful and governed by law. There are laws that govern existence. We are all educated to know the laws that govern the physical universe. We know the law of gravitation, the laws governing the movements of the celestial bodies, the laws which govern atomic and subatomic particles in their relations to one another, the laws of nature, the laws of physiology. Everything seems to be governed by laws, and existence is also governed by laws. Life is not chance nor primordial chaos.

The laws which govern existence are called spiritual laws. Man is an individual manifestation of existence. Man reveals the existence of existence. In order for man to be healthy and find fulfillment in life, he needs to understand the laws which govern existence in order that he may be in harmony with them. When driving on the road we must be in harmony with traffic laws, otherwise we may get hurt, and most people understand that.

In existential psychotherapy we take the laws of existence seriously. We study them, we try to understand them, and we try to help individuals to come into greater harmony with them in order that they may be safe, healthy, happy, and find fulfillment in life. As you can see, this is a much broader perspective than the psychodynamic theory, the interpersonal relationship theory, the libido theory, the adaptational method, or any other approach to the human condition. This is an all-encompassing perspective on man in the context of ultimate reality.

As far as self-understanding is concerned, naturally, if we understand ourselves as manifestations of existence, and if we know our place in the total scheme of things, then we shall have the great advantage of the most perfect self-understanding possible. What does it mean to understand oneself? To understand oneself means to know who we are, what we are, what our purpose is, and what the meaning of everything that we experience is.

It is interesting to contemplate the fact that since time immemorial man has been struggling to understand himself. And he did it this way: He dissected cadavers trying to understand the structure of his own body. He studied physiology, embriology, biology, and sociology, always making man the primary object of his investigation in the hope of understanding himself, and always failing.

No matter how scientific we become, no matter how much we explore, even down to the molecular structure of cells, by studying man we fail to understand man. This reminds me of a humorous definition of a specialist. A specialist is someone who is learning more and more about less and less till he reaches a point where he knows everything about nothing. The more we know about man, the more mystified we are about ourselves, and it seems that there is no way of learning enough about ourselves by studying man. There must be a hitch some place. And the hitch is this—there is no such thing as a man by himself. There is no such thing as a wave without the ocean. Can you imagine a scientist getting a government grant to study waves apart from the ocean? But that is what we do when we study man per se. Just as a wave cannot be understood apart from the ocean, so man cannot be understood apart from God. Therefore, in order to know what we are, we must study God.

By now you may have surmised that existence is a synonym for God, and the laws of existence which constitute the fundamental order of being are the laws of God, spiritual laws which underlie all of life. And the more we understand God, the more we understand man and everything else in the universe.

I must emphasize the word "understanding." It must be understood in its existential meaning and not confused with knowing about something. Theology can offer a lot of information about God, but we cannot understand God just by studying theology. There are two kinds of knowing: there is knowledge that is information, and then there is real knowledge that results in transformation. Whenever we understand something that is truly valid in an existential sense, something happens to us, we become to some degree transformed. Information does not have that existential impact. Information is just intellectual knowing about something. In existential psychotherapy we are not interested in providing people with information about God, or about themselves, or about life. We are endeavoring to bring about the understanding that transforms.

When we get a glimpse of divine reality, it has tremendous importance for health, freedom, and understanding, and we begin to appreciate certain passages and aspects of the Bible in a new light as helpful and very relevant. As a matter of fact, it can become our textbook for intelligent living. But we have to learn to read it in the context of existence rather than in the context of religious dogma or theological polemics.

Question: Would you elaborate upon the controversial word "God"?

Dr. Hora: God is a very controversial word indeed. Many people are put off by it, and even more people are afraid to pronounce the word lest they be labeled religious fanatics. Some people can even be provoked by the word. There are three words that are most misused, discredited, and maligned. One is *God*; the other is *love*; the third is *truth*. These three words have been so badly perverted and discredited that people are afraid to use them. They are especially shunned in the field of psychotherapy. Nevertheless, they constitute the fundamental reality upon which all intelligent life must be based, else we are in darkness. Without God, without love, without truth there is no worthwhile or meaningful existence possible.

Before we go any further, we must familiarize ourselves with two basic concepts which constitute the standard for evaluating everything in life. These are: Existentially valid and existentially invalid values. What do we mean by values? The Bible says: "Where your treasure is, there will your heart be also" (Matthew 6:21; Luke 12:34). Whatever we treasure in life and whatever is important to us constitutes our values. Emerson is quoted as having said: "Beware of what you set your heart on, for you may get it."

It is important to know what values to espouse and to cherish. If we cherish wrong values, we can get into trouble. How do we know which values are right and which are wrong? There are so many values and so many advocates of values. One of the most frequently recommended values in our culture is sensual pleasure. Almost uniformly, the media are advocating the importance of sensual pleasure. This can be such things as sex, clothes, certain foods, or drinks. The basic point they are making is that sensual pleasure is a supreme value.

Comment: They help us to function more comfortably.

Dr. Hora: Here we have just heard of two values: to function and to be comfortable. It is so ingrained in us we do not even realize that we have accepted certain values which the culture is offering. Are these existentially valid or invalid values? For instance, if we function comfortably in life, does that mean that we are healthy or enlightened? Not necessarily; a good machine functions comfortably. The existentially valid value concerns itself with the quality of life as health, harmony, freedom, peace, assurance, gratitude and love. Whatever values will make it possible for us to manifest these qualities of consciousness can safely be considered as existentially valid.

Question: Doesn't conflict have any existential value?

Dr. Hora: What good is conflict? The point about conflict is this: Inasmuch as conflict results in disturbance and suffering, it drives us to seek harmony, and therein lies its value; but conflict in itself is not an existentially valid value.

Question: Is happiness the same as joy and pleasure?

Dr. Hora: As far as happiness is concerned and the relation between happiness and joy, it is good to know that joy is a quality of consciousness which underlies true happiness. But happiness must not be confused with excitement and emotionalism. Joy is not a feeling, it is a quality of consciousness.

The point about pleasure is that we are frequently victims of an elementary mistake, namely, we are all longing for happiness and settling for pleasure. And when we mistake pleasure for happiness, we get hooked on something. That is the tragedy of drug addiction and of various misdirected modes of being-in-the-world. We desire happiness but instead wind up seeking pleasure, not knowing the difference. Sensualism provides pleasure which is shortlived and is invariably followed by an unpleasant aftertaste. Our culture is emphasizing sensual pleasure in every department of life, not because it is malevolent, but simply because there is not sufficient clarity on the issue of happiness.

Session No. 13

THE RIGHT QUESTION

Question: How widespread is metapsychiatry?

Dr. Hora: It is not very widespread, but what is the value of statistical evidence in the area of the quest for truth? It is interesting to observe that the closer we are to the truth, the less popular it is. Just consider all the various fads which have sprung up in our culture and spread like wildfire. We could ask the question: How is it possible that invalid ideas gain such rapid acceptance, that new ideas and new fads are coming along, and that people are eagerly jumping on bandwagons and repeatedly winding up disappointed?

It is interesting to recall what Jesus said: "Heaven and earth shall pass away; but my words shall not pass away" (Mark 13:31; Luke 21:33). Is this an arrogant statement? How could he make such a statement? What did he mean? He meant that the phenomenal world comes and goes, but truth is eternal. Truth is seldom popular but it validates itself existentially. How do we know whether something is existentially valid or not? Truth is health-promoting, life-enhancing, harmony-inducing, liberating, healing, happiness-inspiring.

Excitement is popular. Excitement is counterfeit happiness. Most people want to have an exciting life and yet excitement, when considered phenomenologically, is a disturbance. It is something that disturbs the homeostatic balance. What is homeostatic balance? It refers to the harmonious order of physiological processes in the organism. Excitement, which is believed to be an aspect of the good life, is actually a disturbance.

How can truth be proven and appreciated? By its effects. The main existential impact of truth is freedom. Freedom is an essential element of the fundamental order of existence and of health. Here again, Jesus beautifully defined truth as that which sets man free. Free from what? What kind of freedom does truth confer? The freedom to be what we really are. What is preventing us from being what we really are? Is there anyone who can unequivocally make a statement that he is actualizing in his daily life the truth of his being?

We have heard here an implied definition of freedom: To be able to act as we feel. Acting as we feel is not freedom, it is license. This was the fallacy upon which encounter groups were founded. Those too passed away in spite of their great popularity. Some people define freedom as freedom of choice. But in order to choose freely, we would have to be able to cognize correctly. Do we have the faculty to cognize correctly? Are our perceptions reliable? If they are unreliable, it is illusory to talk about free choice We have also heard here an implied definition of reality: What society says, that is reality. Is that true? Society is neither reality nor the arbiter of reality; it just represents the demands of the culture. Society only requires us to be realistic, society does not claim to know what reality is. To be realistic is to pretend to be real. Realistic man pretends to live in reality.

What is a person? Are we persons? "Person" is not what we are, it is what we pretend to be. The question, "What are we really?" is at the core of existential psychotherapy. Every one of us has to find the answer to that question, and when we do find it we are enlightened.

Now if "person" is something we pretend to be, and if we have interpersonal relationships, what is going on? What is going on in an interpersonal relationship? A friction is going on. Two fictitious characters are trying to interact with one another. If we consider this fact about interpersonal relationships, we can sit in amazement, contemplating the multitudes of people investing time and energy using interpersonal transactions for therapeutic purposes. How is it possible for one fictitious character to improve the health of another fictitious character? Interpersonal relationships can only improve the pretense, not the health of the persons.

The real issue in an interpersonal situation is the altering of pretensions, which is called functioning or adaptation or relating or getting along or adjustment. What is being adjusted? How well we play the game. We learn to play the game in a socially acceptable manner, but we are still alienated from the truth of our self-identity. It stands to reason that there is no hope whatsoever of discovering the truth of our self-identity by focusing our attention, deploying our energies into improving the fiction we believe ourselves to be.

Now when we consider truth as the fundamental factor in liberation, and when we consider the objectives of existential psychotherapy as the realization of our true self-identity, then we see how precious and how important it is to be after the truth, rather than after an improved pretense.

What is the method whereby we would endeavor to attain the goal of authenticity? Actually, it is very simple. All we have to do is to learn to ask the right questions. The entire field of psychotherapy is victim of an unfortunate choice of questions. What are the questions that are asked most often in this field of endeavor?

The first question is: Why did it happen? This is a *cause-and-effect* question. It is assumed that something has happened, it must have had a cause or a reason. This sounds very logical, but unfortunately it is not valid in a broader context.

The second question: Who is to blame for what happened? This is a *personalistic* question. Nobody is really to blame. There is neither cause nor culprit.

The third question: What should we do? This is an *operational* question. It presumes that we can fix whatever went wrong. Man is not really an operator.

The fourth question: How should we do it?, is a *process* question. It presumes that the repair that seems necessary entails a certain process.

These questions are tragically misleading. Whenever we successfully answer any of these questions or all of them, we have embarked on a "wild goose chase" which has no hope of profitability.

To speedily attain the goal of realizing the truth, there are two valid questions which we may ask.

The first is: What is the meaning of what seems to be?

The second is: What is what really *is*?

What do these questions help us to understand? First, if we are to know the truth, we have to awaken to that which is not true. We need to understand the meaning of what seems to be. This, in turn, will help us to realize what really is.

Phenomena, as we know, are appearances, things that seem to be but are not. Phenomena are thoughts externalized as perceptible manifestations. When we ask: "What is the meaning of what seems to be?" we are inquiring into the mental equivalent of phenomena. Suppose someone gets angry at his wife. He gets red in the face, his blood pressure rises, he is ranting and raving, he is upset. The naïve thing to say about him would be that he got mad at his wife, that he seems to have had a temper tantrum. But this would just be judging by appearances. Now the temptation would be to ask: Why is he mad? But as we said, that is a wrong question to ask, it would not help us to really understand him. The second question would be: Who is to blame for his having gotten mad? But this would also not be helpful, it would only lead to further recriminations. Then we could ask: How could we calm him down, and what should we do so that he wouldn't be so mad? This would seem to be the natural question to ask but it, too, would not help us to understand.

If, however, we ask: What is the meaning of his seeming upset? then we are seeking to understand the mental equivalent of this phenomenon. We are actually asking: What are the thought processes that underlie this particular appearance? If we sincerely want to know and are willing to resist the temptation to figure it out, then it will come to us. It may come to us that this man was thinking about what his wife should have or should not have done. That he entertained certain mental assumptions about what should be or what should not be. And when these assumptions were frustrated, he had this reaction, which is really nothing else than that this man insisted that his assumptions be fulfilled.

Most of the time when we are frustrated, it is not because someone else did something or didn't do something. It does not have a cause at all, it only indicates that we are in the habit of thinking in certain ways, most of the time in terms of what should or should not be.

In inquiring after a meaning of a phenomenon, the mental processes which underlie that phenomenon are revealed to us. And once we understand the meaning of a phenomenon, we can ask the final

question: What is what really *is?* In order to get an answer to the
final question, we need to understand something about the context
in which the real man lives. From what was said until now, we can
see that the real man does not live in the context of interpersonal
relationships, nor does he live in the context of society. The real man
lives in the context of reality, absolute reality. What is absolute
reality? A wave lives in the context of the ocean. Real man lives in
the context of divine reality. Real man is as inseparable from divine
reality as the wave is from the ocean. Divine reality is the existential
context of man. "In him we live, and move, and have our being"
(Acts 17:28).

Session No. 14

THE REALM OF THE NON-DUAL

Question: Would you please clarify for us the following concepts: What is real? What is good? What is love? What is value?

These concepts will not appear so difficult if we will remember what phenomena are. Phenomena are appearances, externalizations of thought processes. When thought appears as an experience, an event, or a symptom, this is called a phenomenon. Phenomena are nothing real, they just appear to be. All appearances tend to disappear. Real is that which is immutable. Reality cannot disappear, only appearances can disappear. Whatever is immutable is real. We live in a world of phenomena and our patients are constantly presenting us with a variety of phenomena as symptoms, experiences, events, and problems which fill their lives and which appear and disappear.

The aim of existential psychotherapy is to help the patient to awaken from the world of phenomena and attain a consciousness which is in contact with reality. In the light of this, we can consider the next concept, namely: What is good? It stands to reason that whatever will enhance the prospect of coming into contact with reality is good. Good is that which enhances our contact with reality.

Love can do this for us; therefore, love is the paradigm of good. Love is good, but only real love is good. There is much counterfeit love. How can we differentiate real love from counterfeit love? Counterfeit love takes us away from reality, whereas real love enhances our movement toward reality.

And now we may consider the fourth concept in the question asked: What is value? The issue of value is very important and we have touched upon it previously. Value is that which we value. Everyone values something. What is a hang-up? A hang-up is something we secretly cherish. It can be the most ordinary thing or very outlandish; there is an infinite variety of values which we can come to value. In existential psychotherapy we distinguish existentially valid values from existentially invalid values.

Suppose someone cherishes the idea of success. Is this an existentially valid value, or is it existentially invalid? It is important to know what we consider to be success. Let us consider a patient who is very desperate because he is under investigation and is receiving a great deal of attention from the district attorney. But all his life he was cherishing the idea of publicity. To him success meant to be well known. It is necessary to point out that existentially invalid values are dualistic. A coin always has two sides. If someone cherishes the idea of having a lot of publicity, it can be either good or bad publicity. And that is exactly what is happening to this man. For many years he was receiving a lot of good publicity and now, although he still has a lot of publicity, it is turning sour.

Publicity is not an existentially valid value. There is, however, existentially valid success. Peace, love, and assurance are the fruits of existentially valid success. If we want to define what is supremely desirable to cherish as a value, we must say it is the attainment of conscious at-one-ment with reality.

Question: Could you comment on the Buddhist idea that the supreme value is cherishing emptiness?

Dr. Hora: The supreme value in Zen Buddhism is the attainment of the realization of the Buddha nature. The Buddha nature is attained through an experience of what they call *sunyata,* emptiness. When emptiness is realized, the Buddha nature emerges in the consciousness of the trainee. It can come with a bang or it can come slowly, gradually. If it comes with a bang, it is called *satori;* if it comes slowly, it is called *kensho.* What is the Buddha nature? It is nothing else but the Christ consciousness. What is the Christ consciousness? The Christ consciousness is a quality of awareness which is capable of discerning absolute reality. What is the nature of absolute reality? Love, truth, intelligence, harmony, peace, assurance, gratitude, joy, perfect health, freedom, infinite compassion, inspired wisdom. We are used to thinking of health in physical terms, but health is much more than that. It is the quality of consciousness which we have just described.

Existential psychotherapy aims at helping people attain this kind of health, which could be called spiritual health. It is all-inclusive.

Question: How does an existential therapist act in his work, like Roger or like Jung?

Dr. Hora: As far as the modus operandi is concerned in the therapeutic session, it is neither psychoanalytic, transferential, Rogerian nondirective reflecting of emotions, nor Jungian probing for archetypes and such. It is simply discovering the misdirected mode of being-in-the-world which the patient reveals, and endeavoring to clarify to him the true nature of reality and how to attain contact with it. It is essentially phenomenological and hermeneutic. The activity of the therapist consists of shedding light on what really is. He is endeavoring to shed light on the true nature of reality in order to help the patient get in touch with this reality. And it is the truth of reality which heals the patient. The healing power is not in the therapist, it is not in the relationship between the patient and the therapist; the healing power is in the nature of truth.

For instance, if we notice a mathematical error in a computation and correct it, the power to make the correction is not in us but in the mathematical truth. We only bear witness to the truth. This is important to know because it provides the therapist with an essential quality of humility which cannot be faked or pretended. Unless we really understand that the power to heal is not in man but in the truth, we cannot be genuinely humble.

It is fascinating to consider these two words: witnessing and reflecting. They are both passive and active at the same time. When we are witnessing something it may mean that we are watching something, we are seeing something. But when we are witnessing *to* something, it means that we are giving testimony to something. Similarly, reflecting may indicate that we are focusing our attention on some content of our consciousness. We can reflect upon a thought that came to us. But we can also reflect these thoughts *to* somebody. That is an interesting semantic curiosity. What meaning can we derive from considering this? These words convey something which is neither doing nor not doing.

These are significant words and, strangely enough, they transcend everything we are used to thinking of in terms of activity and passivity. These two words are both active and passive at the same time, and yet they are neither. For instance, the concept of doing or not doing does not apply to these words. When we are witnessing, we are not doing anything in either the active or passive sense. And when we are reflecting, we are not doing anything. The Taoist sages, or at least the translators of the Taoist texts, were hard put to convey the significance of words that exist in Chinese but not in our dualistic language. In the texts of Taoism we read sentences such as: "It is action which is nonaction." "It is doing which is a nondoing." These words transcend our dualistic language.

Now is it worthwhile for us to waste time on this linguistic analysis? Yes. If we take the trouble to consider these two words, and consider how it is possible for a dualistic language to have two non-dualistic words, then we shall come to realize something of the fundamental nature of reality. You see, reality is non-dual. Human experience is dualistic.

In the realm of the real there is neither doing nor non-doing. In reality, action and non-action fuse in events taking place in consciousness. Witnessing and reflecting are events taking place in consciousness. Reality is consciousness being conscious of itself.

Now perhaps the question, "How do you do this therapy?" may become somewhat clearer. The answer is, we don't exactly do it. It is not something we do, it is something we participate in by allowing what really is and what seems to be to reveal itself. What has revealed itself is being reflected in terms of clarification. Reality is non-dual and timeless.

Perhaps this would be the right time to say a few words about timelessness. Unenlightened man is a prisoner of time. He is either an obedient slave of it, or in constant conflict with it. In either case his thoughts are time-bound. Time has three existential dimensions: The past, the present, and the future. In metapsychiatry this is referred to as temporality.

Interestingly enough, time-bound man reveals three characterological frailties. These are: pride, ambition, and vanity.

1. Pride is always in reference to the past. For instance, I am proud of what I have accomplished; I am ashamed of what I did; I am

proud of my ancestors. Pride and shame are two sides of the same coin, and they are both in the past.

2. Ambition always refers to the future. Ambitious man thinks about what should be and what shouldn't be. Fear is the faithful companion of ambition.

3. The present is the domain of vanity. Vanity is wedded to embarrassment. As you see, the difference between shame and embarrassment lies in their temporality.

Pride—shame.

Ambition—fear.

Vanity—embarrassment.

These are dualities of human characterology emanating from the temporality of unenlightened existence.

Since time immemorial people have been trying to overcome these human frailties but with little or no success. Metapsychiatry offers the possibility of healing the human character and freeing man from his involvement with time.

Enlightened man, being in conscious contact with non-dual reality, is completely free. God is not in the past, He is not in the future and not in the present. God is in the realm of the timeless. When timelessness is realized, human characterological frailties disappear. Man lives in conscious harmony with Love-Intelligence which governs his affairs. Interestingly enough, he gains dominion over time, which ceases to be a problem to him.

Session No. 15

PERSONHOOD

Question: What is the difference between neurotic anxiety and existential anxiety?

Dr. Hora: We could start out by saying that <u>neurotic anxiety is social anxiety</u>. <u>Existential anxiety is fear for one's life</u>. <u>Neurotic anxiety is simply fear for one's status in society, in a group, or in a family</u>. <u>In existential anxiety the issue is survival</u>.

If we are to talk about neurotic anxiety, we have to talk about pretending. Pretending has a lot to do with neurotic anxiety. What is pretending? Pretending is the most common way to operate in the world. Anybody who thinks of himself as a person, is of necessity automatically pretending to be something other than he really is. There is no such thing as a person. A person is not what we are, it is what we pretend to be.

Question: Can't this pretending overlap closely?

Dr. Hora: This question reminds me of a patient, a young lady, who came in looking somewhat bizarre. Suddenly, it occurred to me that she was pretending to be a woman. When I confronted her with my impression she was a bit shocked, but after a while she confided that she secretly thought of herself as a man. But in order to hide this secret desire, she played the game of pretending to be a woman. So here was a young lady who lived her life as a female impersonator. Her pretensions were overlapping with what was anatomically true.

The aim of existential psychotherapy is to help people attain authenticity of being. In order to know what is true, we have to face up to what is not true. The strange thing about human existence is that, unexamined, existence tends to be inauthentic. What is the derivation of the word person? It is *per-sona* (mask). In Greek tragedies the actors held appropriate masks in front of their faces. They were literally putting up a front. In reality there is no such thing as a person. Yet we are all conducting ourselves in life as if we were certain kinds of persons. We speak about personality make-up, and we study it and try to improve it. What is make-up? Isn't it pretending to be what we are not? A make-up can either enhance the appearance of an individual, distort it, or detract from it. We do not say that this shouldn't be or that it should be, but let us understand what is, what really is.

The issue of anxiety has puzzled psychotherapists for years, and there are many theories and speculations about it. Various techniques were evolved as to how to help people cope with it. But as long as we are, unconsciously or ignorantly, living inauthentic lives, pretending to be something other than what we really are, there will be always anxiety. Anxiety is fear of being found out that we are not what we appear to be.

Neurotic anxiety can be contained, can be controlled, can be suppressed, can be hidden, can be drugged, but it cannot be healed until man becomes authentic. It is easy to know what a person is, but what is what really *is?* What are we, really, underneath the mask? Is it so horrible that we have to hide it? Are we so awful that we have to put on personality make-up to make ourselves acceptable to our fellow man? What is the meaning of this game of hide and seek we are playing throughout life? What are we hiding?

Existential anxiety was spoken of by Heidegger as the "dread of nothingness." Heidegger's main theme is worth considering, especially in the context of what we have touched upon here. He said: "Nothingness by contrast to all that seems to be is the veil of being." What did he mean by that? We mentioned the dread of nothingness. Children often express an ambition to be somebody. "When I grow up, I want to be somebody." What is the meaning of that? Now this would indicate that we want to feel that we are something. In psychology we speak of role-playing and functioning, but when are we what we really are? And what is it? We can go through life never having met with ourselves, never having found out the truth of our own being. Is it important? Is there any advantage to it?

Existential literature frequently refers to alienation; what is alienation? Mostly it is separation from the truth of what we really are. We have become so involved with our pretensions; we expend so much energy on improving our masks; we are so much concerned with functioning, role-playing, influencing, and being influenced, that as time goes on we become more and more alienated from the awareness of our true self-identity.

Comment: Sometimes I feel as if I am nothing, and sometimes I feel as if I am everything.

Dr. Hora: Unfortunately, we cannot rely on our feelings. St. Paul said: "If a man think himself to be something, when he is nothing, he deceiveth himself" (Galatians 6:3). God is nothing. How can we make such a blasphemous statement? We can if we understand the word "nothing" as "no thing." What do we mean by that? Thing is matter. When we say, God is no thing, we say that God is not a material, physical, anthropomorphic personage. When Heidegger speaks of nothingness, he isn't fooling, he is a profound thinker. He speaks of no-thingness. No-thingness is nonmaterial reality. God is not material. Jesus said: "God is a Spirit: and they that worship him must worship him in spirit and in truth" (John 4:24).

If a person is a material pretension, a lie, or a counterfeit, how can he worship God? Apparently Jesus believed that he cannot. Whatever a "person" does is never true, it is always a lie, because a liar can never say the truth. If personhood is a social pretension, then every person is a liar and a lie at the same time. Did Jesus have something to say about this? Yes. He said: ". . . he is a liar and the father of it" (John 8:44). That sounds like one of those dark sayings, but if we understood what has been said until now, we can see that he was talking about pretensions, persons. Personhood is a lie and every person a liar. St. Paul said: "Let God be true, but every man a liar" (Romans 3:4).

Question: Must we accept these religious concepts?

Dr. Hora: Let us make it clear again, we are not talking about religious concepts. What are we talking about then? We are talking about reality. It happens to sound religious because of the biblical references, but we are exploring the nature of reality as far as man is concerned and in the context in which he exists. Social life takes place in the context of society which is the realm of pretensions, but existence is reality.

Pretensions do not really help us to function better, they burden us with anxiety. The great value of conscious authenticity of being is the freedom to actualize our true potentialities which are oppressed and not permitted to flourish. Jesus said: "Ye are of your father the devil. . . . He was a murderer from the beginning, and abode not in the truth, because there is no truth in him" (John 8:44). The religious interpretation of this passage is that he is talking about the devil, but today the devil has a new name. What is this new name? Inauthentic selfhood. What is this devil murdering? Who is getting murdered here? Our true selfhood is getting murdered. Can something immortal get murdered? Only temporarily. Sooner or later existence demands to be realized and that is called existential crisis. We cannot go on pretending ad infinitum. The truth refuses to allow itself to be murdered, it demands resurrection, it demands fulfillment, it demands the right to manifest itself in the world.

Dante Alighieri describes how, at the age of forty, he began to be aware of a certain inner upheaval which he could not understand. But he yielded to its pressure and allowed this inner upheaval to express itself in his life. And what was the outcome of it? He became transformed into his true self-identity and gave birth to *The Divine Comedy,* the greatest literary work that has ever been presented to mankind.

Existential psychotherapy endeavors to help man liberate himself from the confines of his social pretensions so that he may become what he truly is and what he always was—not another person but another self.

Session No. 16

IGNORANCE

Question: Would you please talk to us about the problem of sin, guilt, and evil?

Dr. Hora: Even though these issues sound theological, I shall be glad to say a few words about them because they play an important role in existential psychotherapy. In order to help people with these problems, it is necessary to have a clear understanding of what they really are. These categories of human experience can be part of normal existence, so-called. They can, of course, take on exaggerated proportions, and they enter into the system of psychopathology.

Evil, sin, and guilt have a common denominator—ignorance. Ignorance of what? Of reality. Ignorance of existential reality. What is sin besides ignorance? *Sine Deo* means to be without God. We can be godless deliberately or unwittingly, right? Not really, it only seems that way. There are really no deliberate sinners. If a man would really understand his complete at-one-ment with the fundamental principle of existence, it would be impossible for him to be a sinner, just as it would be impossible for a wave to be apart from the sea.

Religious usage distinguishes between simple sinners, hardened sinners, deliberate sinners, and all sorts of sinners. But to be a sinner is not really a sin, it is just one aspect of the human condition where man is born in ignorance and educated to increased ignorance. "Father forgive them; for they know not what they do" (Luke 23:34). Normal education is existential miseducation. The simple sinner or the hardened sinner are but victims of positive or negative ignorance.

What is the difference between positive ignorance and negative ignorance? Which is better? The Zen Master says: "Knowing comes from not-knowing." In fact, he says that the negatively ignorant individual has a greater chance to be redeemed than the positively ignorant individual.

Previously I told a story of a professor who came to Japan to study Zen. A Zen Master invited him to tea. As the Zen Master was pouring tea into his guest's cup, he kept on pouring even though the cup was already full and the tea was spilling over. The guest said, "You are spilling the tea." The Zen Master said, "Yes, that's true. You see, you have just learned your first lesson in Zen. You say you want to study Zen, but your head is so full of all sorts of misinformation that there is no room for anything to be received." Which means that to learn something we must approach it with an open, uncluttered mind. The Zen Master immediately saw that his guest was a positively ignorant man, which is the most difficult student to teach. So a sinner is someone who is the victim of his insufficient understanding of man's complete at-one-ment with his creative principle, God.

Now what about guilt? We have a tendency to feel guilty about almost anything. It is amazing what predilection and willingness, even eagerness, we have to feel guilty. Any system of religion which encourages us to feel guilty will quickly become popular. From the study of psychopathology we are used to thinking of guilt as a terrible affliction which torments people. Guilt, however, is very devious; it pretends to be an affliction but is actually a passion. Contrary to appearances, we just love to feel guilty. What is it about guilt that makes it so attractive to man? When we say, I feel guilty, I am bad, it is not different from saying, I am great. What is the common denominator? The common denominator is the "I am," the self-confirmatory essence of guilt. When we feel guilty, our sense of selfhood is increased.

It is interesting to consider that we have two choices. We can either plead guilty or admit to ignorance. When we claim to be guilty, we are really giving ourselves a compliment. We say, "Oh, I know these things, I am just bad. I know everything and I should not have done it because I know better, and I feel guilty." People like to confess publicly to their guilt. We love to go to confession. Feeling guilty and confessing to it is a hidden form of boasting; it is a self-confirmatory mental involvement with ourselves. It is presumptuous to feel guilty, even if we seem to suffer from it.

What is it that makes us feel good when we are given a chance to confess? What happens after we have relieved ourselves through confession? No sooner do we relieve ourselves, we want to be relieved again. Freud, who discovered the cathartic method of relieving guilt, noted that the well-being which appears after a catharsis does not last long. Pretty soon the patients want a repeat performance; it really has no therapeutic value.

The only way that guilt can be healed is by facing up to the truth of ignorance. Whatever wrong we did or thought we did can only be avoided in the future if we become enlightened on the issue involved. Feeling better is no therapy, that's entertainment. The aim of therapy is not feeling better. If we want to feel good, we can have a drink, or take a pill, or go for a vacation. Often people enter psychotherapy with the preconceived idea that they will be helped to feel good, that the doctor's job is to make the patient feel good. Sometimes the doctor believes that also. I remember a young psychiatrist who came to consult me for a problem. His problem was that he was being harassed by telephone calls from his patients. They were complaining that they didn't feel good; they felt good when they left his office, but later they felt bad. This doctor, of course, quickly discovered that he is neither an entertainer nor a pill peddler.

What is the aim of the therapeutic work, if feeling good is not good? What is the aim of therapy? To relieve ignorance and to enlighten. If a patient comes to us believing that he knows everything, how can he be helped? This reminds me of a young lady who never asked a question during a session. When this was pointed out to her, she said: "What's there to ask? I already know everything!" She was told: "This brings up a good question to ask: 'How can I be cured of all my knowledge?' "

It is helpful to try to get the patient to achieve negative ignorance as soon as possible because then rapid progress can be made. How do we achieve negative ignorance? Sometimes patients are embarrassed to become negatively ignorant, they do not have the humility for that. Is there a famous personage in the history of wisdom who publicly proclaimed his negative ignorance? Socrates proclaimed: "I know that I don't know anything." Sometimes, if we show a patient that Socrates was negatively ignorant, he may be willing to consider it. There are often claims of ignorance but they are not sincere. Some people will say they don't know something that they really think they do know. It can become a cliché, a sort of mannerism.

We are all familiar with the widespread mannerism among teenagers and hippies who repeatedly say, "You know, you know." It really means, "I know." It is a self-confirmatory, would-be intellectual mannerism.

Now what about evil? Evil is a great bugaboo of theology, isn't it? I remember working once with a clergyman who was so imbued with the idea of evil that he lived in terror. To him evil was an absolute reality. He believed in two powers, God and evil, and that these two powers were contesting, and that evil seemed to be winning all the time.

Previously we said that the devil's new name is inauthentic selfhood, a false sense of self. Suffice it to say that in reality there are no sinners, there are no guilty people, and there is no evil. In the phenomenal world there are endless manifestations of ignorance. And these manifestations can be individual, collective, national, and international. The cataclysmic evil of the Vietnam war was a clear historical manifestation of ignorance acting itself out on an international scene.

There is only one problem which mankind has and **that** is ignorance. Fortunately, ignorance is not incurable, it can be healed. What is the healing remedy for ignorance? Knowledge. Right knowledge. Knowledge of the truth of what really is.

"To this end was I born, and for this cause came I into the world, that I should bear witness unto the truth" (John 18:37).

Psychotherapy is an endeavor to relieve the suffering which man is prone to through his ignorance. "This is life eternal, that they might know thee the only true God, and Jesus Christ, whom thou hast sent" (John 17:3). The purpose of life is to attain conscious union with ultimate reality. Man must seek, ask, and knock, and he must search all the time to come into conscious at-one-ment with the creative source of his being. No system of knowledge, be it ever so sophisticated and elegant, will ever take the place of this existential imperative under which we live. The creator cannot be left out of his creation. And as a wave cannot exist without the sea, man cannot exist without God.

Question: Doesn't the Bible clearly imply the culpability of man and his condemnation for being guilty of sin and evil?

Dr. Hora: If we read the Bible as a religious book, then we do get the impression of the condemnation of man as a sinner, and for being evil. But if we read the Bible in the light of existential philosophy, then all condemnation of man disappears, man is then the loved son of God, pure and perfect because he is spiritual and perfect, even as his Father is perfect and spiritual. The Bible is here viewed as a record of the evolution of human consciousness.

Question: What gives the apparent power to evil?

Dr. Hora: Evil is no power, it is an apparent power, as you correctly said. What is meant by the word "apparent?" It appears to be a power and it is experienced as a power as long as man does not know what real power is. Once mankind will understand real power, evil will lose all power. It would seem that darkness has great power. For instance, in darkness one can stumble and break a leg, and other things can happen. But when light appears, we see that darkness never was a power even though it was experienced by man as a power. Actually, darkness is nothing, it is just the absence of light. I think it was St. Augustine who defined evil as *"privatio boni,"* which means the absence of good. Darkness is the absence of light, and evil is the absence of the good. We know, however, that light is never really absent, and the good of God is omnipresent. The power of evil is not a reality, it is only an experience.

Session No. 17

THE HEALING OF VIOLENCE

Question: What is violence and what can be done about it?

Dr. Hora: To heal any problem, its meaning needs to be understood. Meaning must be differentiated from cause. For instance, if we wanted to deal with the causes of violence, we would find ourselves in the law enforcement field or in the field of social engineering, and our efforts would not result in healing but in containment, which in itself is a form of violence.

Healing implies making whole what appears to be disturbed, damaged, violated. A good way to begin to understand the meaning of a problem is by starting with the etymological root of the word that designates it. For instance, we can say that violence is that which violates the integrity of something whole (holy). Violence tends to adulterate the essential nature of its object. It tends to commit an act of adulteration (adultery).

There are various forms of violence depending on the area of its action. From the human standpoint, it is helpful to distinguish four basic forms of violence:

1. Sensory violence, the aim of which is physical sensation, assault on the senses.

2. Emotional violence, resulting in affective or mood disturbances, as, for instance, depressions, rage reactions, or emotional states of excitement.

3. Mental violence, producing disturbed states of consciousness and disturbances of the ability to reason coherently.

4. Chemical violence (drugs), affecting the total organism from within.

These forms of violence can be alloplastic (inflicted on others), or autoplastic (self-inflicted). It is commonly assumed that violence invariably involves aggression and hostility. This, however, is not necessarily so. Consequently, it is desirable to separate these issues. Aggression is a heightened form of activity the aim of which may be positive (rescuing a drowning man) or negative (flight from danger). Aggression gives the impression of violence but, in fact, it is not. Hostility is frequently considered to be an aspect of violence, however, it is only malicious intent. Anger is an emotional state characterized by a desire to be vengeful.

Violence is also often thought of in connection with crime. Of course, there are many forms of non-violent crime; therefore, violence must be considered separately from crime, aggression, hostility, anger. It is also noteworthy that there are many upright citizens, even religious individuals who express or invite violence. The Bible stories abound with violence. It appears that violence is a phenomenon of the human condition which was part of man's experience ever since Cain slew his brother Abel. In the history of Western civilization, as far as we know, Jesus was the first one to exemplify total freedom from violence. "Put up again thy sword into his place: for all they that take the sword shall perish with the sword" (Matthew 26:52).

Freedom from violence must also be distinguished from "nonviolence." Nonviolence (Ghandi, Martin Luther King) is a passive mode of participation in violence. Here the question presents itself: What about the crucifixion? How could Jesus have died a violent death if he was so completely free from violence? The answer seems to offer itself in the resurrection and ascension which point toward a transcendence of violence. True freedom expresses itself as transcendence. Einstein is reputed to have said: "Arrows of hate have been shot at me many times, but somehow they never touched me because they came from a world with which I had nothing in common."

A careful phenomenological analysis of violence reveals that the real issue in violence is excitement. Excitement is generally and mistakenly thought of as having positive existential value but, in fact, it is a form of sensualism, emotionalism, or intellectualism experienced as pleasure—pain, vigor, and vitality. Excitement is coun-

terfeit happiness. Ontogenetically, violence appears to be the out-
growth of infantile masturbatory stimulation. Masturbation can take
the form of sensory, emotional, intellectual, or chemical (drug induced) orgasmic experience. What in childhood appears to be innoc-
uous masturbatory play, in adulthood assumes the forms of a variety
of self-confirmatory activities. Among these, drug taking is at this
time becoming a most devastating problem. The striking ineffectual-
ity of the attempts to alleviate these problems indicates that the
"cause-and-effect" reasoning with which they have been hitherto
approached does not get to the heart of the issues.

The common denominator of all these forms of stimulation is the
fact that they tend to anchor human consciousness in the physical
realm of self-awareness. St. Paul tells us: ". . . whilst we are at home
in the body, we are absent from the Lord." "We are confident, I say,
and willing rather to be absent from the body, and to be present with
the Lord" (II Corinthians 5: 6, 8).

Natural man lives with the assumption that he is a physical personality, naturally at home in the body. Therefore, he is subject to
a mental dynamism which requires him to continually engage in
self-confirmatory ideation. This self-confirmatory ideation expresses
itself in a universal desire to maintain an awareness of oneself as a
physical entity or ego. The ego maintains an awareness of itself
through pleasure and pain. The ego man is hungering and thirsting,
not so much after righteousness as for pleasure or pain as self-
confirmatory stimulation, that is, proprioceptive awareness. These
stimuli may be sensory, emotional, intellectual, pleasurable, or painful according to their intensity. For instance, a caress may be pleasurable, while a slap is painful, yet both have the same existential
meaning, namely, they affirm the cherished assumption that one is
a physical ego. The sad fact is that man craves violence in proportion
to his ignorance of spiritual values and his spiritual self-identity.

Thus when we see vandalism, street crimes, graffiti, the squalor of
drug addiction, we may understand these as visual forms of violence.
When we hear rock music blaring from loudspeakers in high decibels
and other noises assaulting us, we are experiencing acoustical violence. When we smell the exhaust fumes from greasy luncheonettes
or city traffic, for example, we are victims of olfactory violence. And

if we marvel at the fact that many people actually enjoy being thus assaulted (stimulated), we can realize that the experiencing of violence is not altogether involuntary. It has self-confirmatory value; it reassures man in his erroneous but cherished belief about the nature of reality and his own existence. The bizarre phenomena of sadism and masochism are thus revealed to us in a context which broadly transcends the narrow and questionable theories of traditional psychoanalytic teaching about their sexual-libidinous dynamism and origin. It must be said, however, that in his later years Freud began to postulate a theory of death-instinct (Thanatos) which, if examined from an existential perspective, may very well reveal an awareness on his part of the strange tendency in man to destroy himself in the process of self-confirmatory pursuits.

To illustrate: A middle-aged, gifted writer with an excellent family background and a high cultural attainment sought psychiatric help for what he thought was a problem of homosexuality. In the course of his visits, he confided to his doctor that he had a secret habit. Occasionally, he would leave his wallet at home and take a stroll on the waterfront with a great sense of pleasurable anticipation and excitement. Invariably, he would find himself the target of some violence in the form of physical assault and robbery. This case, and of course many others, would suggest that there exists a mysterious link between victim and victimizer. The nature of this mysterious link is here presented as the universal tendency of man toward self-confirmatory ideation and self-confirmatory involvement. Self-confirmation is self-destruction, and self-destruction is self-confirmation.

It is thus safe to say that violence will be part of the human experience as long as man will have an unconscious desire to confirm himself as a physical ego-person, autonomous, self-existent, apart from his creator. "For they that are after the flesh do mind the things of the flesh; but they that are after the Spirit the things of the Spirit" (Romans 8:5).

From what has been said until now it may become clearer that violence can only be healed by helping man to transcend his self-confirmatory materialism. He needs to learn to "walk in the Spirit" in order not to "fulfil the lust of the flesh" (Galatians 5:16). To walk

in the spirit involves more than traditional religiosity or moral recti-
tude, it entails attaining a realization of existence as essentially
spiritual in nature, and the concept of man as a spiritual manifestation (image and likeness of God), an expression of divine intelligence
and love.

Such realization brings with it a radical transformation of man's
character and a more harmonious mode of being-in-the-world. He
sees himself as dwelling in consciousness (the secret place of the most
high). The violent and exciting ways of the carnal mind have no more
attraction for him. "None of these things move him" any more.
Knowledge of the truth of being leads him to freedom, wisdom, and
love. He becomes a beneficial presence rather than an ego-person. He
is now in the world as a blessing.

Session No. 18

THE COMFORTER

Question: Is there a way of being a beneficial presence to an individual who is in the hospital with a terminal disease?

Dr. Hora: You are asking, in other words, how to confront the issue of death, and how we can possibly be beneficial in a situation where someone is under the belief of a terminal disease. Well, of course, as in all crises, in a case of so-called terminal disease it is particularly comforting to know that there is no such thing as death. Life cannot die and there is no such thing as terminal disease. How can we say that? Well Jesus could say that. What did Jesus say about death? Whatever he said, we better believe it because he really knew whereof he spoke. He said: "I am the resurrection, and the life: he that believeth in me, though he were dead, yet shall he live." "And whosoever liveth and believeth in me shall never die" (John 11: 25,26).

What did he mean? How can somebody who is dead be alive, and how is it possible never to see death? Unless we understand what he meant, we can never be of comfort to anyone in a situation such as the questioner has described. Ordinarily we are concerned about how to behave in such an awkward situation. The operational idea is: How to act in such a way that would be most appropriate and least anxiety provoking, or at least in some way comforting. But now we are not concerned with behavior or operationalism, we are concerned with gaining such understanding of life and of what is called death, that our very presence would be comforting to the individual in need. Only what we really know has the power to comfort.

It is described in literature that Zen Masters have a custom of inviting their friends to a party just before they are about to die. And they know it ahead of time, perhaps a few days or a week or two, while yet in perfect health. They invite their friends and have a farewell party, very peaceful and perhaps even joyous. A situation is described where a disciple was crying at such a party and the Zen Master rebuked him and said: "What are you crying for? I am going to paradise and you are crying. There is no reason to cry." They seem to know something we don't know yet, and that Jesus also seems to have known and alluded to. Namely, that there is a radical difference between dying and passing on. Unenlightened man may have the dreadful experience of dying perhaps in more ways than one. Enlightened man, having attained the conscious understanding of transcendent reality, may have a peaceful awareness of transition into another dimension of consciousness.

Now the question is, how could we approximate such understanding? The basic issue here again is the question, what is man? The difference between an enlightened Zen Master or Jesus Christ and ordinary people is that they know something about what reality is and what man is. They know that if someone seems to be dying, he may not really be dying. What is happening is that an appearance is disappearing. They know that physical existence is a phenomenon, that man is a phenomenon. A phenomenon is thought in visible form. Appearances appear and disappear, but realities are immutable. Whatever is real cannot die.

Therefore, it would be a tremendous advantage and a great comfort to all of us if we could understand the reality of man, what he really is rather than just what he appears to be.

To be a beneficial and comforting presence in a situation where someone seems to be dying, one would need to know the answer to the question, what is what really is? It was mentioned here that man is an individual consciousness. What is consciousness? Can consciousness die? Could we find out what consciousness is? We know that physical man is a phenomenon, but is consciousness an epiphenomenon?

Medical science, notably brain physiology, claims that consciousness is the epiphenomenon of the structure of the brain and the electrochemical processes which take place in the brain. These processes produce consciousness. If we look at it this way, then consciousness would be the epiphenomenon. But then we could not account for life. But when Jesus said that even if man were dead, yet he shall live, he must have had in mind a different concept of what life is. He must have pointed to consciousness, which is independent of brain physiology.

To unenlightened man what matters most is experiencing, but to enlightened man the most essential issue is the truth of being. I heard a story once about a terminally ill woman who was expected to die any hour. A whole retinue of physicians was standing around her bed having a conference and expecting her to pass on. As she looked around at all those people, suddenly she had a vision. She saw herself standing with the doctors and looking at herself lying in the bed about to die. This was a very strange experience and had never happened to her before. The vision lasted just a few minutes. The doctors left and a few hours later, she sat up in bed and said, "What am I doing here? There is nothing wrong with me!" She got up, got dressed, and was healed. Is this possible?

Comment: It happens every day.

Dr. Hora: Could you tell us what you mean?

Comment: I have read of such instances.

Dr. Hora: So then, what would be important is to gain increasing realization of what consciousness is, and of what is what really *is*. To unenlightened man what he feels is what really *is*. We know what fear is because we can feel afraid; we know what pain is because we can feel pain; we know what pleasure is because we can feel pleasure. The more unenlightened we are, the more we use our feelings as criteria of reality. But anyone who has ever seen a hypnotist tell people what to feel and how to feel, can see that one can feel anything he wants and it has nothing to do with reality; it has to do with suggested thought.

Question: Don't feelings serve a useful function?

Dr. Hora: In the context of physical existence they serve a useful function, just as bowel movements serve a useful function. It is helpful to understand that feelings are by-products of thought processes. Many psychologists give primary consideration to feelings, and they say: "First you feel and then you think about what you feel. Then you can lean on your feelings to guide you to know whether you are on the right track or not." But I think that is not correct. I found it helpful to consider feelings as by-products of thought processes, just as bowel movements are by-products of digestive processes.

Interestingly enough, those who overemphasize the importance of how they feel tend to become very anxious, hedonistic, self-indulgent, and even hypochondriacal. People who are very interested in the frequency, consistency, and quality of their bowel movements tend to develop gastrointestinal complications such as colitis, ileitis, gastritis, cholecystitis. We can say that where a man's treasure lies, there shall his problems be also. We said earlier that there are three things which give us trouble in life: what we cherish, what we hate, and what we fear.

Question: Are you talking about physical feelings or emotions?

Dr. Hora: What is the difference between feelings and emotions?

Comment: I was thinking of intuition as an emotion, what is referred to as "gut feeling." Is that also a by-product of thought processes?

Dr. Hora: There is absolutely no connection between "gut feelings" and intuition. Isn't it interesting that the phrase "gut feelings" has entered into our linguistic usage. What is a gut feeling? In reality a gut feeling is a cramp, a bellyache, an intestinal spasm. The gut feeling indicates anxiety. When we are afraid, we get spasms in the intestines; and when we are anxious, we get "butterflies" in the stomach, which is the so-called solar plexus. But intuition is of an entirely different order. What is intuition?

Comment: Intuition is a nonrational apprehension of reality.

Dr. Hora: How can we account for that? Is it possible for us to understand intuition in some way?

Comment: I don't think intuition is irrational.

Comment: Irrational means automatic.

Comment: Rational is also automatic.

Comment: Machines are rational.

Dr. Hora: Machines are logical. What is the difference between logical and rational?

Comment: Logic is a strictly mechanical process.

Dr. Hora: What is rational? Rational is that which is within the context of our worldview. Whatever does not fit into the context of our worldview appears to be irrational. We are all thinking within a certain context of presuppositions. There are many schools of psychotherapy that are all based on certain particular presuppositions about man. To the extent that they vary, the rationale and rationalizations will vary, and what seems to be rational in one school of thought may appear to be irrational in another. To say that man is alive even though he has died, seems totally irrational from the material viewpoint on life. But it is not irrational from a spiritual viewpoint on life. When Jesus made these fantastic statements of paradoxal nature, he was not being irrational or crazy. He knew that what to unenlightened man appears to be death, to enlightened man is just an advancement to another phase of life.

Whenever we are committed to certain preconceived ideas about reality, we will find things which other people are talking about irrational because they do not fit into the context within which our reasoning is habitually taking place. Intuition is not irrational, it is synonymous with creative intelligence, inspired wisdom.

In existential psychotherapy we are aiming at liberating man from his epistemic limitations. What are the epistemic limitations in which most of us live? Epistemic limitations are limitations of our knowledge about what we are able to know.

Session No. 19

INSPIRED LIVING

Question: I would like to ask your comment on the positive aspects of fear. For instance, I have observed that children enjoy being afraid on Halloween nights; there seems to be some self-confirming quality to experiencing scary things. They get a thrill out of it and it makes them feel alive. This seems to be fairly universal. Would you please comment on the constructive aspects of fear?

Dr. Hora: Fear has no constructive aspects at all. There is a peculiar tendency in man, one of the many I must say, that he mistakes excitement for vitality and has a strange taste for excitement. Unenlightened thinking is dualistic, which means that we tend to think in opposites. There is a universal fear of death, we do not want to be dead. We all want to feel alive. Unwittingly, we assume that peace is synonymous with being dead and life is synonymous with excitement. So, from childhood on we like to whistle in the dark and make noise to assure ourselves that we are not dead.

Comment: That may explain the transistor radios on the subway.

Dr. Hora: Right, the phenomenon of rock music and high decibel stereo reproductions belong here as well. The more primitive man is, the more he will enjoy noise, crowds, excitement, and all sorts of sensory stimulation. Adolescents even do their homework with the radio blaring. The more noise, the more excitement; the more external stimulation, the more seeming aliveness. There is actually a fear of peace and quiet. It is the dread of nothingness which the existential philosophers have brought to our attention. There is even an enjoyment of fear. Fear itself becomes a stimulation and can take on fantastic proportions. People pay money to go to the movies to see disasters and get all up tight. As of late, there is a vogue in catastrophic movies, such as *Towering Inferno, Jaws, The Exorcist.*

Halloween is a national holiday for enjoying fear. People are trying to feel alive and going about it the wrong way. Excitement is counterfeit happiness. Many are complaining about anxiety and fear, but actually they are also courting it.

There is a story about a spinster who had a habit of checking under the bed to see if it is safe to go to sleep. For years she went through this ritual of checking to make sure nobody was hiding there. After many years of doing this, one day she looked and, lo and behold, there was a man hiding under her bed. She screamed from excitement and fear and said: "Finally you are here!"

Isn't it strange how these thought processes operate? How important it is for mankind to understand what real life is. We all want to live life fully and we do not know how because we don't know what life is. We think that life should be exciting, otherwise we are dead. One of the great objections one can hear against existential philosophy and spiritual interests is that it is "quietistic." This is a pejorative term, as if to say: Only fools want to be quiet. Real people want to feel alive, excited, have fun.

Now if excitement is recognized as a mistaken effort to feel alive, what would be the healthy alternative? Boredom? No. Boredom is the opposite of excitement, boredom and excitement are two sides of the same coin. What is the healthy alternative to an exciting life?

Comment: Peace and harmony.

Dr. Hora: Yes, but isn't that boring? That could be labeled as quietism and then our detractors would have a point. Surely, we appreciate peace and harmony but that in itself is not enough. The alternative to a life of excitement is inspired living. What is inspired living?

Comment: This brings to mind the story of the woman who met Jesus at the well, and his remarks about the water of life.

Dr. Hora: What did Jesus mean by the water of life springing up from within? Do you all know the story of the woman at the well?

Comment: No.

Dr. Hora: Jesus was sitting at Jacob's well. A Samaritan woman came to draw water and they had a conversation. And Jesus recognized that this woman lived a life of excitement. She was promiscuous. She was seeking fulfillment through promiscuity. Jesus told her that if she drank of this water, she would thirst again. He meant: If you seek excitement in life, you will always be getting bored and, in turn, will seek more and more excitement. Then he told her to drink of the water of life which he would give her and she would never thirst again. It would be "a well of water springing up into everlasting life." In a way, Jesus was telling her about what we are discussing. Namely, that the life of excitement is unsatisfactory, but inspired living is truly satisfying.

What is this well of living waters which Jesus is speaking about? Excitement is external stimulation, inspired living is an inner flow of intelligent, creative, and loving ideas. What is the source of inspired wisdom? "Whence cometh it?"

Question: Does it come from God?

Dr. Hora: What do we mean by God? God is just as much a word as the "well of living waters."

Comment: Love-Intelligence.

Dr. Hora: Love-Intelligence is another phrase pointing in the direction of this mysterious source of wisdom, energy, power, love, creativity which is continually flowing into consciousness and seeks expression in wholesome harmonious living if man succeeds in connecting up to it. And that's what Jesus was teaching us, how to establish contact with this source, and how to live out of this source rather than from external stimulation, which is only excitement.

The method of establishing, maintaining, and increasing our contact with this source is prayer and meditation, or beholding, and the right understanding of the difference between an exciting life and inspired living. Now Jesus did not say to this woman: "Don't be promiscuous!" He told her he had something better for her. What traditional religions fail to do is to help people discover something better. They just say, don't do this and don't do that. But unless we discover something better, we cannot give up what we consider of vital importance.

It is also helpful to understand that enlightened man is not a thinker. Most of us flatter ourselves with the idea that we can think.

The philosopher Heidegger brought out the fact that there is two kinds of thinking: calculative thinking *(das vorstellende Denken)* and inspired thinking *(das andenkende Denken)*. Ordinarily, unenlightened man is forever calculating, manipulating, figuring, weighing the odds; he "uses his head," he has a personal sense of life, he sort of seeks to manipulate life with his brain. Enlightened man abandons calculative thinking, he allows inspired wisdom to obtain in his consciousness and provide him with creative ideas which then take care of his needs.

So another approach to the well of living waters is understanding the difference between calculative thinking and inspired wisdom. In prayer and meditation we endeavor to become available to this source of wisdom and seek to let it inspire us with the right ideas which we need for effective living. The more we are able to live this way, in constant conscious awareness of creative intelligence, the more enlightened we become. At first, it only happens occasionally, sometimes by chance; later, when we have learned prayer and meditation, we can sort of plug in on it. After a while, it may become a habit of thinking through *listening* instead of through *calculating*.

Question: Would you explain the difference between what you are speaking of and detachment?

Dr. Hora: Gladly, but let me just finish the thread of this thought first. The ultimate goal is surrender to this source. Here we are continually living from this center; all calculative, manipulative, and influencing tendencies have fallen away and we are in at-one-ment with this source. Jesus, when he achieved this point, said: "I and my Father are one" (John 10:30). "I am in the Father, and the Father in me" (John 14:11). His personal sense of self has disappeared and from then on he lives as an emanation of Love-Intelligence. And that, of course, is ultimate freedom attainment.

Now what is detachment? Who can define detachment?

Comment: Closing oneself off from feelings that one finds unpleasant. In that sense, it would be an escape.

Dr. Hora: Detachment is the opposite of attachment. When we are attached, what are we attached to?

Comment: Persons, things, places, ideologies.

Dr. Hora: What are these things?

Comment: Needs.

Dr. Hora: An attachment is clinging to something that we consider vitally important for happiness, safety, and life. It can be person, place, thing, ideology, or psychotherapeutic school. Man wants to feel secure and alive and, not knowing the source of true life, he has the tendency to attach himself to something. Conventional psychological thinking says: In order to be healthy, you have to be attached to other people; it is called involvement in relationships. If you are sick, it is because you don't know how to handle these attachments to other people and, in disgust or defense, you detach yourself from people. And you are a loner and that's bad. But what is not understood is that to be attached or detached is the same. Is that clear?

Comment: Vaguely.

Dr. Hora: What makes it the same?

Comment: They are two sides of the same coin.

Dr. Hora: Essentially it is an erroneous way of viewing life and reality. What is it that you don't understand?

Answer: Two things that are very different are suddenly called the same. I can see it more in terms of dependency than in seeing both words as meaning the same thing.

Dr. Hora: What is the difference between attachment and dependency?

Comment: Both suggest clinging.

Dr. Hora: In other words, to be attached or detached is the same. To be dependent or independent is also the same. For instance, I knew a young lady of very wealthy parents who ran away from home and was driving a taxi in New York City and living in Greenwich Village in terrible squalor, a miserable life. She said, "Well, I wanted to be free, I left home to be free." I was able to show her that she was not free, she was only independent, which means she was still dependent because she was fighting against her parents by driving a taxi and living in poverty. That's not freedom, it is a struggle for independence, which is a state of dependency. If one were not dependent, one wouldn't have to fight for independence.

So to be independent is the same as to be dependent. Yes is no, and no is yes. And to be detached is the same as to be attached. But what about freedom? How did Jesus define freedom?

Comment: Freedom is knowing the truth.

Dr. Hora: The truth of what? The truth of what really is. What do we mean by "is"?

Comment: That which truly exists.

Dr. Hora: When Moses asked God: "Tell me your name," God said to him: "I AM THAT I AM" (Exodus 3:14). What does that mean? In present-day language we could say that God said to Moses: "I am what *is.*" Moses was seeking enlightenment, he was seeking to understand reality and he found it by understanding that God is reality, the source of infinite intelligence, vitality, love, inspired wisdom. This center which we spoke about, this well of living waters, this is what really *is.* So God said to Moses: "I am what is." And in another place the Bible says, "God is all in all," *Omnis in omnis.* Tillich called it ultimate reality. Freedom comes from knowing reality, the truth of what really is. In reality there is neither attachment nor detachment, there is neither dependency nor independence.

Comment: And then there is neither subject nor object, and God is not the Holy Other. There is no dualism and there is no split.

Dr. Hora: Yes, "I and my Father are one." Once we realize that, what happens? What is the healthy alternative to attachment and detachment? What could that be which is neither this nor that? The English language offers us an approximately acceptable word: "nonattachment." Nonattachment is synonymous with freedom. Enlightened man lives in conscious union with the source of infinite wisdom and love; therefore, he is neither attached nor detached, neither dependent nor independent. None of these categories apply to him, he is just free to be a blessing in the world. The quality of his consciousness has a healing and harmonizing radiancy wherever he is.

What practical relevancy does all this have to psychotherapy? If we understand what constitutes freedom and healthy living, what constitutes the real good, what is existentially valid, and what is existentially invalid, we shall be spontaneously very effective in our work. The Hora principle of psychotherapy is this:

"If you know what, you know how."

Session No. 20

WANTS AND NEEDS

Question: How do I reconcile my need for excitement with all the things you have told us about inspired living?

Dr. Hora: Is there such a thing as a *need* for excitement?

Comment: If he feels a need, he must have one.

Dr. Hora: It is very important to have a clear understanding in our consciousness of the difference between a need and a want. This subtle differentiation may have far-reaching consequences for practical living. Recently, a young lady thought she wanted to buy a car and she had a very hard time finding a car. She didn't know what kind to buy, what model to get, how to go about it; all her attempts were unsuccessful. She had the money, she had the time, she had everything, and yet she couldn't buy a car. In talking to her, it struck me that she kept talking about wanting a car. I heard her say, "I want a car and I don't seem to be able to buy it. I don't know what kind of a car I should want." She was told, "Maybe if you would consider whether you really need a car, things would become clearer to you and perhaps it would be easier to get a car."

What happens if we don't clearly understand the difference between "I want" and "I need"? The Bible says, "It is your Father's good pleasure to give you the kingdom" (Luke 12:32). That is something that we really need. When we are aware of a need, we can usually get it. Whatever we really need, we have little difficulty getting, but we have to be sincere about it. However, what happens when we are not thinking in terms of needs but in terms of wants? What is it about these little words that seems to make such a difference?

Comment: It is an ego thing.

Dr. Hora: Exactly. When we think about what we want, we exclude God from our consideration. At that moment we are on our own. It is like disregarding the force of gravitation. That is not a wise thing to do. We are only making things hard for ourselves. There are people to whom everything comes very hard. Some people have a hard time in life, for them even the smallest thing seems hard to come by. On the other hand, there are people for whom everything seems to be easy. Surely that's not just due to some capricious fate. There must be some underlying principle here which is being either consciously or unconsciously obeyed, or flaunted. When we learn to understand, appreciate, and cherish the difference between wanting and needing, we may be successful in tuning in on the principle of an infinite supply of good. There is a higher intelligence underlying reality, and this intelligence is essentially benevolent. We call it the principle of Love-Intelligence. We endeavor to understand this principle, tune in on it, and let it bless us with what Jesus called "the abundant life." "I want" is an arrogant position, is it not? What does the word arrogant mean?

Comment: Proud, haughty, presumptive.

Dr. Hora: What is the etymological root of "arrogancy?"

Comment: To arrogate?

Dr. Hora: Right. It is to arrogate to ourselves something that is not rightfully ours. If we are in the habit of thinking in terms of "I want" and "I don't want," we have assumed an arrogant position toward existence, and our mode of being-in-the-world has become existentially invalid. Without realizing it, we are making things difficult for ourselves.

There is a family that consists of two grandparents, a divorced mother, and two little girls. The girls are absolutely unmanageable, frighteningly rebellious, destructive, and out of control. The grandparents are desperate and the mother, who goes to work, is afraid to come home. In talking to the mother and the grandparents, one thing became very clear. They never say to the children: "Here is your milk." They always say: "I want you to drink your milk." An unfortunate habit has taken over the whole family and most sentences start with either "I want" or "I don't want." "I want you to go to sleep." "I don't want you to watch television." And what do the children

say? "I don't want to want what you want me to want." "Whatever
you want, I don't want." This builds up into stormy scenes. These
are loving people, but they don't know the difference between a want
and a need. Such a seemingly inconsequential issue can have far-
reaching consequences. In that climate of tyrannical coerciveness
there are frequent psychosomatic breakdowns, somebody is always
getting sick. It is interesting that when this was brought to the
attention of the family, they had a hard time switching over from "I
want" to what is needed.

There is something in man which resists humility, we would like
to believe that we are in control. The more we cherish the idea of
being in control, the more troublesome our lives become. Some
people cherish the idea of being in control to such an extent that,
when they are being shown and taught about God and about prayer
and about spiritual values, they may begin to use God in subtle ways
as a tool of controlling the world around them.

One such lady has two big dogs. These dogs are hard to handle.
They don't obey her, and when she takes them out for a walk, they
are pulling her so hard that she cannot walk with them. The other
day she said: "I prayed to God that these dogs should be well-
behaved. Nothing happened. Instead, they act like two idiots." Can
we get a "handle" on God and religion in such a way as to control
our affairs with the help of God? Can we tell God what we want and
that he should get it for us? What do you think? Again, it is the same
secret desire to believe in a personal power to control our affairs and
run them according to what we want, even to use God as our servant.

With the help of prayer and religiosity we may attempt to use God
to do our bidding. Then we seek to control God. Then we would be
greater than God. Of what good is a god if you cannot tell him what
he should do, right? What is the general idea about prayer? Isn't
prayer a way of telling God what he should do for us? The prayer
of supplication is often nothing more than telling God what we want.

There is a story about two brothers. One was very religious, the
other didn't bother much about God. The religious one was very
poor and afflicted, while the other fellow was doing well, thriving in
his business. One day the religious one came to his brother and asked
him: "How is it possible that you never pray and are not religious

and yet you are doing so well? And I pray so much and nothing good ever comes my way?" His brother said, "Well, maybe you nag him too much."

Question: What is the right approach?

Dr. Hora: What happens when we begin to think in terms of needs instead of wants? These tiny little, seemingly insignificant, details have surprising ramifications.

I recall that recently a young lady told me a story. She and her girlfriend were subjected to verbal abuse by a supervisor at the place of their work. The lady who told me the story got terribly upset and felt deeply hurt; she couldn't get over it that this man talked to her in such a manner. Her girl friend, who was equally subjected to that tirade of abuse, was not upset at all. She said: "He just needs to talk to somebody." We see here the difference in two ways of responding to the same situation. One was thinking that she wanted to be treated right, while the other was thinking of what the need was. When we think in terms of needs, we can be loving. Parents who think in terms of what their children need can be spontaneously loving. But if they think about what they want—well, everything is suddenly different.

Now what about therapists? Suppose we are in our office and one of our patients is hostile, aggressive, abusive. We can react badly or we can remain calm and loving, depending on whether we are thinking about what we want, or what the patient needs. An entire *Weltanschauung* is at issue, a way of seeing life, a mode of being-in-the-world. There can be a radical change in our experiences and in our responses according to certain habits of thought. "For as he thinketh in his heart, so is he" (Proverbs 23:7).

Comment: I was just wondering how you can think in your heart. I find this a contradiction.

Dr. Hora: To think in one's heart is a metaphor. What is a metaphor?

Comment: A symbol.

Dr. Hora: It is a symbolic way of communicating an idea. A metaphor is a word which carries a meaning beyond itself. *Metaphor,* to carry something beyond. Let us clarify this metaphor. What does the Bible mean by saying: "For as he thinketh in his heart, so is he?"

Comment: It is what one cherishes in thought.

Dr. Hora: That's right. What we cherish in thought, determines our mode of being-in-the-world. Now let us come back to the original question and ask: "Do we *need* excitement, or do we *want* excitement?"

Comment: It seems to me that people want excitement, and most of the television programs cater to that.

Comment: I believe that there is a need for, say, stimulation, if not excitement. What this brings to mind is the experiment on infants who were deprived of stimulation. A large number of them developed depression and, as a result, even died in institutions.

Dr. Hora: These experiments you are talking about were conducted by Rene Spitz, a well-known psychiatrist, and they deal with so-called anaclitic depressions. What is anaclitic depression? What does the word "anaclitic" mean? The word anaclitic refers to a need to lean on somebody, to lean on someone who is a representative of nurturing love. These infants were deprived of mother love. They were given perfect scientific infant care by noncaring, well-trained nurses. There was stimulation from the environment; they were fed; they were diapered; they were kept in clean rooms; their medical needs were provided for scientifically; but they were deprived of nurturing love. They developed anaclitic depression and a certain percentage of them died of intercurrent complications. Those who didn't die were probably very troubled for a long time. Of course, the right kind of stimulation is important, but it is not synonymous with excitement. What is the difference between stimulation and excitement?

Comment: The degree of intensity.

Dr. Hora: Right. And purposefulness. The healthy reaction to stimuli is response; this is, of course, needed. But excitement is a form of entertainment, a way of trying to be happy and feel alive through the titillation of the senses.

In inspired living there are internal and external stimuli in harmonious balance providing for an optimum unfoldment of consciousness; there is restful activity. Has anyone ever experienced restful activity? Activity which does not lead to fatigue?

There is a story about two Zen monks who were famous for their joy and happiness. People from far and wide came to talk to them. They asked them about the secret of their happiness and their joy. The monks answered: "Isn't it marvelous, chopping wood and carrying water all day long?" What did they mean? What do you think that means?

Comment: I would say that they were not thinking about what should be.

Dr. Hora: What do you mean by what should be?

Comment: What one wants.

Dr. Hora: Yes. It seems that, with such a mental outlook, it is possible that the most difficult physical labor would not be fatiguing. Actually it would be stimulating. Very much depends on our mental attitude toward life and toward the work itself. Our mental attitude depends, of course, on the values we cherish.

Session No. 21

FAMILY THERAPY

Question: I was wondering whether you do family therapy, and what your ideas might be about it, whether they are different from what we learned until now?

Dr. Hora: I don't work with families, but I do work with parents and with couples. I really don't believe that we can help a child apart from the parents. The way I see children is that they are extensions of the consciousness of the parents.

Question: The bad consciousness?

Dr. Hora: Fortunately, the good too. And if parents worry about their children, then it is helpful to show them that the most important factors in the life of their children are not the school, the television set, the playmates, or the neighborhood, but what the parents cherish, what they hate and what they fear. These three factors seem crucial. Any parents who are seriously concerned about being good parents, would be well advised to take stock of their secret thoughts and reach a point where they would be willing to be embarrassed about themselves and alter their mental preoccupations.

For example, recently a lady came with a problem of a *tic douloureux.* Do you know what a *tic douloureux* is? It is a painful twitching of the face. This condition plagued the patient for over ten years. She consulted many physicians about it. Novocain injections and other forms of treatment were tried but with no relief. It is known that this problem does not yield easily to any kind of medical treatment. In exploring the patient's ideas, we discovered that she had one prevailing thought—to be better than her daughter. There was a secret competition going on for many years between herself and her daughter. Both of them had become very successful in life; the mother in business and the daughter socially. The patient never admitted this to herself. She always thought of herself as a very good, self-sacrificing mother who loved her daughter and admired her, except that there was always some unexplainable tension between them. Not long ago she went to visit her daughter, who has a little boy. When she arrived at their home, the little boy started yelling and screaming and said to his mother, "Get out, I want to be with Grandma alone." This was a tremendous triumph to her; it made her extremely happy. Here she was told that she was better than her daughter, the child recognized her superiority over her daughter.

It took quite some time and considerable self-confrontation for her to begin to admit that she looks upon her daughter as a rival. At one point she remarked that her daughter, though she writes books, has never sold any. When it was pointed out to her that she said this with a certain amount of glee, she became very embarrassed. After this she had a twenty-four-hour period of severe guilt reaction. It was pointed out to her that this guilt reaction was just an attempt to cover up her embarrassment. She relaxed in time, and finally said: "I guess it is true, I was always competing with my daughter." At that point the *tic douloureux* disappeared. She was able to "face up" to this great secret, this cherished idea. You can probably surmise how competitive the daughter is, and even the grandchild.

So if we want to be good parents, it is important that we cherish the right ideas, existentially valid ideas, and be free of hate and of fear. Then we can be good parents, good spouses, and our mode of being-in-the-world will be harmonious and wholesome.

Recently a family problem involving twin boys came to my attention. One of them was an excellent scholar. He was getting good marks, reading well, was good in arithmetic and in everything else. The other one was failing. He couldn't read, he couldn't do math, he was having trouble in the same school and in the same class where his brother was so successful. How is it possible? Can you explain it? Who is the casting director in this play?

Comment: They are seeking attention, each in his own way.

Dr. Hora: You have just demonstrated the conventional reasoning in psychology, which is based on cause-and-effect thinking. But if you remember some of our previous sessions, we have discarded cause-and-effect reasoning as invalid, narrow-minded thinking. Would you like to know what happened to these children when the parents began to face up to their problem? The poor student became a good student, and the good student developed asthma. What happened here?

Comment: It seems to me that this was a new way of getting attention.

Dr. Hora: Would you like to know what was really going on? After having clarified the problem to some extent, the parents altered their thinking about the failing child, and they began to think well about him. But they were not willing to alter their thinking about the successful child. You see, being successful seems good, so why bother? Why change a good thing? They let the successful child be successful. Success then just increased a little bit until he was losing his breath. So there is more here than seeking to get attention through success or failure or illness. There is something more that needs to be considered.

Comment: The idea of ambition and competition in the parents' thoughts.

Dr. Hora: Right. The dualism of thinking in terms of ambition and success, the love of success and the fear of failure. Being a failure is a particular form of success. One can be ambitious in opposite directions; one can be ambitious to fail and one can be ambitious to succeed. And it is the same. And if ambition is carried a little beyond a reasonable degree, one can get sick. The successful child is losing his breath, he is running so hard that he cannot breathe.

So if we want to help these children, what must happen? Certainly the parents' idea of what is good, what is desirable needs to be brought in line with what is existentially valid. Aren't ambition and success existentially valid? Don't we all want that? Aren't we all striving for success in life? Can we discover on our own the existentially valid ideas which we need in order to be healthy, and to be good parents? What would be the existentially valid way for parents to think about their children? What is really important? Clearly, the values of the parents are expressing themselves in the children as troublesome, and these values need to be changed. How can the parents achieve this?

The danger here is of slipping into cause-and-effect thinking which is very common. If we slip into that error, then we are talking about responsibility when we really mean blame. And then there is recrimination and trouble. Let me give you another illustration.

There was a couple who had a pet dog. Every time they had a fight, this dog developed a prolapse of the rectum. When the fight was over, the prolapse disappeared and the dog was all right. This happened repeatedly. Whenever the couple started blaming themselves or each other, the prolapse would get worse until such time when they could see that this was not a cause-and-effect situation. They didn't cause the prolapse to happen, the prolapse was a manifestation of the discord in their consciousness. A home is really the mental climate of consciousness. In a mental climate of discord and mutual recrimination, certain pathological phenomena occur. As long as these people were blaming themselves for the poor dog's suffering, they couldn't solve the problem; instead of solving the problem, it was getting worse.

Question: Dr. Hora, I don't understand the difference between manifestation and effect.

Dr. Hora: I will explain. As long as we are in the habit of asking the four futile questions—Why did this happen? Who is to blame? What should we do? How should we do it?—there is no hope of finding a solution. But when this couple was led to ask the two intelligent questions, then there was healing. Their marriage was healed and the dog was healed. To the first intelligent question— What is the meaning of what seems to be going on here?—the answer is: There seems to be discord in the house. To the second intelligent question—What is what is really going on here?—the answer is love and harmony and peace and mutual regard, because in divine reality that is the status quo: peace, harmony, assurance, gratitude, and love. As the couple began to see their situation in the context of jointly participating in the good of God, the fights disappeared, the discord disappeared, and the dog was healed. The prolapse of the rectum was not caused by the discord between husband and wife, it was indicating the presence of discord. It is presumptuous for anyone to think that he can, through his thoughts, produce a prolapse of the rectum in the dog. That would be magic thinking. The phenomena are indicating the presence of certain emotionally charged thoughts. Thoughts in general have a tendency to express themselves as phenomena. Phenomena are thoughts in visible form.

Question: Aren't thoughts also phenomena?

Dr. Hora: Invalid thoughts are phenomena in manifest form. And the same principle applies to the condition of both children and pets. Pets are also living in the noosphere, which is the mental climate of the significant adults around them. What is needed is to outgrow cause-and-effect thinking. Then we will be able to see phenomenolog-ically and the right healing solutions will be possible. As long as our thinking is within cause-and-effect reasoning, the harder we try to heal something the worse it gets. A healing cannot be caused to happen; it unfolds, as a shift in consciousness occurs, due to im-proved perception.

Session No. 22

ETHICS
OF PSYCHOTHERAPY

It is a principle of psychotherapy that we must respect the patient's explicit desire for help in certain areas. We cannot tell him what he needs, we must wait until he reveals his need. So when we sit with a patient we are waiting until he makes his need known to us, and then we try to understand the issue. Having understood it, we proceed to make relevant comments. Unsolicited solicitude is trespassing. This principle applies not only to psychotherapy but to all of life. The ethics of psychotherapy apply to all of life. We don't impose anything on people, not even on animals or plants. We seek to discern the need and proceed to respond to it in a constructive and helpful way. Would you call that being passive? It is neither active nor passive. What is it? It is being responsive. What is responsibility? Most people think of responsibility as liability.

Comment: Responsibility is blameworthiness.

Dr. Hora: In general usage, when someone says to us, you are responsible for this, what do they mean? They mean you are to blame for it. But this is a mistaken usage of the word. What is the meaning of the word "responsibility"?

Comment: The ability to respond.

Dr. Hora: That's right. God gave us the ability to respond to our fellow man, to nature, to animals and plants, to whatever the need appears to be. Thus, man is able to be a beneficial presence in the world. Only man has the gift of response-ability.

Question: Isn't it a burden?

Dr. Hora: It is only a burden if we misunderstand it in terms of liability, but it is a divine attribute if we understand it as a God-given assignment to have "dominion over the fish of the sea, and over the fowls of the air, and over the cattle, and over all the earth, and over every creeping thing that creepeth upon the earth" (Genesis 1:26). Only man has this ability to respond, animals don't respond. What do animals do?

Comment: They react.

Dr. Hora: Right. Now in our clinical work, we seek to be responsive to the patient's manifest need in such a way that it might have beneficial consequences. When the concept of responsibility is not understood in its ontological context, then it becomes problematic. What do we mean by ontological context?

Comment: The context of being.

Dr. Hora: Right.

Question: Doesn't responsibility imply a dialogue in contrast to reaction?

Dr. Hora: Certainly, it is dialogic. Reaction is unthinking. It is not based on understanding, it is not based on transcendence. It is just based on sensory or emotional gratification. When we react, we are concerned about our own needs. When we respond, we are concerned about the needs that reveal themselves beyond ourselves. We transcend ourselves in responding. When a patient comes to us, he is not interested in how we feel, and he is not interested in what we want, he is interested in finding answers to his problems. So we must transcend ourselves and be available in a responsive way to whatever needs reveal themselves from moment to moment.

Sometimes, when we are partisans of some school of thought or some philosophy, we can lose sight of this and instead of responding to the patient's need, we fall into the error of advocacy. What is advocacy?

Comment: Selling something.

Dr. Hora: Right. Selling a particular cherished idea or point of view. I remember in my younger years, I was in a therapy group as a trainee and the psychoanalyst who was conducting the group had a Marxian bias. At that time, there was a taxi strike in New York City, so our group sessions revolved around the question whether one should take a taxi or not, whether one should support the strike or be a strikebreaker. We were being indoctrinated in Marxism, and that was called group psychoanalysis. Our good doctor didn't even realize that he was out of order. We must be very careful not to commit the sin of advocacy. How is it possible not to sell our favorite ideas? Is it possible to be objective?

When we are advocating something, we are being subjective, we are speaking about what we like. There are certain subjects which we like to talk about. We are being subjective. Is it possible to be objective for anybody?

Comment: Yes, I think so, if you are listening to the need of the patient.

Dr. Hora: But when we are listening to someone's need, are we being objective? No, we are being transjective. What is that?

Comment: Sounds like something on the way to being objective.

Dr. Hora: No, it is beyond that.

Comment: It sounds as if you have just eliminated another dualism.

Dr. Hora: Yes, that's what we are doing all the time. Would you like to know what transjective is?

Comment: It is from an ontological perspective.

Dr. Hora: Yes, it is neither subjective nor objective, it transcends these categories. It does not concern itself with what we like, what we want, or what the patient likes or wants; it concerns itself with what really is.

Question: Isn't that a definition of "objective"?

Dr. Hora: No, reality is not an object. Reality is neither subjective nor objective, it is existential, it is what really is. How can we tell that it really is?

We are not advocating anything, we don't want anything. We have the capacity to respond, the ability to respond. And that makes man divine in contrast to all living creatures on the planet. But what happens when our responses are biased? Is that also a response? Is a biased response a response? It is neither a reaction nor a response. What is it?

Comment: It is an interpretation.

Dr. Hora: What is an interpretation?

Comment: Something learned.

Dr. Hora: Is that a response? It is not a response, it is a conditioned reaction. Animals react, miseducated man is conditioned, enlightened man responds. Love is responsive. Man is able to react as an animal or as a conditioned creature or as a divine consciousness, in which case he responds. A spiritual being who sees reality in the context of Love-Intelligence is able to respond. When we are learning to be partisans of certain psychotherapeutic schools, we are becoming conditioned. A conditioned reaction is called an interpretation. What is a response called in psychotherapy?

Comment: Understanding.

Dr. Hora: Right, understanding. We do not interpret, we clarify. You remember we said that the existential psychotherapeutic work is hermeneutic, that means clarifying, elucidating, shedding light, helping to make things clear. So there is a fundamental difference. When we sit with a patient we wait for something to reveal itself. And when something reveals itself we try to understand it, not in the context of a particular theory but in the context of existence. And when we have understood it, which means that what *is* has revealed itself to us, then we proceed to shed light, to clarify what has revealed itself to us. That helps the patient to understand, and when we know what, we know how. Then everything becomes very simple. Our work becomes complicated when, instead of understanding, we are interpreting things in the light of preconceived ideas and trying to fit the patient into a Procrustian bed. What is a Procrustian bed?

Comment: My teacher used to talk about Procrustian analysis, which meant pigeon-holing patients.

Comment: Procrustes was a famous innkeeper in ancient Greece. He was fitting his guests to the size of the beds, either by stretching them or cutting them short.

Question: We are talking about clinical issues, but it strikes me that the more we focus on therapy, the more we are talking about the consciousness of the therapist where he has arrived at the point of at-one-ment with what is, and that there is no way to be therapeutically present unless the condition has developed.

Dr. Hora: That's a beautiful statement, but what is the question?

Question: I expected to be looking more and more at the client, and we are looking more and more at the consciousness of the therapist.

Dr. Hora: It is in accordance with the biblical admonition: "Cast out first the beam out of thine own eye, and then shalt thou see clearly to pull out the mote that is in thy [patient's] eye" (Luke 6:42). What could be more important than the therapist's consciousness? It is the therapeutic tool. If we don't have the equipment, how can we do the work? The most important aspect of training, it would seem, is the liberation of the therapist's consciousness. Otherwise what happens? According to the Bible—which is a very good textbook of psychotherapy—"the blind would be leading the blind." And what happens then? "Together they fall into a ditch."

Question: That raises another question in my mind concerning supervision. The line between supervision and therapy was always very vague to me, and it seems that this is saying, in a sense, that supervision is therapy.

Dr. Hora: Of course, unless you are being supervised for some technical type of therapy, like behaviorism or something like that where the emphasis is on technique.

Comment: You said before that we must be careful about advocacy, and yet I feel, from what you said about the therapist's consciousness and existentially valid values, that you have been advocating.

Dr. Hora: The impression is, of course, inevitable. But that which is, needs no advocacy, only that which isn't. That which we can all verify in our lives does not need to be advocated, only illuminated. For instance, if you light a candle in a dark room, this candle will reveal to you everything that is in the room. But it doesn't mean that the candle is advocating the furniture, or the decor of the room, it is just shedding light. Incidentally, the etymological meaning of the word "education," *e-ducere,* means to lead out of the darkness into the light.

Comment: I recently read about a study which said that psychotherapy is basically harmful to many people. The good results have more to do with the character of the therapist than the schools of psychotherapy. And what I hear you say is that when the therapist is the light, there is no problem.

Dr. Hora: It is no crime not to be enlightened but it is a terrible waste not to seek enlightenment. The therapist who is a sincere seeker of the truth and the light will inspire the same sincerity and desire in the patient. And the patient will join him on the path.

Session No. 23

WHAT ARE THOUGHTS?

Question: Dr. Hora, you described in several examples how thoughts tend to appear as phenomena. Would you please explain the power which produces these phenomena?

Dr. Hora: The second law of thermodynamics essentially says that energy cannot be created or lost, it can only be transmuted into other forms of energy. Thought is energy, and we can observe that thoughts tend to become transmuted into phenomena. In the process of transmutation of energy from one form to another, no power is lost. In the entire universe nothing is the effect of something else. There is no such thing as cause and effect, it only seems that way. Certainly, if in our ignorance we assume that when something happens there must have been a cause to make it happen, then we are postulating a power which can cause things to happen. The physicist Heisenberg received the Nobel prize for showing that there is really no such thing as cause and effect. He called it the theory of indeterminacy.

Comment: It seems that cause and effect are just illusions.

Dr. Hora: Right. And it is a mistake to believe that man has personal mind power with which to cause things to happen. One of the most outstanding phenomena we are confronted with in daily life is hypnotism. Hypnotism is a phenomenon where thoughts seem to have power to produce symptoms. There is autohypnotism and allohypnotism. What is allohypnotism? When one individual seems to induce symptoms in another with what appears to be the power of his thoughts, that is allohypnotism. But, of course, this is a misinterpretation. Thought is a type of energy which has a tendency to manifest itself as form. The Zen Master Suzuki used to say: "Form is formlessness and formlessness is form." He didn't say formlessness causes form to appear, or that form causes formlessness to become. He said: "Form is formlessness and formlessness is form." What did he mean? What happens in hypnotism?

In hypnotism certain thoughts are allowed to manifest themselves as symptoms or behavior. In other words, certain formless ideas are allowed to take form. It is not the power of the hypnotist's thought that causes these forms to appear, it is the energy of the thought itself which tends toward transmutation into another form.

Question: What determines the course of the transmutation?

Comment: It is the intentionality of the thought.

Dr. Hora: Intentionality is also a thought. If thought is intentional, then it is an intentional thought, or it is a thought which has the quality of meaning and direction.

Question: But who is this individual who is having these thoughts?

Question: What is the origin of thoughts?

Question: Is there a thought without a thinker?

Dr. Hora: These are fascinating and mystifying questions. Whenever thoughts are exerting some influence on us, overtly or covertly, we are involved with some form of hypnotism. It is very helpful to understand hypnotism in its broader manifestation, and to develop the perceptivity to be conscious under all circumstances of the variety of thought processes which obtain in consciousness, so that we might have dominion and not be unwittingly subjected to invalid ideas lodging themselves in our consciousness and taking form as phenomena.

A lady I knew, a young mother, bright, well-educated, had a peculiar quality about her. Wherever she went people would start fighting and hating each other, and nobody knew what was happening. In therapeutic interviews we discovered that she harbored fantasies of sowing dissension and stirring up strife between people. Her favorite phrase for this was: "Let's you and him fight." Here was a hypnotist *malgré soi* (in spite of herself). This fantasy had a way of communicating itself subliminally and hypnotizing people into acting out discord and strife. People usually didn't know what hit them.

She didn't cause these things to happen, she didn't even know that they were going on. Phenomena communicate themselves through a process called hypnotism, and they manifest themselves either as behavior or as a symptom.

We cannot ask why these things are happening. We cannot say who is to blame for these things. We cannot ask what we should do about it. And we cannot say how we should do it. We can only ask: What is the meaning of what seems to be? And what is what really *is?* When we find the answers to these two questions, refraining from asking the four futile questions, then there is a solution. In the Bible there is a passage where God is asking Satan: "From whence comest thou? And Satan answered the Lord, and said, From going to and fro in the earth, and from walking up and down in it" (Job 2:2). This is a strange answer, what does it mean? Previously one of you asked the question, where do thoughts come from? This gives him the answer. What did Job do when he reached the end of his reasoning ability? He put his hand on his mouth and he shut up. And what happened then? At that point there was a radical shift in his mode of being-in-the-world. From an intellectual he changed into an inspired thinker. He said to God: "I have heard of thee by the hearing of the ear: but now mine eye seeth thee" (Job 42:5).

Previously we spoke about inspired living. What happens when we attain the understanding of how to live on the basis of inspiration rather than on the basis of calculative thinking? There is a change in the quality of thoughts which come into consciousness; our thoughts begin to flow from a different source. This source can be called God, cosmic mind, or Love-Intelligence. At that point we are beyond hypnotism; the thoughts which are floating around in the world—up and down and to and fro—have no place to take root in our consciousness. When we attain the point of inspired living, we become unavailable to hypnotism, and we are also not inflicting hypnotism on others. We become what is called beneficial presences in the world. And that could be called a therapeutic personality.

A beneficial presence in the world is, of course, more than a therapeutic personality because it involves all aspects of one's personality rather than just one's professional activity.

Coming back to the question about the individual who has those thoughts—those hypnotic thoughts—the Zen Master says: "The thinker and the thought are one." This just looks complicated but actually it is simple. The Bible says, "As he thinketh in his heart, so is he" (Proverbs 23:7). Carrying this a little further we could say that the thoughts prevailing in our consciousness constitute our sense of self-identity. If we reach the blessed condition of inspired living, then our thoughts flow to us from infinite mind, which is God, and then our identity takes on the character of an image and likeness of God. Then, that's what we are. "The thinker and the thought are one."

Question: Are you saying that God is a state of consciousness?

Dr. Hora: God is cosmic consciousness and we are emanations, reflections, manifestations, expressions, witnesses of this divine consciousness. Intelligence and love, peace, assurance, joy, gratitude, freedom, perfect life constitute our being.

Session No. 24

CONSCIOUS UNION WITH GOD

Question: What is pragmatism?

Dr. Hora: Does pragmatism mean that we ought to be able to do something?

Comment: That's the general idea.

Dr. Hora: Often when we want to be pragmatic about a problem, we just mess it up. Suppose we had a plant, and the plant had a problem and we wanted to do something about it. So we would start watering it, giving it vitamins, and the chances are it would get worse. The most pragmatic approach is the one that would be most helpful, isn't it? And what is most helpful is understanding what really is.

Suppose we do the right thing for a plant; then who is it that is doing it? Suppose we discern that the plant needs more light and we place it somewhere where there is more light. Suppose we discern that it needs less water, so we give it less water. Suppose we discern that it needs more nourishment and so we give it more nourishment. Who is it that is doing these things?

Comment: Either the plant or nature. You are not imposing your will on the plant, you are providing it with what is needed. Therefore, the situation is doing it. It isn't a who, it is a what.

Dr. Hora: It is both a who and a what, depending on whether our concept of God is a personal one or an impersonal one. But essentially, it is intelligence that does everything that is being done right, wherever it is being done. And who does it when it is being done wrong? Ignorance. The Bible says: "All things were made by him;

and without him was not any thing made that was made" (John 1:3).
Now this is a dark saying; is there anyone here who can shed light
on this dark saying?

Comment: What comes through is the idea of total ultimate dependency on this God.

Dr. Hora: On Love-Intelligence. It is Love-Intelligence that does
everything that is being done right, and it is ignorance that is responsible for whatever is being done wrong. Where does it leave us?

Comment: We have to tap into Love-Intelligence.

Dr. Hora: Suppose we have an electric light, the lamps in this
room, for instance. Do they give light? What is this light which we
enjoy? The lamps by themselves couldn't give us light. What gives
us light?

Comment: Harnessing the energy in the right way.

Dr. Hora: Electricity gives us light. What do the lamps do?

Comment: Provide an outlet.

Dr. Hora: They manifest electrical energy in the form of light.
They do not do anything, they are there to manifest this fantastic
event called the transmutation of energy. Now if we were ignorant
of this basic elementary law of physics, we would probably think that
the lamps give us light, and then if they would fail to give us light,
we might try to fix the lamps instead of plugging in the electricity.
And isn't it somewhat along these lines that pragmatism tends to
work? Or if something goes wrong with a man, we may try to fix him
and think that we can do it. No amount of fixing of the lamps would
give us light. In order that light could come through the lamps, we
need to understand the basic principle of the flow of electricity from
its source. And we would have to know that it is not the lamps that
give us light, it only seems that way.

Comment: It sounds like a parallel with idolatry.

Dr. Hora: What do you mean?

Comment: We hold up this idol and believe that it's God.

Dr. Hora: Now what is the great idol which pragmatic man is the
victim of?

Comment: That there is some kind of rational solution to problems which is called self-sufficiency.

Dr. Hora: Self-sufficiency, independence from the source of life, intelligence, vital energy, and love. The basic error is the misapprehension of reality in terms of man's autonomy, apart from God. "I can fix it," we say. "I can do it." "I figured it out." "I did it." "I have cured him." "I found the solution." Let us not kid ourselves; there is no such thing as personal intelligence, there is no such thing as a lamp giving light without being plugged into the electric current. Therefore, the more perfectly we shall learn to be plugged into the source of vital energy, intelligence, and love, the more effective we shall be in every area of endeavor, whether it is psychotherapy, fixing a tractor, or shoveling snow. It is important for us to be plugged in all the time, otherwise we cannot function in an intelligent way.

We all know how lamps get plugged into the electric current, but do we know how people are plugged in?

Comment: Everybody has a different theory about how to discover that particular source. They have rules and regulations which they believe work. But, ultimately, they all have something in common, they all have plugged themselves in at one point or other. This reminds me of something I read about Buddha. He figured out that the best way to do this is to sit down under a tree and do absolutely nothing.

Dr. Hora: When Buddha sat down under the bo tree, crossed his legs, folded his hands, and sat there motionless for forty days, was he doing nothing?

Comment: Nothing apparent.

Dr. Hora: What was he really doing?

Comment: He was plugging himself in.

Dr. Hora: You are right. But what was the action which was taking place in that situation?

Comment: He got in touch with himself, with his higher self, and with Love-Intelligence, as you refer to it. It was probably meditation of some sort.

Comment: I find the idea of this extrapersonal source of energy and intelligence quite comforting, but how does one plug in?

Dr. Hora: Jesus said: "God is a Spirit and they that worship him must worship him in spirit and in truth" (John 4:24). What relevancy does this have to the issue of establishing contact with the source of all intelligence? When Buddha sat under the bo tree crosslegged, apparently that's what he did, he established what is called in Christianity conscious union with God. How did he do it?

Comment: I would say he did it by mind-fasting, not letting himself be distracted from that central consciousness.

Dr. Hora: What is mind-fasting?

Comment: Mind-fasting is not holding to, or attaching oneself to, ideas, thoughts, or anything not beneficial that comes into consciousness.

Dr. Hora: Does everyone understand the concept of mind-fasting? You remember, Jesus said at one point: "This kind goeth not out but by prayer and fasting" (Matthew 17:21). Most people jump to the conclusion that he was talking about not eating food. But what would that contribute to man's enlightenment? A little perhaps, but not much. The Taoist sages speak of mind-fasting and, as it was correctly said, there are certain ways of thinking which interfere with our realization of conscious union with God. In prayer and meditation we refrain from these ways of thinking in order to be available to divine intelligence to reach our consciousness. What are these thoughts that interfere with realization? There are quite a few of them, but there are certain ones which we have touched upon already in previous talks.

In the field of psychotherapy the greatest obstacles to this realization are the futile questions. Does everybody know the futile questions by now?

Comment: What is wrong? Why did it happen? Who is to blame? What should we do about it? How should we do it?

Dr. Hora: Right. These questions interfere with the process of enlightenment. Then there are fantasies and various mental preoccupations, like ambition, envy, fear, jealousy, hostility, criticism, ideas of what should be and what shouldn't be, and what we want and what we don't want. Such "pragmatic" thinking interferes with establishing conscious contact with Love-Intelligence. So anyone who sincerely desires to come into conscious union with God and reap the blessings of inspired living, has to practice mind-fasting.

Sometimes when we have to plug an electric light into an outlet, we have to make sure that the plug is not rusty or covered with paint, so that the contact may be clean. And similarly, consciousness can be messed up with many invalid thoughts which can interfere with contact with Love-Intelligence. Where do these invalid thoughts come from?

Comment: Up and down the street?

Dr. Hora: Yes. They come from "going to and fro, and up and down in the world," as Satan put it. But much of it is due to miseducation, we greatly suffer from miseducation. And sometimes we get attached to the erroneous ideas education has provided us with, and we encounter difficulties in revising them or letting go of them. As a matter of fact, we can be very resentful sometimes if that becomes necessary under the pressure of circumstances. But of course, life has a way of forcing us to revise the cherished notions we have accumulated over the years, because they are existentially invalid and tend to get us into trouble in many, many ways.

If we are willing to be sincere seekers of this conscious union with Love-Intelligence, then things will become clearer and clearer over the years, and at the same time our lives will become more and more harmonious. Naturally, our helpfulness to our patients or clients will become increasingly more effective with less and less effort. As the saying goes: "No sweat." The Zen Master says: "No fuss."

It is characteristic of divine mind, divine intelligence, that everything tends to become simpler and simpler all the time, in contrast to the wisdom of the world which has a tendency to be more and more complex.

Comment: The Apostle Paul said: "The good that I would I do not: but the evil which I would not, that I do" (Romans 7: 19). He seems to be saying that the problem is not only ignorance, but that there are forces in the cosmos which interfere as well.

Dr. Hora: Well, not really. It just seems that way. For instance, let us take darkness as an example. Darkness seems to be a universal experience of man. In the darkness one can stumble and break a leg. All sorts of bad things can come into experience in darkness. Would we say that darkness is a power which can inflict disasters on man? No, it seems that way, we can experience it that way, but actually darkness is not a power. What is it?

Comment: The absence of light.

Dr. Hora: Yes, it is nothing. It is just the absence of light. Simi-

larly, ignorance can inflict a great deal of suffering on us as individuals and as groups, families, and nations. It seems to be a tremendous
power, yet it is no power, it is nothing.

Question: Three questions come to mind: 1. Why do they miseducate us this way?

Dr. Hora: "Why" is the first of the four futile questions.

Comment: The second is: Why do we allow this to happen to us?
And the third: Why are we willing to give up our natural contact and
lose it? I am thinking about the socialization process and how, in a
sense, we all become alienated from the world. This is something that
has always confused me. Why are we taught to be ignorant?

Dr. Hora: Isn't this a marvelous demonstration of the futility of
asking the wrong questions? Interestingly enough, within the question "why?" there is implied the second futile question, "Who is to
blame?" Whenever we ask "why?" something happens to us, we have
a tendency to become angry. That is not good for anybody and it will
certainly block the flow of intelligent ideas. But let us do an experiment and refrain from asking why we are miseducated and who is
to blame for it. Let us ask, what is the meaning of what seems to be
a universal condition of miseducatedness among us. What is the
meaning of it?

Comment: It seems to be the idea of autonomy. Somewhere this
idea has taken root, and we come to think of ourselves as separated
from this source, and having to go and do something to get it. This
idea is rooted in the culture and is passed on from generation to
generation. The Bible says that the sins of the fathers shall be visited
upon the children for four generations.

Dr. Hora: Would you all like to know the meaning of miseducation?

Comment: Sure. Tell us, please.

Dr. Hora: It is very simple. It is called "judging by appearances."
This is the source of all miseducation.

Session No. 25

THE EPISTEMOLOGY
OF BELIEVING

Comment: Lately, when I am confronted with the aggressive question: Do you believe in God? my answer has been: How can you not believe in God? I found this answer very helpful.

Dr. Hora: That is answering a question with a question.

Comment: A very important question.

Dr. Hora: Which makes it OK? Is it a good idea to believe in God? I would like to warn against it. Believing in God can be a stumbling block on the way to understanding God. Millions of people believe in God and it doesn't do them much good. What happens when we believe in something? It puts us to sleep. Karl Barth, the famous Swiss theologian, said: "The greatest obstacle to understanding God is religion." Now what's the trouble with religion? Religion is based on the comfortable, complacent idea that all that is needed is to believe.

If someone asks us if we believe in God, it is better to say: I am trying hard to understand what God is. If we want to be complacent and smug, then believing will be enough. But we are only taking a partisan stand and we will feel comfortable that way. If we are disbelieving, we are taking an antagonistic stand because that may be in vogue at that particular time. You see, to believe or to disbelieve is really the same, it is being nowhere. Man is given the possibility of understanding. Jesus said that we must *know* the truth in order to be free. He did not say, *believe* in the truth. He said we must know the truth. Which means, we must struggle and work and aspire and reach out and stretch ourselves to understand. And if we understand, we do not have to believe. If we settle down to believing or to being believers, we will never bother to understand. That is the difference between a religious man and an enlightened man. Religious man is comfortable and smug in his beliefs, and an irreligious man is comfortable in his disbeliefs.

So let us understand that we are not talking here about believing anything. Let me repeat what we have said on previous occasions, namely, that there are three ways of getting nothing out of these seminars. One is if we believe what is being said, the other is if we disbelieve what is being said, and the third is if we are daydreaming.

Is it good to be skeptical? It is better than to believe, but it is not a constructive attitude. The most promising attitude is sincere discriminating interest, with the aim of eventually understanding. In the Bible there are many instances where believing is being recommended. Jesus said, "I am come a light into the world, that whosoever believeth on me should not abide in darkness" (John 12:46). But I think that the word "believe" here and in other places in the Bible is an inexact translation from the Greek, the Aramaic, or the Hebrew, and it really refers to understanding rather than believing in today's sense of the word. Surely, Jesus knew that believing makes people complacent and smug.

In another place the Bible says, "Wisdom is the principal thing; therefore get wisdom: and with all thy getting get understanding" (Proverbs 4:7). So let us not be satisfied with believing; it is not enough. As a matter of fact, not even faith is enough, even though faith is more than believing. Faith is believing with commitment.

If we want to learn mathematics, is it enough for us to believe that two and two is four? Or is it enough for us to have faith in it? No, we will never be mathematicians until we really understand the principles of mathematics. And, of course, if God is a cosmic principle of Love-Intelligence, it is not enough to believe in it, we must come to understand it. If I were to talk to you about believing in God, I would be an evangelist. But I am not an evangelist, I am a teacher. A teacher does not advocate any systems of belief, a teacher is a facilitator of understanding.

Question: What is the meaning of Jesus recommending that we be as little children. How does this reconcile with what you were just saying?

Dr. Hora: It is usually interpreted as being gullible, but it means wanting to know how everything works. Children are extremely curious, interested, enthusiastic, and teachable in the right way. And it also means not having preconceived notions and false motivations beyond wanting to understand. As we grow up, we develop attachments to certain ideas. These attachments to certain ideas and notions are called preconceived ideas. These preconceived notions are cherished, consciously or unconsciously. And when they collide with some new facts, some new information, we may get very upset and we don't like the idea of having to revise, or perchance even drop, something that we have become attached to. It is this strange tendency of man to form attachments to persons, places, things, and ideas that is the source of much suffering, fear, and conflict in the world.

To be open-minded is not easy. It takes a willingness to allow for the possibility of discovering that we may be wrong, or that something that we have cherished—perhaps spent years developing—is not really valid. But without this willingness there is no possibility of progress or of learning anything new. The whole world, for instance, believes that believing is good, and now someone says that believing is not good. That's shocking, isn't it? It "blows the mind." We have to be willing to consider the possibility that maybe the world is mistaken. If we are to grow and expand our knowledge, we have to be willing at any moment of life to ask ourselves: Is what I am attached to mentally really valid? Or is it possible that perhaps it never was valid? And if there is this humility and willingness to part with our cherished opinions and possessions, there will be learning, progress, and growth. And that's the essence of psychotherapy, isn't it? What are patients suffering from?

Comment: Attachments to their ideas.

Dr. Hora: Exactly. It is called dependency, attachment, possessiveness, obsessiveness, fear, anxiety, willfulness. It has many names, but essentially it is a tendency to cling to something. And anybody who would challenge the validity of what we are clinging to, will immediately loom up in our minds as a threat.

Question: Dr. Hora, one of my patients is a very confused young woman, and I don't know how to help her. One of her most frequent phrases is: "I don't know what I want." Another is: "I don't know what I should do." And I feel the same way about her.

She is married but promiscuous. She doesn't know whether to leave her husband and live alone. She doesn't seem to enjoy anything and is confused about her place in society. Her life seems to be an aimless floundering.

Dr. Hora: What do you think is the basic issue in this young woman's life? She seems to be asking two questions, "What should I want?" and "What should I do?" What is the meaning of these two questions?

Comment: She doesn't take responsibility for anything.

Dr. Hora: Do you think she can? These two questions indicate a basic position of miseducatedness. As you know, we all suffer from miseducation. The young lady assumes that one has to know what one wants in life, and that one has to know what one should do in life. And then everything will be all right. But will it? What is needed in life? What are the requirements for a well-established existence?

Comment: To know who you are and to know what really is.

Dr. Hora: Unfortunately, these questions are seldom heard. This patient would like to find a footing in life. She is disoriented, confused, and she doesn't know how to find a sense of assurance, contentment, happiness, and fulfillment. She seems to be trying many things. What would the Bible recommend to this young lady? "Commit thy works unto the Lord, and thy thoughts shall be established" (Proverbs 16:3). "Delight thyself also in the Lord; and he shall give thee the desires of thine heart. Commit thy way unto the Lord; trust also in him; and he shall bring it to pass" (Psalms 37:4, 5).

Comment: Isn't there a danger that she might misunderstand and become religious, join a church, or something like that?

Dr. Hora: Of course. But we are not saying that she should be told this directly. We are saying that the therapist needs to know this. The point is that the patient has been educated to believe, and the world is saying to her: You have to know what you want and you have to know what you should do. That will give you a sense of direction and a foundation in life and you will find happiness and fulfillment. Of course, many people would agree with her that this is the way things are. However, reality and existence are not based on what we want and what we do. It is based on what *is,* on *what really is.* Coming into alignment and conscious harmony with the fundamental order of existence can give us a sense of purpose, direction, assurance, and fulfillment.

Now what would happen if we threw this information at the patient? She might think we were crazy or that we were selling religion; she might believe us and join a church, or she might disbelieve us and go look for something else. We are not saying what to tell the patient. We are not talking about a technique of psychotherapy. We are talking about what a therapist needs to understand for himself in order to be able to respond in a helpful way from moment to moment to a patient. Once we understand the existentially valid principles upon which to base our lives, then we can be appropriately responsive to our patients when they come to us confused, frightened, driven.

Would you like to know the value of exploring the historical data of the patient's background? It is less than nothing. Historical data are only important if we want to find out why the patient is the way she seems to be today, and if our reasoning is in terms of cause and effect. And then we might want to know who is to blame for the way she seems to be, and what we should do about it, and how we should do it. Here again are the futile questions; they get us nowhere. It does not matter who taught us to believe and how it came to be that we believe that two and two is five. The important thing is to discover that it is four.

Comment: My feeling is that it is helpful to know the system of miseducation by which we operate.

Dr. Hora: It is either irrelevant, or it may provide the patient with an excuse to feel sorry for himself, to think of himself as a victim of childhood circumstances, and to blame someone. What happens if we have an excuse for being sick?

Comment: I can see that some people could get stuck and never move beyond that point. But that is not necessarily so.

Dr. Hora: But why take chances with that if it is not essential? If we don't blame anyone, if we don't try to figure out why we are in trouble, then we don't waste time feeling sorry for ourselves and we confront the fact that we are ignorant and are in great need of being enlightened. We quickly reach out for the truth which makes us free.

Psychotherapy becomes speeded up considerably this way. Don't you think there is a lot of time wasted in psychotherapy?

Question: Dr. Hora, how does a person incorporate the feelings he or she has into the new way of life?

Dr. Hora: What does it mean to incorporate feelings?

Comment: It seems that this woman is divorced from her feelings, and I would think that she would have to incorporate her feelings into her new life as opposed to incorporating just some new ideas.

Dr. Hora: You seem to have a notion, which is very widespread among various therapeutic schools, that there are three entities: one is called feelings, the other sensations, and the third intellect. And that these somehow have to be brought together to make a whole man. The assumption here is that the patient is disintegrated into constituent parts. But that is an assumption. Man is whole. He may be confused, ignorant, and frightened, and he may spend himself in futile endeavors struggling for some kind of stability and even fulfillment in life, and in the course of that discordant and uncoordinated struggle he may manifest a prevalence of emotionalism, intellectualism, and sensualism, but that does not mean that he is disintegrated and has to be pasted together.

It reminds me of a man who said: "After I am through with this therapy, I am going to have sex with emotions attached to it." He had also read some books on psychology, engaged in "psychobabble" at cocktail parties, and he had the idea that in psychotherapy feelings are being hooked up to the intellect. This, of course, is nonsense.

Question: How do you deal with repressed emotions?

Dr. Hora: When we come into conscious harmony with the fundamental order of existence, everything falls into its proper place and we are whole. It is not the therapist who patches up a personality, it is the truth, which, when perceived in consciousness, liberates the patient and reveals his intrinsic wholeness. Psychotherapy is not a patch-up job, it is liberation. Liberation from what? From ignorance. The healing power is not in the therapist, it is in the truth, which becomes revealed and integrated in the consciousness of the patient. And it is this truth which brings everything together if it does not seem to be together. But it is together.

Session No. 26

A CASE OF PHOBIA

CASE PRESENTATION

A young woman, twenty-six years old, separated from her husband for a year. Her main complaint is a fear of traveling and a fear of leaving home. She gets panicky in traffic jams in the direction away from home, but not in the direction going home. She also has difficulty sleeping at night, and she is also afraid to stay at home alone. I have a problem with her because she comes on as a very strong person. She is well dressed, her demeanor is quite incongruous with the pathology she is describing.

Commentary on Case Presentation

Dr. Hora: What is the diagnosis?

Answer: I really don't know.

Comment: Would anxiety neurosis be an appropriate diagnosis?

Dr. Hora: She is not really anxious. She is panicky in certain special situations. Before we start thinking about the diagnosis, I would like to bring to your attention a very interesting feature of this case, namely, the incongruity of the patient's countenance and demeanor with the gravity of the problem she describes. Her problem is not evident during the interview. Quite to the contrary, there is practically no evidence of psychopathology.

Comment: She seems to be a well-controlled, strong personality.

Dr. Hora: What is the difference between panic and anxiety?

Answer: Panic is a quick thing; anxiety is more lasting.

Dr. Hora: We could put it this way: in anxiety we are still in control, but in panic there is a sense of loss of control. It is important to differentiate between fear, anxiety, and panic. What is fear?

Answer: Fear has an object, you fear something.

Dr. Hora: We could put it this way: Fear is a thought of what might be. Anxiety is a thought of what should not be. Panic is a sense of having lost what should be. This patient gets panicky in traffic jams. What is it that happens in a traffic jam?

Answer: We have no control of the situation.

Dr. Hora: Yes. We seem to be at the mercy of circumstances. No matter how powerful, how influential, how smart we are, there is nothing we can do; we seem to be helpless. Most people can endure this with not too much distress, but this patient says she gets panicky. Interestingly enough, on her way home she does not get panicky. What could be the meaning of that? As you know, we are not looking for the cause of a problem but for its meaning.

Comment: Only at home does she have the feeling of control.

Dr. Hora: That's right. Home means being in charge. At home we are in charge, in control, we are the boss. And if we are the boss, we can be comfortable. This case can help us understand the dynamics of a very important syndrome which is called phobia. Here we can learn to differentiate phobic reaction from anxiety neurosis, or fearfulness, or any other kind of syndrome. We find phobias in people who want to be in charge of their destinies. Phobias often have puzzling specificity.

Everyone can easily understand that the phobic fear is irrational, but not many people can understand that being in charge is also irrational. The phobia is just the other side of that irrational coin which wants to be in charge. Traditional psychoanalysis was working for the achievement of ego-control. Originally the therapeutic aim in psychoanalysis was the attainment of genital primacy. The idea was that if someone can function well in bed, he is healthy. Later this was changed and the idea of ego-control was substituted for it. And this seems very rational. It seems very desirable for man to be in charge of his own affairs. We certainly appreciate leadership qualities, executive abilities, command presence, managerial skills. Our culture affirms these qualities. And that is why it comes as a surprise to realize that to be in panic and to be in charge are equally irrational, that they are two sides of the same coin. How else then is life to be lived? It seems that we can be neither in control nor out of control. So what else is there?

Comment: Just being.

Dr. Hora: What is that? That is not a solution. The behavioristic school of therapy would propose to help this patient to get control over the phobia, and to expand the area of her controllingness to include situations in traffic jams. Suppose we would succeed in training this patient to be in control even in traffic jams heading away from home, what would happen? Seemingly this would be very good to achieve, it would seem very desirable. With this she wouldn't be afraid in a traffic jam in any direction.

Comment: She would become a tyrant.

Dr. Hora: Yes. We would then be supporting the irrational striving for control. And, of course, what we would then see is the up-cropping of new phobias. No sooner would she get control of one phobia then another would appear. The phobias come in proportion to the intensity of the desire for control. What would then appear as a great therapeutic success through behavioral therapy would actually mean an aggravation of the irrational striving for control. "The good that I would I do not: but the evil which I would not, that I do" (Romans 7:19).

Question: What accounts for the specificity of the phobic symptom?

Dr. Hora: It is based on the interpretation which the patient assigns to certain situations in which she believes herself to be deprived of control.

Question: I worked with a man whose main fear was going through bridges and tunnels, but he would lose his fear if he could get himself to be angry. What accounts for that?

Dr. Hora: It is very simple. What is anger? It is a violent form of emotional self-assertion. Of course, that is not a healing. It is good to know the difference between symptom removal and healing.

There is another way phobias are sometimes treated, namely, through hypnotism. What does hypnotism do? With the help of posthypnotic suggestion, it is possible to suppress a symptom. What does a hypnotist do? A hypnotist says: "You are not strong enough to control your panic; therefore, I am going to control your controllingness. With the help of my controllingness I am going to control your controllingness to such an extent that you will be able to control your symptoms. Now what do we have when this happens? We have what is called *folie à deux*.

The more we believe in the importance of being in control of our lives, the more fearful we are of losing the power of being in charge. We can now clearly understand that any therapy that would focus only on relieving the patient's fear would be insufficient. If a therapy is to be lastingly effective, what is needed is to heal the patient of her erroneous belief that to be healthy one must be in control. Now how can that be? Such a patient may fight tooth and nail against the idea of relinquishing control. Such a patient will be very interested to be relieved of her panic and incapacitating fears, but she will not be much interested to be healed of her delusion of personal competency. The questions we need to consider are: How can anyone survive without personal control? Is it possible to live without being in control?

Comment: It would probably be helpful to show the patient the connection between her fear and her assumptions about life.

Dr. Hora: Yes. Another question is: If we are not in control, then who is or what is?

Comment: God is in control.

Dr. Hora: Do you really mean that?

Answer: I guess, if we could help her to tune in to universal intelligence, maybe that would help. I know that this is one of the futile questions, but how do you do it?

Dr. Hora: I remember a lady who was incapacitated for years due to her fear of traveling on the subway. She was brought to me for one visit by her husband, and in the course of the interview, I remarked that God is in control of the subway. She looked at me incredulously, but this remark stayed with her and from then on she had no fear of traveling on the subway. Of course, she had many other problems to be healed of, but this seemed to have been an instantaneous cure.

Question: Do you believe that God is driving the subways?

Dr. Hora: It is possible to be aware of God's sustaining and harmonizing presence under all circumstances. It is important for a therapist to know this, not as a belief but as a realization. We have to know that we are not self-existent and that without Love-Intelligence we have no power and no intelligent thoughts. We have to know that God is our life, God is our energy, God is in charge of all our affairs. Love-Intelligence is in absolute, complete, and permanent control.

Question: But what if the therapist cannot say these things because he himself has not realized them?

Dr. Hora: Then he is limited in his ability to benefit the patient. This is the great advantage of knowing the truth, the truth which makes man free.

FULFILLMENT

CASE PRESENTATION

Patient is a forty-eight-year-old married woman, overweight, complaining of unhappiness, depressions, marital discord, general dissatisfaction with life, promiscuity, intermittent employment, neglect of household, and generalized alienation from family and friends.

Commentary on Case Presentation

Question: What does she want from therapy?

Answer: She wants to feel better.

Dr. Hora: If a patient says she is depressed, does that constitute a diagnosis? Do we have to accept the patient's diagnosis of herself?

Comment: That's the way it feels to her.

Dr. Hora: What seems to be the diagnosis?

Answer: Depressive neurosis and passive-dependent personality.

Dr. Hora: That's quite an indictment.

Comment: I have a feeling there is a lot of immaturity.

Dr. Hora: Is that a feeling or just an impression?

Answer: An impression.

Dr. Hora: Right, it is not a feeling. All right, we have heard the diagnosis. A diagnosis always sounds like an indictment, doesn't it? What is the mode of being-in-the-world of this woman?

Comment: "I cannot do anything for myself, somebody has to do it for me."

Dr. Hora: What evidence is there for this?

Answer: She keeps telling me that.

Comment: She feels unloved.

Dr. Hora: On what do you base that observation?

Answer: She is getting no love from her family.

Dr. Hora: Suppose she were to get it, would that change things?

Answer: I don't know.

Dr. Hora: So then it is not really a central issue.

Comment: It is an attitude of flight.

Dr. Hora: What do you mean?

Comment: She keeps changing her situation, going from one thing to another.

Dr. Hora: Is she a naughty girl?

Answer: She likes to think so.

Comment: Is it possible that her problems are caused by menopause since she is forty-eight years old?

Dr. Hora: If you are reasoning from that standpoint, then you are really asking yourself the question, why is she the way she is?

Comment: The next question then would be, what should we do about it?

Comment: Perform a hysterectomy, perhaps?

Dr. Hora: When we diagnose a patient we are indicting the patient; when we try to find a cause we are trying to blame somebody or something. When we try to repair the patient we are being arrogant or presumptuous. So what is left? We have here a woman who is looking for happiness. She is running hither and yon trying this and that and is unable to find it. She is not alone in this, millions of people are trying to find happiness. How do people usually seek happiness? The first idea we all tend to have about happiness is that maybe some person could give us happiness. "If I am not happy with this person, I have to try somebody else." The most elementary idea about happiness is that it can be gotten from somebody else. Then there are some people who are seeking happiness in an acquisitive way. For instance, by acquiring a friend or collecting something like antique furniture, cars, or horses. That is also a way of trying to find happiness. This woman is trying the conventional approach to happiness through interpersonal relationships and through activities. Another way to seek happiness is to try psychotherapy.

As you see, there is really no justification here to label this woman

as a depressive neurotic or a passive-dependent personality. All we
see here is joylessness, frustration, a frantic search for the meaning
and happiness which seems to elude her. In order to help such a
patient, it would be desirable for the therapist to have found happiness in his own life, to know the secret of fulfillment. For how can
we give somebody what we do not have? It is therefore important for
therapists to be happy, to be fulfilled in their own lives, and to know
what is the existentially valid basis for fulfillment. You are all on the
way to becoming therapists and, therefore, it is not only that you
have to learn a theory and a technique, you also have to become
fulfilled and realized individuals. It is not like learning carpentry.
One can be miserable and yet be a good carpenter, but we cannot be
unhappy and be good therapists. The patient is coming to us to find
guidance toward a happy and fulfilling life, and we have to be able
to show him the way. What is the way to happiness and fulfillment?
Has anyone ever formulated the secret of a happy and fulfilling life?

Comment: That seems to be a futile question.

Dr. Hora: No, it is not. Would you like to know the secret approach to fulfillment and happiness?

Comment: Yes.

Dr. Hora: There was a man who formulated this great treasure.
His name was Jesus and he said: "Blessed are they which do hunger
and thirst after righteousness: for they shall be [ful]filled" (Matthew
5:6). What did he mean?

Comment: That sounds like an indictment, too. It sounds more
like an admonition than the secret formula for happiness.

Dr. Hora: No, it is a formulation of the existentially valid principle
through which to attain health, happiness, and a meaningful life.

Question: What does the word "righteousness" mean in that sen-
tence?

Dr. Hora: Righteousness in this context means right usefulness.
The secret of fulfillment and happiness is to be useful in a constructive way in this life. You notice that this patient is not very useful
in her home; she does not take good care of her husband or household, she is not useful in the community. She does not live a constructive useful life. She is only struggling to feel better. So the first
principle of happiness, health, and a fulfilling life is to have a great

desire to hunger and thirst to live a useful, constructive life, to participate in existence as a beneficial presence in the world. Jesus has told us the secret, it is available to everybody, there is no great mystery, it is very intelligent and understandable.

We cannot find happiness by looking for it, we cannot find fulfillment by running around trying to use people to make ourselves feel good. In existential psychotherapy this is called a misdirected mode of being-in-the-world. Due to ignorance and miseducation we are pursuing happiness in futile and frustrating ways. We don't know how to get it because we do not take the valid principle seriously. We tend to think that Jesus was only talking about religion when he was annunciating the Beatitudes, the Sermon on the Mount. However, he was not talking about religion, he was talking about existentially valid principles which are universally applicable, and which indeed can help a patient quickly and effectively, provided the therapist has actualized it in his own life. "Blessed are they which hunger and thirst after right usefulness . . ."

Comment: I wish you gave us the secret of how to remember all this. I feel spiritually uplifted and inspired, but when I leave here the whole thing deserts me.

Dr. Hora: It is a mistake to try to remember anything that is being said here. Remembering is just as undesirable as believing. What happens when we try to remember?

Comment: We forget.

Dr. Hora: What we remember is stored in our mental filing cabinet. What we have in a filing cabinet is alien to us, it is not part of us. Only what we *understand* is existentially effective. Neither believing nor disbelieving, remembering nor forgetting is helpful. Some may have memorized the Sermon on the Mount in childhood, but never took the trouble of understanding its relevancy for everyday living. Believing and remembering are two stumbling blocks to benefiting from whatever is valid and good in the Bible or in wisdom coming from any source. We must realize that what we remember or believe we do not bother to understand. And what we understand, we do not have to remember or believe. Therefore, it is much easier to profit from everything in life if we make it our central concern to understand. "Understanding is a wellspring of life unto him that hath it: but the instruction of fools is folly" (Proverbs 16:22). Who are the fools?

Comment: Those who try to remember or believe.

Dr. Hora: Right. Understanding is a very interesting epistemological principle. For instance, it is impossible to understand that two and two is five, one can only believe it. Only the truth can really be understood. If we think that we understand something that is existentially invalid, then we are deceiving ourselves. We are really dealing here with belief. Only the truth can be understood, error can only be believed. Conversely, it is possible to believe the truth, but it is not possible to understand error.

This epistemological curiosity has practical implications, especially in psychotherapy. In the common usage of our language we say, I understand what is wrong with somebody or something, but this is really just observation, error came to our attention. Our linguistic use of the word "to understand" is somewhat loose, but that does not mean that this epistemological principle is not very important. It is helpful to pay a great deal of attention to understanding and to differentiate it from belief, conviction, speculation, and observation. Error comes to our attention and we observe it. And if we want to use more precise language, we could say: "I can observe that this patient has a misdirected mode of being-in-the-world," but that is not synonymous with real understanding.

Question: Would you say that understanding is the experience of the truth?

Dr. Hora: No, it is more than experience, it is realization.

Comment: Krishnamurti writes that it takes understanding of the truth to be able to discern error.

Dr. Hora: The Bible says: "Wisdom is the principal thing; therefore get wisdom: and with all thy getting get understanding" (Proverbs 4:7). There is great emphasis in the Bible on understanding, and wherever it speaks of believing, it is, in fact, referring to understanding.

In view of what has been said until now, what would be the best way to help this patient?

Answer: We could ask her: What is it that you are looking for and where are you seeking it?

Dr. Hora: That's pretty good. And eventually, when she would be ready to hear—and patients are seldom ready to hear initially—we might even explain to her the principle of fulfillment.

Comment: She mentioned that when she works, she feels much better.

Dr. Hora: Of course, work has to be really defined as being useful. There is much work which is just a waste of energy, or is ego-gratifying.

Comment: That's the good part of work.

Dr. Hora: Is ego-gratification desirable?

Comment: It feels good.

Dr. Hora: It is very important to outgrow the widespread idea of ego-gratification, through work, personal relationships, or through games. What happens when we pursue ego-gratification? We are in trouble if we get it and we are in trouble if we don't get it. What kind of trouble do we have if we get it?

Comment: We need more.

Dr. Hora: We need more and we are getting more and more proud, conceited, and vain.

Comment: It sounds like an addiction.

Dr. Hora: Yes, of course there can never be enough. What happens when we are used to ego-gratification, when we believe that it is absolutely necessary for survival? If we don't get it, then we go into real depressions and we are unbearably unhappy. Our joy is precarious. The more ego-gratification, the more precarious our joy. What else is there besides ego-gratification? There is *existential fulfillment.*

Session No. 28

EGO-GRATIFICATION OR EXISTENTIAL FULFILLMENT?

Comment: In the previous session you promised to explain to us the difference between ego-gratification and existential fulfillment.

Dr. Hora: All right, let us consider this issue. It is an interesting point and rather important. What would you say is ego-gratification? What do we mean by that?

Comment: Ego-gratification is self-seeking motivation.

Dr. Hora: Anything that makes us feel good is ego-gratifying. What's wrong with feeling good?

Comment: Nothing.

Dr. Hora: In the early history of religion, both Eastern and Western, some individuals began to notice that the quest for feeling good tended to have bad consequences. Therefore, it occurred to them that perhaps God does not approve of it. There seemed to be no way of seeking to feel good without it having ill effects. Which, of course, is quite a valid observation, but the conclusions they drew from these experiences were not valid. These religious seekers had the impression that God does not want man to feel good, therefore, they naturally assumed that maybe God might be pleased if man felt bad. So they developed various practices of inflicting suffering upon themselves in the hope that perhaps God would be pleased. What is that religious system called?

Comment: Asceticism.

Dr. Hora: Right. These ideas occurred quite independently in both the East and in the West. There were ascetics who thought that by inflicting suffering and deprivations on themselves, they would come closer to God. As a matter of fact, even Buddha, when he began his search for enlightenment, joined some group of nature people. He went into the woods and lived a harsh ascetic life of severe deprivations. But after several years of this, he concluded that it was not the right approach. Now there still are certain religious groups which continue to believe that deprivations and suffering may bring man closer to God. Jesus, however, never recommended suffering as an approach to God. As a matter of fact, he recommended the abundant and triumphant life as a fruit of right understanding.

Ego-gratification is really a naïve idea that the good life is based on pleasure. It is interesting to note that while people seek pleasure, and even pain, they are not primarily interested in pleasure or pain. They are really interested in confirming the sense of self. And that may proceed under a religious rationalization or any other kind of psychological presumption. However, the central preoccupation of man, whether in the East or West, whether civilized or uncivilized, educated or uneducated, cultured or uncultured, sophisticated or unsophisticated, is the unconscious pervasive quest for self-confirmatory ideation and experiencing. Pleasure and pain have a common denominator. Pain is also ego-gratifying. How is that? How can pain be ego-gratifying?

Comment: It confirms the existence of personal selfhood.

Dr. Hora: Right. Exactly. When we are hedonistic or ascetic, masochistic or sadistic, passive or aggressive, depressed or elated, we are always pursuing one urgent agenda, namely, the quest for confirming ourselves. Trying to comfort ourselves or convince ourselves that we really are here, that we really exist in the form in which we appear to be. That we are persons living in a physical body with minds of our own. This is the all-pervasive preoccupation of unenlightened life. What could be the meaning of such a foolish pursuit? Isn't it self-evident that we are here? Isn't it self-evident that we are physical persons with minds of our own? Do we have to keep convincing ourselves all the time? Are we perchance doubting this? How can anyone doubt something that seems so natural and self-evident?

Question: Isn't it a claim of Eastern philosophies that this life is an illusion and that reality is on a higher plane?

Dr. Hora: There are all sorts of theories in the East and West, and we could go into them, but it would be more fruitful to work our way through the concept of ego-gratification. Those of us who consider ourselves healthy are pursuing ego-gratification; those of us who are not healthy are pursuing ego-destructive experiences. It seems healthy to feel good, and it seems unhealthy to feel bad. This thought is very simple but naïve. Normal people are pursuing ego-gratification, abnormal people are doing all sorts of other foolish things. But the trouble with ego-gratification is that the more successful we are in gratifying our egos, the sicker we become and the more we fail in gratifying our egos. What happens then?

Comment: The sicker we become.

Dr. Hora: We seem to be damned if we do and damned if we don't. Isn't that interesting?

Comment: So many of your sayings are pointing to the two sides of the same coin, but this seems to be a coin with only one side.

Dr. Hora: How is it that ego-gratification is pathogenic? Ego-gratification is based on the simplistic idea that what feels good must be good; that the most important thing in life is to feel good. And if we feel good, we are healthy and everything is all right. And we feel good when we can say: "I am"; or if someone can say to us: "You are really something." St. Paul, however, said: "For if a man think himself to be something, when he is nothing, he deceiveth himself" (Galatians 6:3). So if feeling good is not good, and feeling bad is not good, what then is good?

Comment: Just feeling.

Dr. Hora: Is "just feeling" good?

Comment: Just being probably is.

Dr. Hora: Being is not enough. Just being is vegetating; it would not lead to fulfillment. We have put ego-gratification in juxtaposition to existential fulfillment. What is the difference between ego-gratification and existential fulfillment? We said that in ego-gratification the issue is self-confirmation. What is the issue in existential fulfillment?

Comment: Confirmation of the reality of Love-Intelligence.

Dr. Hora: Yes. In existential fulfillment the issue is fulfilling and becoming aware of the truth of our being. We could also put it this way: In ego-gratification the aim is *feeling* good, in existential fulfillment the aim is *being* good. Now what's so good about being good? Are we to be "goody two shoes"? What do we mean by being good? Helping old ladies across the street?

Comment: If we, as therapists, help people to feel good, that seems to be self-defeating. It seems more important to help them to become beneficial presences in the world.

Dr. Hora: Now what's so good about being a beneficial presence in the world? Why would anybody bother with such things?

Comment: It makes you feel good.

Dr. Hora: So we are back full circle. Isn't this remark illustrative of man's basic orientation? We are quite willing to be good in the hope of feeling good. There must be some other rationale for being good than just feeling good. What's the good about being good? Is being good synonymous with being a do-gooder?

Comment: I don't think so.

Comment: A do-gooder is gratifying his ego.

Dr. Hora: Yes. When a tree has its roots in contact with the source of its nourishment it is in harmony with its own nature and, as a consequence, it is a beneficial presence in nature. What is man's essential nature? If man were an ego-person, then ego-gratification would make him healthy because then he would be true to his essential nature. But we see that ego-gratification does not make man healthy, it makes him sick, so there must be something wrong with this idea. But being a useful, beneficial presence in the world makes man healthy; and vice versa, a healthy man is a beneficial presence in the world. He cannot help it. He is naturally good, which would point to a different basic nature of man. In existential fulfillment we are concerned with being true to our essential nature, fulfilling our mission and purpose in life. Isn't it surprising to consider this "outrageous" idea that man's essential nature is goodness? When we look around in the world how much goodness do we see? Of course, if we know how to look, we shall see. It is really something very encouraging to discover that our essential nature is goodness, intelligence, beneficence, usefulness, love, harmony, beauty, freedom, power, and joy. Have you ever seen such a man? How few people are really true to their essential natures? Isn't it strange? As a matter of fact, man's

essential nature is so rare, so obscured by distortions that it comes
as a surprise to hear someone say that this is what we really are.

Comment: It comes out through religion that man is the image
and likeness of God.

Dr. Hora: The problem is the misperception of what is good.
Ignorant man assumes that the basic good is feeling good. Enlightened man discovers that the basic good is being true to his essential
nature.

Comment: It seems that everything else in nature is true to its own
nature. A tree is a tree, a rock is a rock, a lake is a lake, and man
is the only thing that is out of harmony.

Dr. Hora: Man seems capable of ignorance. What is ignorance?

Comment: Not knowing.

Dr. Hora: Yes, it is really the absence of knowing. What is darkness?

Comment: The absence of light.

Dr. Hora: Right. What is the substance of absence?

Comment: It is the absence of substance.

Dr. Hora: Right, it is nothing. How can nothing play such an
important role in our lives? Isn't it surprising that nothing can be so
important and have such far-reaching consequences? Ego-gratification is the pursuit of nothingness. It is an attempt to make something
out of nothing. But existential fulfillment is the pursuit of reality, of
what really is. Existential fulfillment will not only make us feel good
but it will bring out our essential nature and we shall know what is
good, and we shall know the truth of being. We shall discover that
we are spiritual manifestations of God, Love-Intelligence, that our
essential nature is the expression of God's being, that we are individual divine consciousnesses, reflecting and actualizing in the world the
good of God. This gives meaning and purpose and content to our
lives, and this is the secret of being healthy, both mentally and
physically and in every way.

One of the case presentations which we heard earlier was about
a woman who was floundering, seeking to gain a foothold in life and
not knowing how because all she had to go by was what everybody
else was doing, which is called "the blind leading the blind." When
we are ignorant we are always looking left and right at what other

people are doing and trying to imitate them. The tendency in man to follow blindly various trends which keep changing with the times indicates that people are seeking, searching for something. They don't know exactly what and they don't know where to look, so they look at each other. They go from one error to another. Jesus said: "Heaven and earth shall pass away; but my words shall not pass away" (Mark 13:31; Luke 21:33). Is that an arrogant statement?

Comment: Yes.

Dr. Hora: It may sound that way. The Bible also says: "For he taught them as one having authority" (Matthew 7:29). What does that mean?

Comment: He was speaking for someone else.

Dr. Hora: It also means he knew what he was talking about. In other words, if we have come to understand something in our lives, then we can speak authoritatively; not as authoritarians but with authority. What is the difference? The authoritarian speaker is dogmatic, he imposes certain ideas on people which he himself does not really exemplify. But when we speak authoritatively, we speak on the basis of individual realization. Jesus knew that the principles he was formulating and expressing in words were existentially valid principles. What does that mean? It means that they constituted fundamental laws of reality and therefore there will never be a time in the history of the world when these principles will not be valid. They are fundamental building blocks of reality and he has understood them. He wasn't just talking about religion, he was annunciating existentially valid principles.

Everything else is constantly changing; psychotherapeutic schools come and go, but existentially valid principles do not change; they are timeless. They are not dependent on culture or civilization or economic and social conditions. They are existential, which means that they are basic elements of reality.

So when we seek existential fulfillment, then we are really on the right track. But ego-gratification is a mistake, notwithstanding its popularity.

Session No. 29

ROMANTIC LOVE AND SPIRITUAL LOVE

CASE PRESENTATION

A middle-aged woman, married for eighteen years, complains about her deteriorating marriage and presents a history of a lifelong sense of being maltreated as a stepchild in her childhood, later on in life, and in her marriage. She often thinks of herself as a Cinderella, vainly expecting her Prince Charming to rescue her so she could live happily ever after.

Commentary on Case Presentation

Dr. Hora: It is not rare to find people who are discontented with their lives and are seeking solutions.

Comment: It is very common; it is so common that we have fairy tales about it.

Dr. Hora: Right. Everyone would like to be happy and find fulfillment in life. The problem is that not many people have a valid idea of what happiness is and what fulfillment is. The Cinderella story contains within itself a certain concept of happiness. What is the Cinderella's concept of happiness? The Cinderella's concept of happiness is based on the idea of romance. "You will be happy if you find a Prince Charming who falls in love with you and sweeps you off your feet. A romantic love relationship will bring you happiness and will make your life meaningful, and you will live forever after without complications."

Now the question is, is the Cinderella solution existentially valid? What is romantic love? Romantic love is a form of insanity.

Comment: It was created in the Middle Ages.

Dr. Hora: Well, I don't think that romantic love was created. God never created romantic love, and God is the only creator. What kind of love did God create? God created spiritual love, the only love that really is, and is the foundation of sanity and of true happiness. On what basis can we make the startling statement that romantic love is a form of insanity?

Comment: It is all about the ego and its involvements.

Dr. Hora: It is illusion. It alters our perception of reality and brings about a state of pathological elation. In contrast to romantic love, what does spiritual love do to us? And what is it anyway? Spiritual love is not horizontal, it is full-dimensional. What do we mean by horizontal?

Comment: Interpersonal.

Dr. Hora: Right. And what is spiritual love?

Comment: I would think of it as concern for the well-being of all who come into the scope of your experience.

Comment: It is not self-centered; it is other-directed.

Comment: Caring without attachments.

Dr. Hora: Essentially, spiritual love is a quality of consciousness which is open and receptive to inspired wisdom, joy, and benevolence; therefore, it is the harmonizing principle of existence. It has healing power, it liberates man from involvement with petty preoccupations and gives him a broad perspective on reality. It makes it possible for him to fulfill his potentialities to the utmost and thus find existential fulfillment rather than just ego-gratification. The good of romantic love is based on ego-gratification, where Cinderella changes from a downtrodden, dirty little stepchild to an elegant and beautiful princess. Well, that's a boost to the ego and that feels very good. But whenever the ego feels good that is a dangerous thing because it leads to a hypertrophy of the ego. So to feel good is bad, and to feel bad is also bad. We get more egotistical when we feel good, and we get more and more egotistical when we feel bad. The ego has it both ways: it grows when it feels good, but it also grows when it feels bad.

Spiritual love is existentially valid, whereas romantic love is a

precarious form of well-being. Many people believe that love and
hate belong together. Experience shows that love can very quickly
turn to hate. Only ego-gratification can turn into hate because ego-
gratification is very vulnerable to ego-frustration, and the more we
enjoy ego-gratification, the more vulnerable we become to ego-frustration. The more we seek to feel good, the more we are vulnerable
to feeling bad. So when there are two people in love with each other
and flying high on wings of romance, they are in danger of crashing
very quickly.

Now we don't know much about this patient but, of course, it is
true that she has this Cinderella complex, this idea about happiness
in life. And we will have to find a tactful way of disabusing her of
her preconceptions about happiness, which may not be easy because
we just love to believe the validity of our preconceptions. And sometimes it takes a great deal of suffering before we become willing to
revise our ideas about what is good and desirable and valid. And the
unhappiness, self-pity, griping, running hither and yon from one
therapist to another, going to various movies, reading all sorts of
romance magazines, watching soap operas—all these indicate that
people are desperately searching for an answer to the question: What
constitutes the good life? What will give me happiness and fulfillment? And the media and the novels offer various solutions—a ca-
reer, romance, fame, money, and power.

All sorts of ideas are being offered and accepted and put into
practice, by both men and women. Marriage is the proving ground
where ideas are tried and fought over. Now what happens to a terrain
where there is a lot of warfare going on? It suffers. It gets destroyed
in the process. Therefore, when we try to find the existentially valid
solutions to the problem of happiness and fulfillment, it is important
that we turn to some expert guidance, isn't it? Otherwise we will be
just trying invalid solutions over and over again and blaming others
if it does not work. Husbands blame their wives, wives blame their
husbands, children blame their parents. But essentially, it is the blind
leading the blind, and together they fall into the ditch. When it comes
to problems of living, it is helpful to go to the source of all wisdom
and all valid ideas. And what is that source? Freud? No. Jesus Christ,
the Prophets, and some of the oriental sages. They had existentially

valid viewpoints on life and these will never be outdated, there will never be a time when Jesus will be irrelevant.

Now is a time when Jesus is tragically misinterpreted and distorted and rendered almost irrelevant. Except that he cannot be rendered irrelevant; the misinterpretations are irrelevant. Right understanding always validates itself existentially. So there is no need to believe anything or accept anything on the basis of religious dogma; what we cannot prove in our experience, we don't have to believe and we don't have to disbelieve. We can postpone it until such time that we are able to actualize it in our lives.

Now it is interesting that the most important ingredient in life, which is spiritual love, has elicited so little response. Most people are familiar with romantic love, but spiritual love, strangely enough, has not been part of their education. And yet it is the cornerstone of all rational, intelligent, and wholesome living. Some of these people are men of the cloth. But, of course, religion has little to do with it, spiritual love is not a religious idea, it is an existential value. And when we say that a patient needs to be guided toward understanding that spiritual love is the only basis on which happiness and fulfillment can be achieved, we don't mean to say that we will recommend her to join a church, or be converted to one religion or another. We just try to show her what is existentially valid and what is not valid. "The stone which the builders refused is become the head stone of the corner" (Psalm 118:22). And this stone is called spiritual love.

Question: Could you, please, explain inspired wisdom?

Dr. Hora: Inspired wisdom is synonymous with creative intelligence. What is creative intelligence? Is man capable of creative intelligence?

Question: Isn't creative intelligence seeing what is?

Dr. Hora: Seeing what is is correct perceptivity. But creative intelligence or inspired wisdom is something else. What is it?

Comment: It must be something that bears fruit.

Dr. Hora: But everything bears fruit, even romantic love bears fruit.

Comment: But not necessarily good fruit.

Dr. Hora: This is reasoning according to the principle of *post hoc ergo propter hoc,* which means reasoning after the fact. It is possible, however, to define creative intelligence and inspired wisdom for what it is.

Comment: But can you define it? Don't you have to discover it? There is a difference between that; I mean, intellectually I can define many things.

Dr. Hora: First, somebody has to define it and then we can discover it. If Jesus hadn't given us those various insights into divine reality, we would still be two thousand years behind in spiritual evolution. By the fact that he gave us these insights, the whole human race has made a leap forward in spiritual evolution (except psychotherapists, they seem to have been left behind). Creative intelligence consists of intelligent ideas which are not of our own making but which obtain spontaneously in consciousness, and they come from the source of all life, love, truth, and intelligence. And that source is God, cosmic mind. There are some individuals who have great receptivity to creative intelligence in certain areas of their interest. These people are called artists. Artists have selective receptivity to creative intelligence in the areas of their giftedness. They produce a beautiful work of art and when it is done they are just as surprised as anyone else. They have a clear awareness that a transcendent impulsion was active in the producing of that work of art. The same goes for some creative scientists.

And then there are individuals who are living a full-dimensional life of creative inspired wisdom. Every moment of their lives they are in the flow of creative ideas. How are these people called? Who are they? They are the "salt of the earth." Have you ever met such an individual? They are the enlightened ones who are beneficial presences in the world. Wherever they go, harmony, peace, wisdom, love, the good of God becomes manifest around them. They are open channels for spiritual love, and they represent what is called the Christ consciousness in the world. Indeed, the world is in great need of such people because there will never be peace in the world until there will be large numbers of such individuals everywhere on the face of the earth.

Session No. 30

"I AM"

CASE PRESENTATION

A twenty-four-year-old woman complains of unhappiness at home and in her social life. She has no boyfriend, is preoccupied with what people are thinking about her, feels inadequate and insecure in most situations. She is employed in a menial occupation, earning a very low salary. She lives with her parents and believes her parents have a low opinion of her. She calls herself the black sheep of the family and she thinks of herself as garbage, as stupid, gullible, and exploited. Occasionally she entertains suicidal thoughts.

Commentary on Case Presentation

Whenever someone comes to us, it is a good idea to ask: What do they want and what do they need? Most often there is a difference between what people want and what they need. And then therapy can start by trying to reconcile what the patient wants and what we understand his needs are. One of the basic problems we have in life is that we don't really know what's good for us and what we really need to be happy.

Before we go any further, let us ask the therapist: "What are your thoughts about this patient?"

Answer: She is miseducated.

Dr. Hora: That's pretty safe to say. What would be your diagnosis?

Answer: Regular or irregular?

Dr. Hora: Both.

Comment: She is paranoid. She is schizophrenic.

Dr. Hora: What makes you think that?

Comment: She is very detached from people, and when she tells me about suicide, she always has a smile on her face. When I ask her about feelings, she says she doesn't have any feelings. When she is angry, she does not appear angry. She has an attitude of hopelessness.

Dr. Hora: All right, now what is the "irregular" diagnosis?

Comment: You mean her mode of being-in-the-world?

Dr. Hora: Right.

Comment: I don't know.

Dr. Hora: Paranoid schizophrenia is a very serious indictment, and we must put it on the shelf because if we get impressed by our own diagnosis, we become sort of handicapped in trying to help someone. It is interesting to consider how unfair we can be to people if we label them as schizophrenic. If a patient is seeking to be liked by people—as this patient is—we say that's bad. If a patient is avoiding people, that's also bad. What is the poor patient to do? We can always find something wrong with him. Usually, schizophrenics are being accused of being afraid of people and avoiding them, forming no relationships with people, being disinterested in people. Here we have someone who is worried about what people are thinking about her and would like to be liked and find out how to relate. She would like to move toward people.

Comment: It sounds as though the only identity she is aware of is that she is a piece of garbage, and that's why she is looking to people to tell her that she is better.

Dr. Hora: But that would be reasoning from the standpoint of cause and effect, saying that because she feels like a piece of garbage, therefore she is trying to get people to tell her something better.

Comment: Could I ask a question? Don't you get the feeling that the patient was never accepted by her parents? I feel that she has felt the effects of that, and that that might have affected her greatly in other areas of her life.

Dr. Hora: Well, if we wanted to find out why she is the way she seems to be, we could speculate about that. But we are not going to try to find out why she is the way she seems to be.

Comment: But wouldn't you have to find out the effects that the parents had on her?

Dr. Hora: Yes, if what we wanted was to find out why she is the way she seems to be. But we don't have to. It is good that you have asked these questions because it brings to light again the fallacy of our education about cause-and-effect thinking. If we were now to follow that trend of thought, we might wind up being pretty angry at those parents and blaming them for what they have done to their child. And what good would that do? Our blood pressure would go up unnecessarily and the patient would in no way benefit by finding out why she is the way she seems to be and who is to blame. Then we would want to find out what we should do; and then someone would ask, yes, but how should we do it? And then we would end up frustrated.

So here we have a young lady whose mode of being-in-the-world appears to be self-deprecatory. And what else characterizes her mode of being-in-the-world?

Comment: Dependency.

Dr. Hora: A better way of putting it is horizontal thinking. She is thinking about what other people are thinking about what she is thinking. So her mental outlook is horizontal and her sense of self-identity is depreciated. Once we understand someone's mode of being-in-the-world, then it becomes very simple and clear to realize what is needed. What do you think this young lady does need?

Comment: She needs to be reeducated about the feelings she has about herself.

Dr. Hora: How would you produce better feelings in someone? It is very easy to do it with drugs, but they don't help very much in the long run.

Comment: Could we perhaps try to show her that her feelings about herself are not very realistic?

Dr. Hora: That reminds me of a story about a patient who was lying on a couch and the analyst was sitting behind her. She said, "Doctor, I have an inferiority complex about myself." And the analyst said, "Don't kid yourself, you really are inferior." Of course it is unrealistic. God never made inferior people, God made us all in his own image and likeness as perfect, loved and loving, intelligent, useful, joyous, and capable. We have been created perfect. The Bible

says: "Lo, this only have I found, that God hath made man upright;
but they have sought out many inventions" (Ecclesiastes 7:29). What
are the inventions in this young lady's thinking? All the thoughts of
inferiority, unworthiness, fear, insecurity—these are the inventions.
Where did these inventions come from? Who is to blame for them?
What is the source of these inventions?

Comment: Dualistic thinking?

Dr. Hora: No, the source of these inventions is the sea of mental
garbage. Have you ever heard of the sea of mental garbage?

Comment: I take a dip in it every day.

Dr. Hora: The sea of mental garbage is the world we live in. It is
very easy to pick up all sorts of garbage thoughts about ourselves and
others. As the Chinese sage says: "We cannot stop all kinds of birds
from flying over our heads, but we don't have to let them nest in our
hair." All kinds of garbage thoughts are floating around us, and we
pick and choose which ones we are going to use. What is the purpose
of picking up garbage thoughts and using them? When we go to a
department store and see all sorts of merchandise—let us say clothes
—what is the purpose of picking out some and not some other?

Comment: We choose what we think becomes us.

Dr. Hora: Right. In other words, we pick and choose things in
order to, as the saying goes, express ourselves; or in our esoteric
language, to confirm ourselves; or to say, "I am." But what do we
really need? Do we need garbage to confirm ourselves with? You see,
there are all kinds of garbage, fancy garbage and rotten garbage.
Some people choose fancy garbage. A young lady I know bought
some very expensive perfume and splashed it on herself and smelled
like a public toilet. And she wondered why people were avoiding her.
We want to sort of confirm ourselves all the time, and most of the
time we don't know how to do it right. This young lady bought
herself this expensive perfume and tried to make the statement "I
am" with it. We are always trying to say "I am" whether it is with
perfume or neckties, fancy clothes, or inferiority complexes, or
through bragging; some people are forever promoting themselves,
showing off, but always they are saying "I am."

Now to help this patient and to help ourselves, we have to ask
ourselves, what is the right way of saying "I am"? Certainly our

happiness, our health, and our success in life will depend on discovering the existentially valid way of saying "I am." What would be the most valid—mind you, not only realistic but real—way to say "I am"? What is the difference between realistic and real?

Comment: One is real, the other seems to be real.

Dr. Hora: Realistic is appearing as if it were real. But, of course, we are not going to settle for realism, we are reaching for reality. We don't want to appear healthy, we want to be healthy, and we want to help this young lady attain perfect health. She is entitled to it, God wants her to be healthy. Jesus is saying: "Be ye therefore perfectly healthy even as your Father which is in heaven is perfectly healthy." So in order to be healthy, we must find out how to say "I am" in an existentially valid way. The world is offering us garbage thoughts with which to make self-confirmatory statements. But what does the Bible offer us? Jesus said: "Peace I leave with you, my peace I give unto you: not as the world giveth, give I unto you" (John 14:27). Jesus gave us the truth with which to make a statement about ourselves. Can anyone guess what would be the existentially valid statement that we could make about ourselves in order to be what we really are? If the therapist will know it about himself, he will be able to help his patient, and that will heal the patient completely, absolutely, and permanently regardless of family ties, economic situation, childhood experiences, or professional diagnostic indictments. What is the existentially valid way of making a statement about ourselves?

Comment: I am a child of God.

Dr. Hora: That's good.

Comment: Love *is.*

Dr. Hora: That's even closer.

Comment: I am a manifestation of Love-Intelligence.

Dr. Hora: Certainly. That's very good. The most precise statement we can make is to say, God is the only I am; I am because God is. "I and my Father are one" (John 10:30). The patient is also a child of God, a perfect manifestation of God's self-revealing presence, unique individuality endowed with all the good, the intelligence, the love which God is. This is an existentially valid self-confirmatory idea. If we understand it about ourselves, we can behold the patient in the same perspective and she will then be seen as she has never been seen before. This will be a most unusual discovery for her and it will wipe the slate clean. Clean of what? Garbage thoughts. And this is the basis on which healing can speedily occur. It is not something we do to the patient, it is something that *we know for her.* All the therapeutic doing is none of our doing, it is the power of the truth present in consciousness that is doing what needs to be done, which is no doing at all.

This may be a little difficult to accept because it hurts our vanity. In a therapeutic situation, whatever good is accomplished is never the therapist's doing; the therapist can do nothing of himself. The power to heal, to correct miseducation, to eliminate mental garbage is in the truth, not in man. And that reminds us of what Jesus said: "I can of mine own self do nothing" (John 5:30); "But the Father that dwelleth in me, he doeth the works" (John 14:10).

Session No. 31

HEALING OF CHARACTER

CASE PRESENTATION

A sixty-year-old divorced woman is living on disability insurance and her daughter's support. She appears very agitated in the course of the interview and keeps taking various pills. She has a son living in Chicago but never sees him nor hears from him. Her husband abandoned her and her daughter threatens to abandon her. She presents a whole assortment of complaints, emphasizing her inability to cope with life. She is also attending group therapy in a hospital and is involved in a so-called recovery program in another place, but says that nothing works for her.

Commentary on Case Presentation

Dr. Hora: Let us first consider the diagnosis. What would be the traditional diagnosis?

Comment: Schizophrenia, because sometimes she gets feelings of unreality, like all this is not really happening to her.

Comment: Maybe she is manic-depressive.

Dr. Hora: Can you think of any other diagnostic possibilities? There is a diagnostic category which could perhaps be applied, and that is: Adjustment reaction to old age. But let us ask, what is this patient's mode of being-in-the-world?

Comment: She claims helplessness and she wants someone to do things for her.

Dr. Hora: How would you categorize this mode of being-in-the-world?

Comment: Passive-dependent.

Dr. Hora: We could best understand her mode of being-in-the-world as a character disorder encountered in certain cultures and neighborhoods, such as the Bronx, or Brooklyn, or other places. What exactly is a "Bronx character"? By the way, does she live in the Bronx?

Comment: Yes.

Dr. Hora: Of course, we have nothing against the Bronx per se. But an individual's mode of being-in-the-world is molded by the perceptions of life processes around him and learning how to survive, for instance in the Bronx. There is a special kind of adaptational skill which some tend to develop in various parts of the world. What does it take to survive in the Bronx? In the Bronx, and in other places of course, one needs the power to move people. If we want to understand a patient's mode of being, we have to learn to perceive phenomenologically what is transpiring in the interview. What happened in that initial interview? Something very meaningful and revealing took place.

Comment: She moved him to listen to her.

Dr. Hora: More than that. She moved the therapist to be solicitous for her welfare. Did you notice that? That requires a special skill, which you acquire in the Bronx if you want to survive; you develop the psychological power to move people to become involved with you and to do things for you, to become solicitous of your welfare. Otherwise, you go down the drain, nobody will give a damn about what happens to you.

In principle, it is not a good idea to try to do therapy with a patient in the first session. How can you do anything for anyone if you don't yet know what the situation is? Sometimes a very skillful patient can elicit anxiety in the therapist right in the first session, and the therapist begins to therapeutize, which means that the patient has him in his pocket. Already the therapist has become the patient and the patient is sitting in the driver's seat. So it would be advisable to be alert to this kind of influence that a patient can exert. We must not rush into solicitous therapeutic activity, no matter how much we are being manipulated. Now if this patient is able to elicit solicitude right in the first session, the poor therapist is in danger of becoming putty in the hands of the patient. Where do you think those pills came from that she kept popping during the first interview? She probably has doctors and pharmacists, hospitals, the recovery group, the therapy group, the welfare department and social agencies hopping on her behalf in solicitous helpfulness. Of course, the more successful someone is in the wrong direction, the greater failure he becomes existentially. As you see, traditional diagnostic categories will help us very little here; they would just blind us to the real issue.

Question: Wouldn't a patient like this quickly abandon a therapist who would see through her ways of dealing with people?

Dr. Hora: Well, we have to take some risks in life.

Question: Wouldn't it be better not to cure this patient, since she is so effective in dealing with her environment?

Dr. Hora: But you see, the real issue here is the "survival" of the therapist.

Comment: We are assuming a solicitous attitude both for the patient and the therapist.

Dr. Hora: When an individual like this comes into therapy, and if the therapist sees through her *modus operandi,* then it is fair to expect that the patient will become very frustrated and will begin to make greater and greater efforts at moving the therapist and getting him into her power to do her bidding. If she succeeds in eliciting solicitude on the part of the therapist, then the therapist will get gray hair from frustration. Whatever he suggests or is willing to do for her will not be good enough. On the other hand, if the therapist is not ambitious to help, the patient may get gray hair, so to speak. No wonder this patient is running out of people to use and is finding herself more and more isolated. There is a diminishing return in this kind of mode of being-in-the-world. The result can be total isolation, and then, when there is no one to push around any more, there is panic.

So this kind of adaptation to life is not a happy one. The patient is losing when she is winning, and losing when she is not winning. Now the question is, can anything be done for such a lady?

Comment: I think she needs supportive treatment from a medical doctor who would give her properly regulated medication.

Dr. Hora: Do you suggest that she be refused psychotherapy and referred to a medical doctor for drug treatment?

Comment: I think so.

Dr. Hora: No, there is a better way. The lady's mental horizon has been circumscribed by life in the Bronx in a certain social class and she really has no idea that it would be possible to see reality in a broader context. It is never too late to try to expand the mental horizon of an individual. Of course, it requires a certain skill and understanding of her tendencies. For a long time she may come to see the therapist for the purpose of getting control of his mind so that she can use him for herself. But the therapist has to see through all this and classify it as what the patient *wants*. The patient wants to control people and to make them solicitous in her behalf. That is what she wants and she doesn't know anything else. But the therapist must know what the patient *needs*. So, while he is not cruelly reject-ing, he must have patience and compassion for this manipulative individual and the various ploys she will use in the sessions. What the patient needs is the elevation of her consciousness, the expansion of her mental horizon toward discovering values in life other than interpersonal manipulations. Now we cannot foresee the details of this process, but it can unfold provided the therapist is patient, has compassion and the strength not to become a pawn in the patient's hands. At the same time, little by little, he endeavors to show the patient that besides manipulating people, there is also such a thing as love and leaning on God, on the goodness of God.

The basic problem is always the horizontal perspective on life. One cannot remain healthy if one only sees people and doesn't see God. Of course, if you would mention God to this lady, she might say, "I go to the synagogue (or church) on the holy days, I know all about God." But, of course, that's nonsense. It is not possible to reach such a patient conceptually. What we can do is to "shipwreck" her system in the course of the therapeutic situation. At the same time, we must be compassionate, and we must wait for an opportunity to open up some new vistas and introduce an awareness of new values.

Question: Isn't it rather late in her life to try to change her rela-tions with people?

Dr. Hora: It would be late to try to change her relations with people at any time, even if she were a teen-ager, but we are not trying to do that. What are we trying to do? We are proposing to expand her perspective on reality. We are only trying to help her see more of life, to go beyond what she has seen until now.

Question: How do you begin this so-called "shipwrecking" of a patient's mode of being-in-the-world?

Dr. Hora: As it was said, we first take note of what the patient wants, and then we need a clear understanding of what her need is. And we have to be very compassionate because we will inevitably provoke a great deal of displeasure in the patient for not giving her what she wants. Slowly, opportunities may arise to show the importance of certain spiritual values. Whenever some spiritual quality reveals itself in the course of the sessions—such as kindness, honesty, aesthetic values, neatness, or love—it is good to point it out. Spiritual qualities are like those pearls in a pile of garbage that we spoke of. We seize a pearl and begin to pull on it. And, lo and behold, pretty soon a whole necklace may emerge. The patient is being awakened to the fact that there are spiritual values, spiritual qualities, and that she too has them because she too is a spiritual being. Once she begins to be aware of the fact that she is not just a horrible old woman who makes a pest of herself, but a spiritual being, she may begin to wake up to an entirely new dimension of reality, and her self-esteem can improve on the basis of realizing that there are spiritual qualities she is capable of expressing. And slowly, slowly, things may open up and surprising things may happen even in such a case. So we look for these spiritual qualities, we look for opportunities to awaken her to new vistas or aspects of reality which were completely overlooked through the years.

In proportion that the patient is awakening to these, she is improving. In this manner, her character distortions may disappear and her life-style may become harmonious. Character and mode of being-in-the-world are interrelated, and they are both based on elementary perceptions of life in certain contexts.

Session No. 32

IDENTITY
AND INDIVIDUALITY

Dr. Hora: Essentially all problems are ego problems. What do we mean by ego problems? What is the ego?

Comment: An image of self.

Comment: Artifact?

Dr. Hora: An image is a thought in pictorial form, an idea. We all have the idea of being persons, persons in our own right. And some seem to be better persons than others, or more important persons, or more talented persons, or more knowledgeable, or, as the saying goes, some are more equal than others. And we are very busily working at making something of ourselves so that we may be better persons than others. And that's where the danger of a bloated ego comes in.

Those of you who attended previous lectures are familiar with the concept of "self-confirmatory ideation." What did we mean by that? Essentially it means thinking about how good we are, how smart we are, how attractive we are, how important we are, how successful we are; or how bad we are, how guilty we are, how worthless we are—always thinking about ourselves in comparison to other people and trying to be better or worse than anyone else. Then there are those who are very democratic; they want to be equal to everybody else, and they are working on that. But whether we want to be better or worse or equal, we are still preoccupied with the idea of self, we are still ensnared in self-confirmatory ruminations about how we stack up in comparison to others.

What is the meaning of the word "identity"? If we look at the root of this word, what do we find? Id-entity. What does that mean? Id means "it." What is "it"? "It-entity?" What does that mean? It refers to an object. When we are preoccupied with our identity, we are reifying ourselves. What does it mean to reify something? In Latin *res, rei,* means thing. If we reify ourselves, we make ourselves into a "thing," an object. Being preoccupied with identity means treating ourselves as a thing in itself, a self-existent object, an "it." Those of you who are familiar with the writings of Martin Buber will know that he makes a big issue of the sin of treating our fellow man as an "it" rather than a human individual.

But today we are talking about treating ourselves as an "it," and trying to work on ourselves as if we were a piece of clay, or a statue, or a tape recorder, and trying to improve ourselves, making ourselves an object of our own self-improvement program. Nowadays we hear people speak of self-enrichment programs, and it is not thought of in financial terms only but also in terms of packaging ourselves externally and intellectually, so as to improve our identity, it-entity. Man is forever trying to improve himself. If he thinks of himself as an it, then he makes himself the object of his attention and tries to produce a better product. And that is sometimes called education, or psychotherapy. So when we are endeavoring to psychotherapeutize ourselves, it is the same sin as when we are trying to psychotherapeutize others. We turn a divine idea into an object of our misguided solicitude in terms of trying to improve what has already been made perfect.

In contrast to the idea of identity, let us consider the word "individuality." If we take part and analyze the word individuality, what do we find?

Comment: That which cannot be divided.

Dr. Hora: Right. We find undividedness. Now isn't that interesting? If we juxtapose these two words, identity and individuality, we arrive at an interesting insight. Identity implies isolation of man as an object. Individuality implies undividedness, the opposite of isolation, the opposite of separation. Well, if man is an individual, it means that he is not isolated, not divided, not separated. From what? From his mother's womb? From the umbilical cord? From the family ties?

Comment: It's a oneness with yourself.

Dr. Hora: What does that mean, oneness with yourself?

Comment: If we are all part of the cosmos, then we are one with the totality of everything.

Dr. Hora: Then you are not saying that man is in oneness with himself?

Comment: No, that sounds redundant.

Comment: You are different but you are not separate from other people, you are in oneness with everybody else.

Dr. Hora: Well, you will go home and you will be separated from everyone here. So what does it mean to be undivided?

Comment: In undividedness there is no self.

Dr. Hora: Then are we just swallowed up into the background?

Comment: I am thinking of certain words, like uniqueness and core, and the quality which is not replaceable. When we get down to these issues, I think we are getting close to the essence of individuality.

Dr. Hora: You are talking now about the uniqueness of the individual, which is very true and very important and which makes it possible for a self to exist even while one is undivided. That's interesting, isn't it? We are undivided and yet unique. Every snowflake is unique, I understand, and among millions of leaves on a maple tree every leaf is unique. In nature we find many analogies. It is a remarkable fact that there is uniqueness connected with undividedness.

Comment: Every maple leaf is an entity to itself.

Dr. Hora: No. A maple leaf is only a leaf as long as it is connected to the tree. The moment you disconnect the leaf from the tree, it is not a leaf anymore, it is trash. But as long as a leaf is connected, undivided from the tree, it has a uniqueness and individuality. The leaves don't form relationships with each other, they jointly participate in that life which is called a maple tree, or an oak tree. They have their individuality by virtue of the fact that they remain undivided, and yet they live their lives as unique selves. They do not disappear into a big amorphous mass, into an "undifferentiated aesthetic continuum."

Now what does this all have to do with us? After all, we are neither trees nor snowflakes. One of you has already mentioned that we are all unique, that we all have unique qualities, characteristics, but we have still not understood quite clearly what we mean by being individuals, undivided individuals.

Comment: To take your analogy a little further, you say that each maple leaf does not have a separate identity but has its unique individuality, and that individuality has something to do with the connectedness to that which is. So I would say that for human beings it would have to be the consciousness of being a part of that, or at one with that which is.

Dr. Hora: What is that which is?

Comment: We can call it God.

Comment: Instead of saying God, you could say Life.

Dr. Hora: Yes, surely. Now a maple leaf will only be alive as long as it remains undivided from the tree. So in order to be alive we must preserve our individuality, i.e. undividedness. For a maple leaf the source of life is the tree. The tree gives life to the maple leaf, and when the leaf is separated from the tree it dies, it ceases to be what it was meant to be. So it is vitally important for the leaf to remain connected with its life-giving source. But what about man? Man says, I have my own identity, I am my own boss, I am entirely autonomous, self-reliant, self-existent, I am only connected psychologically with my friends and divided from my enemies, and I derive my life from my human relationships.

Jesus said something very interesting. Among other things, he said: "I am come to set a man at variance against his father, and the daughter against her mother; and the daughter in law against her mother in law" (Matthew 10:35). What did he mean? Was he a troublemaker? Did he come to disrupt family life? What good is there in breaking up family ties? In traditional psychotherapeutic work there is much talk about family ties—the relationship to one's father, one's mother, sibling rivalry. There is much talk and energy expended in trying to repair family ties. The idea is that if one has good relationships with members of one's family, then one can have good relationships with other people too, then one will be healthy, presumably. And here comes Jesus and says, in fact, break it all up. What was he trying to do?

Comment: You cannot become a whole unique individual as long as you cling to your family; you must stand apart and coexist with others, and until you do that, you cannot develop your full individuality.

Dr. Hora: In the past we spoke about horizontal thinking and full-dimensional thinking. Family ties condition us to horizontal thinking and give us a worldview which is flat. We lay great stress on how we feel about Mom and Dad, Sister and Brother, what they say and what they think, and what we should say, and what's going on. We expand our family ties into our interpersonal relationships and we work on that, and then we have a whole network of relationships with people. This network then becomes more and more complex, and we get increasingly entangled horizontally, and life becomes a big hassle.

But Jesus was working to elevate human consciousness and to open up our mental horizon to perceive a fuller dimension of reality. In order for that to happen, one must lift up one's eyes. As the Bible says, "I will lift up mine eyes unto the hills, from whence cometh my help. My help cometh from the Lord, which made heaven and earth" (Psalm 121: 1, 2). We have to behold man in the context of divine reality and see him as undivided from the true source of life which is God, or Love-Intelligence, or Creative Mind, or Spirit. It is vitally important to understand individuality and uniqueness, otherwise our perceptions are limited, our judgment is distorted, and we cannot live intelligently. If we only have one eye through which to see, we are not as safe as when we have two eyes. If our mental outlook is horizontal, we don't see as well as when it is full-dimensional. In order to live intelligently and to have good judgment and to be healthy, we need the ability to see ourselves and others and everything around us in the proper context. Now you may say: Who are you to tell us what is proper? What's the proper context? How can we know what is proper?

Comment: Whatever is existentially valid, that is the proper context.

Dr. Hora: That's right. That which is existentially valid validates itself as the proper context in which to view ourselves and others. And we know that the proper context is Love-Intelligence which is divine reality—the source of all life, love, intelligence, vitality, vigor, harmony, health, freedom, wisdom, and joy.

Comment: The analogy with the maple tree strikes me as a good illustration of what being a beneficial presence is all about, because the leaf gives life back to the tree as well by mediating the sunlight to the tree, and all is harmonious in which everything is giving to everything else.

Dr. Hora: Right, it is very well arranged. Once we gain this transcendent perspective on life, what happens to psychotherapy? What happens to our work?

Comment: It becomes nonessential.

Dr. Hora: No. But isn't it true that most traditional psychotherapy revolves around trying to improve interpersonal relationships, building up the ego, and helping man to become what is impossible, namely, an autonomous identity? It is like saying to a maple leaf, look here, you have bad relationships with the other maple leaves; why don't you separate yourself from the tree and build up your own ego? Then you will know how to handle the leaves that make trouble for you. This of course is not helpful. What psychotherapy has to achieve is the elevation of consciousness, broadening of the mental horizon to behold man in the existentially proper context.

Comment: It occurred to me that psychotherapy must become a search for the truth.

Dr. Hora: That's right. Very well said. But what truth and whose truth? Freud's? Adler's? Sullivan's?

Comment: Hora's.

Dr. Hora: Hora doesn't have his own truth. The truth that makes man free does not belong to any particular individual, it is freely available to all who are sincerely interested in it.

Session No. 33

THE CLINICAL EYE

CASE PRESENTATION

I would like to tell about an eleven-year-old boy who was brought to me by his mother because of his declining school performance. In the therapeutic interviews the boy manifested a high degree of intelligence and friendliness. He has two younger sisters who had also been in psychological treatment for various problems. The boy at one time related that he has a prized collection of cactus plants, and when asked what he liked about cactus plants, he said: "They have thistles and nobody can get close to them." I was told by the parents that when the boy was two years old, they explained to him everything about sex. The parents appear to be well-intentioned but overanxious and under the influence of literature on "progressive" child rearing. The boy told me that he wants to become a cartoonist, and indeed he has talent for drawing pictures which often portray violence. One of his pictures is that of a dragon spewing fire and killing people. The boy asked me on this occasion, "Is there something wrong with me?" I said, "I don't know."

Commentary on Case Presentation

Question: How does he relate to his sisters?

Answer: He says he likes them, but most of the relating seems to be in the form of arguments. The boy complains that nobody respects him.

Question: What did he mean by saying that?

Answer: He says he makes a fool of himself in school. He says the other children in the school laugh at him and poke fun at him.

Comment: It sounds like he has been looked at as a model and expected to live up to it.

Comment: It is my impression that he has been treated like an adult.

Question: Do you think that he has been given too much responsibility and cannot cope with it at this stage of development?

Question: Do you think he is in a panic all the time?

Answer: He doesn't seem to be in panic but carrying a great burden. That's apparent.

Dr. Hora: How is that apparent?

Answer: Several times he said that he feels like he is eighteen years old.

Comment: It sounds like the boy has no fun in life.

Dr. Hora: What could be the meaning of that? You see, you can actually imagine that this boy is right here in the middle of the room and our questions represent the thoughts of his parents about him. And what do these questions amount to? They amount to one simple dumb question: "What's wrong?" This is the first dumb question most people seem to be inclined to think about. Here is a lovely eleven-year-old child, intelligent and good. The problem is the mental climate in which he lives. The more sophisticated some parents are, the more they are inclined to view child rearing with a clinical eye. The clinical mentality is comprised and defined by six dumb questions. The first dumb question is, What's wrong? It is in the back of the mind of every amateur psychologist. 1. What's wrong with the boy? 2. How does he feel? 3. Why does he feel the way he feels? 4. Who is to blame for it? 5. What should we do? 6. And how should we do it to make him normal? What is normal, anyway?

Comment: Like us.

Dr. Hora: Normal is a clinical idea. People look into books on psychopathology to find out what is normal.

Comment: In books on psychopathology normal is that which is not sick. The only thing that's defined in medical books is sickness.

Dr. Hora: Right. And sickness of course is very interesting, it holds a great fascination for people. We are interested in sickness. When we meet our friends, we are in the habit of finding fault with them, and so we have a certain predilection to the diagnostic approach to life, which of course is a sin. Jesus said: "Be ye therefore perfect, even as your Father which is in heaven is perfect" (Matthew 5:48). And: "Thou shalt love thy neighbor as thyself" (Matthew 19:19; 22:39; Mark 12:31; Luke 10:27). Which means that we have to look for the perfection, the health, the good, the wholeness, the qualities of God in one another, in our families, in our communities; we must look for the good, for the real. To have a psychopathological bias is really a sinful way of living.

Now you may ask: But since we are studying to be psychotherapists and counselors shouldn't we look for what is wrong? How can a Christly outlook on life aid us in being psychotherapists? Will that not blind us to what is needed?

Question: Are you saying that we should find the positive and build on that rather than concentrate on the negative, and perhaps the unhealthy aspects will seem not quite so bad?

Comment: Then the garbage disappears.

Dr. Hora: Then the garbage reveals itself as garbage. We shall not be blind to the garbage—as a matter of fact, our perceptivity will improve, our diagnostic acumen will become sharper—but we will not have an iatrogenic effect on people. What is iatrogenic? *Iatros, iatrein,* means physician. Iatrogenic means illness induced by the physician.

Question: Is it the same as "physician heal thyself?"

Dr. Hora: It is relevant. We could say: "Physician, heal your outlook on life so that you may not induce illness in your patients. And when you get a lovely eleven-year-old child in your hands, don't try to find something wrong with him and pin all sorts of possible symptoms of pathology on him. Because your thinking communicates itself subliminally, and it has an effect, not only on patients but on friends and relatives, on children and adults alike." There is nothing more harmful and vicious than a diagnostic mentality, whether in a professional or a lay individual. It induces fear, and it can hypnotize an individual into believing himself to be sick. "As thou hast believed, so be it done unto thee" (Matthew 8:13).

Once before, we spoke here about hypnotism in its broader sense.

What is hypnotism? Hypnotism is a mental influence exerted, overtly or covertly, by one individual's thoughts on the thinking of another. A diagnostic mentality tends to hypnotize others into believing that they are sick, and so that is really a sin. If we want to be beneficial presences in the world—which is much more important than to be psychotherapists, and of much greater value—then we have to learn, not a positive approach but a valid approach. What is the difference between positive thinking and right thinking? We are not recommending positive thinking, we are recommending right thinking. Right thinking is always positive, but positive thinking is not always right. Right thinking is existentially valid, positive thinking may be existentially invalid.

It is very harmful to think of anyone as sick, even if it is clinically justified. But if we try to find something wrong by hook or by crook, wracking our brains to figure out what's wrong with someone when there doesn't seem to be anything wrong, this is outright foolish or malicious. And, of course, here you have the fantastic tragedy that the children of psychiatrists and psychologists are statistically proven to be more subject to mental diseases and other illnesses than any other children. Ignorant, unsophisticated parents seem to bring up healthier children than sophisticated ones. Isn't it paradoxical and tragic? According to certain statistics, there are more schizophrenic children in the families of psychiatrists than in other families in the country. And there is more physical illness in the families of physicians than in any other families.

Comment: They are constantly thinking sickness.

Dr. Hora: Of course. Now what does that tell us about the nature of illness?

Comment: Illness is a manifestation of thought.

Dr. Hora: Right. "As he thinketh in his heart, so is he" (Proverbs 23:7). So if we want to be more than just psychotherapists, if we want to be beneficial presences in the world, we may want to learn the health-promoting mode of being-in-the-world. And that would reorient us mentally from an interest in psychopathology to an interest in freedom, wholeness, love, joy, forthrightness, gratitude, peace, assurance, beauty, harmony, goodness. In other words, we will be more interested in spiritual values than in anything else.

Let us now come back to what was presented as an indication of pathology in this boy. As to his remarks about cactus plants having thistles, and his drawing of a dragon spewing fire and destroying people, we must not exaggerate the importance of such marginal remarks. They in themselves mean nothing, they are only thoughts prevailing in the culture. Our culture is filled with violent fantasies, and they can be found in the thoughts of almost anyone. As for the school performance of the child, it may reflect more on the teaching methods of the school than on any problems attributable to the child. Let's not jump to conclusions that there is psychopathology.

Question: Could I ask why the therapist was called in?

Dr. Hora: That's a good question. It happened more or less by chance acquaintanceship between the mother and the therapist. When the parents are afraid that a child will not be normal, then the child will get sick. When the parents are anxious that the child should do well in school, then the child will do badly in school. Whatsoever the parents want, in one way or another, it will happen this way. Yes is no and no is yes. Now the question is: what would be a healthy way of parenting?

Comment: The least government is the best government.

Dr. Hora: Love is not synonymous with anxiety, quite the contrary. "Perfect love casteth out fear" (1 John 4:18). When the parents know how to love, they are not anxious over the child. They are confident, assured that the child is perfect because he is God's child. He is a spiritual being and he is cared for, looked after, inspired, governed by infinite Love-Intelligence. So what the parents need is the same as what the therapist needs, namely, to have a more valid viewpoint on life, a more spiritual perspective on life. But the more books the parents are reading, the more anxious they become and the more clinically minded they become toward their children. Some parents read books on psychopathology. Others may read books on nutrition—and what happens then? They become anxious about giving their children healthy diets, they become involved with scientific nutrition, and the result is colitis, gastritis, stomach ulcers, and complications of the digestive system. "The good that I would I do not: but the evil which I would not, that I do" (Romans 7:19).

Session No. 34

CONTEXT

CASE PRESENTATION

A sixty-two-year-old housewife and part-time bookkeeper seeks help at the urging of her daughter. She is under great stress of anxiety over her husband's failing health. Her life revolves around concerns with her extensive family—husband, sons and daughters, sisters and brothers. She is neatly dressed and pleasant looking. She has had psychiatric treatment at various times in the past. She is preoccupied with guilt feelings and conflicts over various obligations in connection with her family relationships.

Commentary on Case Presentation

Dr. Hora: Any questions? There is a strange silence here today. What is the meaning of this strange silence? This strange silence indicates that we have to learn how to present a case in a meaningful way. What has characterized this presentation? It was a very conscientiously prepared and detailed presentation, except we don't know much that would be really helpful.

In the traditional way of presenting a case we start out with the thought that there is something wrong with this person. We try to find out how she feels, and then we try to figure out why she feels that way. Further we try to find out who is to blame. And when we have already amassed these data, we try to think about what we should do. Then we bring it to a conference to find out how we should do it. What we have, finally, is usually a mixture of the present and the past and there is very little cohesion. There is no intelligent cohesive picture as to what we are confronted with.

I would like to recommend a different approach to case presentations. When a patient comes to us, we try to see and describe in detail what seems to be. We pay a great deal of attention to what we see, how the patient appears, how she behaves, how she is dressed, how she sits in the chair, how she communicates, what her mood is, what her censorium is—everything that we are able to observe with the naked eye and with our phenomenological perceptivity. The first session is devoted to the description of the patient in the context of the interview situation, so that we get an impressionistic picture, so to speak. The meaning of what seems to be will be discerned by describing the context in which the patient lives at the present time. So let us repeat, first we describe the patient in the context of the therapeutic interview, and then we describe the patient in the context of his present-day life situation. And from these two data we endeavor to understand the patient's mode of being-in-the-world. When we have understood this we already know everything that is needed for a clear presentation at a conference. In the conference we may then consider whether our impressions were correct, whether our understanding of the meaning of what seems to be is valid, and what the possible therapeutic approach might be. The crucial word here is *context*. Man is never a solitary isolated phenomenon; he exists in a certain context. Now what is the particular context which we were able to discern from this presentation? What is the context in which this patient sees herself as existing?

Comment: In an uncertain world.

Comment: Living in her own social milieu.

Comment: Fragmented concept of self.

Dr. Hora: The context in which this patient seems to exist is family ties, in contrast to the context of the previous patient presented (the lady of the Bronx character) who lived in the context of social institutions. She had a broader context than this one. This particular patient is presented to us as living in the context of family relations. This much we were able to glean from the presentation.

Most of our problems stem from living in narrow contexts. The narrower our context, the sicker we are. What is the sickest, narrowest context in which a man can live? It is narcissism. Total self-involvement to the exclusion of anything else is, of course, the context of the psychotic individual who is turned in on himself. The next sickest context is what? It is the context of family relations. That's why Jesus was so eager to cut family ties. It is essential for mental health to be able to outgrow the context of family relations. Our lady of the "Bronx character" was, in a way, healthier than this one. As a matter of fact, she had what could be called in traditional lingo a "strong ego." It was so strong that she was endeavoring to control the whole social system, and she was managing pretty well. But that is also a sickness. That was an institutional context in which the Bronx lady was living. Now psychology is teaching us to live in the context of social relationships, which is better than nothing, but not much. There are other contexts, of course: ideological contexts, class contexts, racial contexts. But there is only one healthy context in which to prosper and be healed of all our problems. This is the all-transcending context of divine reality. What do we mean by that? What is divine reality? It is the only reality which really is. You see, social contexts, family contexts, institutional contexts, these are all human inventions and are limited. Reality is not limited. Whatever is limited cannot be real. Health requires man to be in contact with reality and not with artificial, limited substitutes of reality.

Man is a spiritual being; therefore, he can only find fulfillment and realization if he is able to live in the context of infinity which is the context of Love-Intelligence, infinite mind, God, Spirit, creative intelligence. There is a universal yearning in man for expanding his freedom, but he usually doesn't know what freedom is. What he does is lash out blindly against limitations.

Then we have freedom fighters who are not really freedom fighters but fighters against limitations. As long as we fight against limitations, we are increasing our limitedness, for whatever we are involved with, that's what we are. When we are freedom fighters we are not freedom realizers. It is not possible to attain freedom by fighting against limitations, because freedom doesn't know limitations, and limitations are in our consciousness. Nobody is forcing our patient to live in a limited context of family relationships. It is not her male chauvinist husband's fault, nor is it the fault of anyone else. Nobody is to blame for a person being a prisoner in a narrow context of existence. Jesus said: "I am come that they might have life, and that they might have it more abundantly" (John 10:10). Some people think he was talking about money, or automobiles, or furniture, or things, or the goodies of life. He wasn't talking about these. What was he talking about?

The abundance of good is in proportion to the boundaries of the context in which we live. If we live in the context of the infinite, then infinite good is available to us in this life, and that's the abundant life which Jesus was teaching. He also said: "I am come to set a man at variance against his father, and the daughter against her mother, and the daughter in law against her mother in law" (Matthew 10:35).

How would we go about helping this patient? Is it practical? Can this help the situation in which our patient finds herself?

Comment: It seems to me that she is a functional woman. She is already sixty-two years old and she has many relationships with her family.

Dr. Hora: Is she really a functional woman? If she were, she wouldn't be seeking help. It would seem that she is a dysfunctional woman. Well, of course, we could say: What can you expect from a sixty-two-year-old woman? Maybe it is too late for her to espouse the lofty ideas that we are talking about. But Jesus didn't say, "I am come to talk only to people under thirty." Sooner or later there comes a time when we are longing to be free of the confines of our contexts, which could also be called existential prisons, and age has nothing to do with it. Some people attain their freedom on their deathbeds in a flash of light. It is never too late to reveal to people the wider context of reality, and it makes all the difference in the world. It is not just an issue of religious conversion. We are not talking about religious conversion, we are talking about enlightenment, about seeing what really is and what has always been. In fact, we exist in infinite reality; we just don't know it. It appears to us that we are in prison, in limitations. So we live our lives in imaginary limitations and we are longing to be set free.

Sooner or later we all have to come to the point of knowing the truth which makes man free. And this truth reveals to us the context of infinity, or Love-Intelligence, which always was and is and shall be. There is no other way to help anyone, because this is what really is. Nobody has made it this way. It is not a human invention. It just is.

Session No. 35

DYNAMICS OF DEPRESSION

CASE PRESENTATION

I have been interviewing a patient recently and I need help in determining her mode of being-in-the-world. This patient has been in a mental hospital off and on for the past ten years. In 1964 she had a mental breakdown following a traumatic experience when her daughter's boy friend intruded into their home, shot the patient's daughter dead, and shot her husband several times, wounding him gravely.

Ever since that tragic incident, she has made a habit of taking two cakes to the graveyard on the anniversary of that event. She has moved out of the upstairs part of the house and lives alone in the basement. She refuses to have anything to do with her husband, her grandchildren, and people in general. She has been diagnosed as a case of severe depression.

Commentary on Case Presentation

Dr. Hora: What is a depression?

Comment: I think it could be anger turned toward oneself.

Dr. Hora: It could be. But you see, anger is just a symptom. It is not the dynamic of depression. What is the dynamism of depression in general? It would be good to know that because of the importance of differential diagnostic considerations.

Coming back to the opening question of the presenter about

the patient's mode of being-in-the-world, it is good to know the difference between official diagnostic categories and the existential determinations of modes of being-in-the-world. Official diagnostic categories are like a Procrustian bed; they endeavor to fit the patient into a diagnostic category, or with certain labels. But when we consider modes of being-in-the-world, we are trying to find the concept appropriate to the patient's condition. Instead of fitting the patient to a preconceived label, we are trying to find the right concept which would be most descriptive of the problem, and thereby give our therapeutic approach a right focus.

This case reminds us of something Heidegger said about mourning. He said: "Mourning is remaining with the dead." What did Jesus say about mourning? He said: "Follow me; and let the dead bury the dead" (Matthew 8:22), which is very appropriate to this situation. But he also said: "Blessed are they that mourn: for they shall be comforted" (Matthew 5:4). This woman is suffering now for about nine years, she has not let the dead bury the dead, and she has not been comforted.

Coming back to the dynamism of depression, we may ask: What is involved in depression? There are two things: First, there must be an attachment to some thing, some place, some one, or some idea. And then there is a loss of that which we are attached to. What is an attachment in psychological terms? We know that we have a tendency to form attachments to persons, places, things, and ideas. An attachment is an overvaluation of some thing, some one, some place, or some idea, as essential to life and happiness. Once I saw a cartoon in *The New Yorker* which depicted a middle-aged couple walking at the seashore. The wife was licking an ice cream cone and the husband appeared to be deeply depressed. The caption said, "But Sam, just because they are out of tutti-frutti, don't let that spoil our anniversary!" Sometimes our attachments can be very trivial. Be that as it may, whenever there is a depression, whether small or deep, short or long, this is an indication that there was some attachment and there is a sense of loss, fancied or real. So the problem is not the tragedy itself or the loss itself, be it ever so great; the real problem is always the attachment.

When a drug addict suffers withdrawal pains, it is not as much a chemical problem as a problem of the attachment which the addict has developed psychologically to the drug. Depressions then are in fact withdrawal reactions.

Question: How can one be attached to ideas?

Dr. Hora: Some people may, for instance, get depressed by attending these seminars because, if they listen, they may lose certain ideas they were attached to. So it is not this seminar that is to blame, but their preexistent mental attachments. What is the value of understanding this? Does it have relevancy to our therapeutic approach? We can see that it is not possible to therapeutize a depression. We cannot cheer up someone by saying to him, "Snap out of it. Don't be depressed." And we cannot explain to this poor woman: "Look here, it is already so long since this tragedy occurred, why don't you just forget about it and cheer up."

It is very hard to help someone who says: "I am disgusted with life, with people, with the judicial system in this country, with the police, with my husband. I don't want to see anyone. I don't want to talk to anyone. I just want to be miserable. I am inconsolable." It is usually a therapeutic conundrum. As a result, doctors have often despaired over helping despairing patients. At times, a depressed patient will generate such frustration in the therapist, that he himself may become depressed.

There is one thing a patient in depression wants to do. He has lost something that was precious to him, and he has a desire to inflict such a loss on others. If, for instance, a therapist happens to have an attachment to his therapeutic skill, then he is in for some painful experiences because the depressed patient may want to rob him of his cherished idea about himself, and may prove to him that he doesn't have this therapeutic skill. Often we hear colleagues complain how difficult it is to work with depressed patients. But it is really not difficult if, instead of working with depressed patients, we work with problems of attachment. The tendency to form attachments is universal in man. It is a mystery in itself, and helping patients to be healed of this tendency is a very interesting therapeutic task. What is the meaning of the tendency to form attachments?

Comment: It probably means a desire to maintain contact with reality.

Dr. Hora: Very good. We all want to hold on to something meaningful which would give us the impression of having a firm footing in reality. But this is all too evanescent.

Comment: There is a story about Salvador Dali, the famous painter, who, when offered a cigarette by someone, said, "Thanks, but I prefer my moustache."

Dr. Hora: So the problem to be attacked is not the sadness, not the resentment, not the despair, not the sense of culpability, not the slowing down of physiological processes, not the apathy—all these things are but symptoms. The root of the problem is the human tendency toward forming attachments. Clearly Jesus had the remedy for depression: "Blessed are they that mourn: for they shall be comforted." What is so great about mourning?

Comment: Mourning is an opportunity to let go of attachments.

Dr. Hora: Yes. It is an opportunity to be liberated from the tendency to form attachments. As long as there is this tendency in man, there is insecurity, and there is no possibility of freedom and true happiness. If we have to hold on to something, we are not free. So, indeed, mourning is an opportunity for liberation. How does one attain freedom from the human frailty of forming attachments? In mourning there is a discovery of the misery of attachments. As long as a drug addict has an uninterrupted supply of drugs, he is only aware of the pleasures this provides him. But when the supply of drugs dries up, he becomes aware of the misery of the craving for this drug. As long as we feel good, we are not interested in being healed, we are not even interested in freedom.

Jesus said: "Ye shall know the truth, and the truth shall make you free" (John 8:32). This truth can heal depressions, liberate drug addicts and alcoholics from their enslavement, help people lose interest in smoking, and bring the joy of freedom into life. The essential point here is that *only attachment can bring freedom from attachment.* Does that surprise you? The fact is that man cannot really live without attachments, and deep down he knows that. There is no such thing as independent man; the trouble is that we are reaching out for the wrong kind of attachment. So we can only be healed by attaching ourselves to that which is existentially valid. The art of psychotherapy hinges on that creative intelligence which always provides us

with the right concept with which to reach the patient in a meaningful way. And this cannot be directly thought; it comes when there
is a sincere desire to be a beneficial presence rather than just a
psychotherapist. It is love itself which makes it possible. So we must
help the patient to shift his attachment from that which is existentially invalid to that which is valid. And what is that? Jesus put it
this way: I and my Father are so closely attached that we are practically one. "The Son can do nothing of himself, but what he seeth the
Father do: for what things soever he doeth, these also doeth the Son
likewise" (John 5:19). In other words, we are attached to God like
the mirror image to the object standing in front of the mirror. We
are inseparably attached to God. But we have to reach a point of
conscious awareness of this fact, and then we will find our complete
freedom. In this absolute attachment there is real freedom. It sounds
paradoxical, but it is true; and it is available for everyone to discover
it for himself.

Now there are all sorts of drugs being used in the treatment of
depression. Will a drug ever be able to accomplish this shift in
attachments? It is a very difficult situation because the moment a
drug helps a patient feel better, he is not interested any more in what
one is saying. On the other hand, he may be so sick that he may not
even be able to hear what the doctor is saying. So what does one do
then? One prays. The better we know how to pray, the more effective
we will be in awakening a patient sufficiently to be accessible to
rational communication.

It is interesting that in the presence of certain people we are more
alive than in the presence of other people. Have you noticed that?
There must be some quality in us which inspires the patient with a
little life, a little vitality, at least to a sufficient degree to help him
to listen and to hear a few words. What does that quality consist of?
How do we acquire that quality, that therapeutic presence? It is
through compassion. When the therapist is imbued with true compassion—which is not sympathy but love based on understanding—
then there is an awakening of receptivity in patients. This quality is
most desirable.

Session No. 36

THE DIVINE MARRIAGE

Question: Could you please talk to us about the existentially valid concept of marriage?

Dr. Hora: We have formulated the existentially valid concept of marriage as a joint participation in the good of God. Do you think this is a workable idea?

Comment: It seems most unusual in our present-day thinking.

Dr. Hora: Of course, statistically speaking, such a concept of marriage is most unusual. But we are less concerned with statistics than with what is valid and what is workable. It is conceivable that this concept could heal the great "affliction" called present-day marriage. It is well known that the institution of marriage is nowadays in a severe crisis and very much under attack. Our psychological notions have contributed greatly to the breakdown of marriage. These introduced complexities and difficulties into marital life. The more sophisticated we are psychologically, the more impossible it is to be and to stay married.

It is difficult to coexist with our fellow man if our worldview is determined by invalid questions (page 197). We are constantly analyzing each other, we are constantly finding fault with each other, we are constantly asking: Why? And we are constantly trying to do something about other people, to improve them to suit our needs, and this leads to complications and a high divorce rate.

What would happen if we could realize joint participation in the good of God? Can you conceive of a marriage based on that principle? In connection with this issue, Jesus said: "But they which shall be accounted worthy to obtain that world, and the resurrection from the dead, neither marry, nor are given in marriage" (Luke 20:35). We could paraphrase this saying by putting it this way: Enlightened people neither marry nor not marry. What could that mean?

Comment: It would mean that they are not involved with each other as persons but they jointly participate in something that transcends them.

Dr. Hora: Right. Is that clear to everyone, or are there any questions? When enlightened people are married, they live together side by side as expressions of Love-Intelligence, and their mode of being-in-the-world is not determined primarily by their relationship to one another but primarily by their relationship to God. Again, we could illustrate this whole issue with our hands. Traditional marriage could be illustrated with the fingers of both hands intertwined. Nonmarriage, or divorce, could be illustrated by the palms of both hands turned away from each other. Enlightened marriage could be illustrated by the palms of both hands approaching each other and touching in what is customarily considered a prayerful gesture. What is required for a harmonious marriage? It is not something that we can decide to accomplish. What is required here is to know something. What must we know that this kind of marriage could come about? Such a marriage can come about through right understanding of what God is and what man is. This is being in the kingdom of God. Here we neither marry nor not marry. We coexist harmoniously. We do not impose our personal wills on one another. We do not form attachments or detachments, nor do we manipulate or influence anyone.

Question: What is the good of God?

Dr. Hora: God is spirit, as you know; therefore, whatever good is from God can only be spiritual. What is spiritual good? Love, joy, truth, harmony, right usefulness, beauty, health, peace, freedom, integrity, gratitude. These constitute the good of God. Right now we are aware of lovely harmony, inspiration, intelligence, assurance. These are all intangible, invisible, nonmaterial aspects of life, seemingly very illusive; and yet without these, life would really be intolerable. Without the good of God—without these subtle evanescent realizations—life would mean nothing, it would be a constant tribulation.

And that reminds us of the word "tribulation" in the statement
Jesus made when he said: "In this world ye shall have tribulation:
but be of good cheer; I have overcome the world" (John 16:33). Now
if he has overcome the world, what does that mean to us? It means
that we can overcome the world, too. All we need is to understand
what it means to be Christlike. What do you think it does mean to
be Christlike? Does it mean to wear a beard? No, the beard will not
do the trick. Understanding and appreciating spiritual good, living
in constant, conscious awareness of the good of God and seeking it
above all else, will make it possible for us to overcome the world and
be delivered from tribulations. You see, tribulations are inevitable
but not necessary. In other words, if we don't understand divine
reality, tribulations are inevitable; it is a common experience. It is
like marital strife; if we have a marital relationship, then marital
discords are inevitable, and it is an accepted fact. People cope with
this and learn from marriage counselors how to handle it. That's
what is called normal. Marital discord is an accepted form of tribulation and considered inevitable; but it is not necessary because, if we
come to understand marriage in the context of divine reality, then
there will be no marital discord ever. And we don't have to do
anything to avoid it, we only have to know something and that will
overcome everything that is considered normal.

Question: What if one of the partners doesn't like harmony?

Dr. Hora: That is an interesting question. There are people who
believe that happiness can be found in excitement, in winning or
losing, in strife, in having power over another, in being overpowered
by another, even in hurting another or being hurt by another. This
is so widespread that statistically it could be considered rather normal. How do we understand that?

Comment: All that is ego-confirmatory.

Dr. Hora: Right. There is a prevailing erroneous belief that the
good of life can be found in self-confirmatory experiences, or in
ego-boosting or ego-degrading experiences. And if we have this erroneous belief of what constitutes the good life, then marriage becomes
a means to that end, and we will use the so-called marital relationship
either to gratify our tendencies of boasting and ego-inflation or,
obversely, in ego-deflation and seeking to be abused. Now clearly,
there are pathological variations on what is called marital relation-

ship, and they are all based on the assumption that happiness consists of excitement and ego-gratification. This, of course, is an erroneous idea. What gives us the right to make such a statement in face of the fact that so many people choose to live that way? Who are we to say that this is an erroneous assumption about what is good?

Comment: It proves itself to be invalid because of the suffering which results from it.

Dr. Hora: Yes, it is pathogenic, it is illness-producing. Happiness which is illness-producing cannot possibly be the right idea. After all, we are not created and put into this world to produce illness in one another, or in ourselves. Just because something may feel good it does not necessarily mean it is good. One of the most nefarious things which can happen to us is admiration. If we are being admired, we feel very good. One could say: "So I feel good. What's wrong with that?" It is dangerous to enjoy admiration. What is the danger?

Comment: Ego-gratification.

Comment: You want more and more and more.

Dr. Hora: It enhances our pride. However: "Pride goeth before destruction, and an haughty spirit before a fall" (Proverbs 16:18). There is a scene described in the Bible where a man came over to Jesus and expressed a great deal of admiration for him. He began: "Good Master. . . ." But Jesus told the man not to call him that. He was protecting himself against the temptation to accept compliments. He knew that what feels good is not necessarily good. As a matter of fact, it can be very bad. For it is ego-gratification and self-confirmatory ideation which is really the universal meaning of all pathology. Let us repeat this: Self-confirmatory ideation is the universal meaning of all pathology, be it mental, emotional, physical, economic, marital, political; individual, or collective. What is self-confirmatory ideation?

Comment: Could it be a consistent desire to make oneself into a primary and ultimate reality?

Dr. Hora: Right. Essentially, what was just said is that self-confirmatory ideation is a constant silent assertion going on in consciousness and consisting of two little words: "I am." We are constantly saying to ourselves, "I am." For instance, when we think of how we feel, what people think of us, what is happening to us, what we are saying, there is one pervasive theme in the back of our minds which says, "I am." This basic thought is the universal troublemaker to be found everywhere. Now what is so troublesome about such a seemingly innocent statement? As it was pointed out, we are endeavoring to make ourselves the primary reality. What's wrong with that? There is nothing wrong with it except that it is a lie, it is not valid. If it were valid, it would be all right, but it is a lie. How can we know that? Because, as we said previously, it is pathogenic, it causes problems. Then we can ask: What then is valid? If we cannot say, "I am," and it is not even advisable to think it, then what is the existentially valid statement? The only true and existentially valid statement that has ever been made and is of enormous portent for the whole world, was made on Mount Sinai when Moses suddenly understood that God is the only "I AM." God was telling Moses: "I am the only 'I am.' In the whole universe there is no other 'I am.' " This throws an entirely different perspective on our lives. Man is not entitled to and cannot possibly say, "I am," but he constantly does it and suffers the consequences.

When man understands that God is the "I am" of everyone, then he can suddenly see that there is no existence apart from God. And he comes to know that great secret which makes it possible for him to overcome the world and escape its tribulations. He sees reality in a broader context. The broadest possible context is the context of God.

Session No. 37

THE SERPENT

Question: Dr. Hora, would you please elaborate on the statement that man is an idea of divine mind. What is the divine mind?

Dr. Hora: The Bible says "Let this mind be in you, which was also in Christ Jesus" (Philippians 2:5). Are you familiar with this passage?

Comment: Yes.

Dr. Hora: What kind of mind is being referred to here? What kind of mind was in Christ Jesus?

Comment: I don't really know.

Dr. Hora: "The word which ye hear is not mine, but the Father's which sent me" (John 14:24). "As I hear, I judge: and my judgment is just: because I seek not mine own will, but the will of the Father which hath sent me" (John 5:30).

The implication of all these is that God is a cosmic intelligence, a mind. God and the mind of the universe are synonymous. Mind is the source of all intelligent ideas; and all creative power, all creativity is the faculty of this cosmic mind. And since we are creations of God, it is this mind that has conceived us.

The word "conception" is also very interesting, on the human level it has a double meaning. When a woman conceives, we understand that she has become pregnant; but when God conceives, we mean to say that a creative idea was born. When an artist conceives a creative work, we don't say he has become pregnant—even if it is a lady artist —we say he has been inspired by a creative idea that has become a concept in his consciousness, which then has its own dynamism requiring expression.

It is interesting to consider what power divine creative ideas have. Some artists were known to sacrifice everything, like Gauguin for instance, who was so powerfully driven to express his artistic ideas and concepts that he forsook everything and went to Tahiti. Having given up everything, he became an instrument of his artistic drive, and finally his life ended in tragedy. Truly creative ideas have a powerful dynamism requiring expression.

So God is that mind which is the source of all powerful, creative, intelligent ideas. Enlightened man is constantly mindful, receptive, and aware of inspired wisdom flowing into his consciousness from this infinite source of Love-Intelligence. The Zen Buddhists say: "An enlightened man has great wisdom, but he looks like an idiot." What do they mean by that? He doesn't appear to be cogitating. Simplicity, unpretentiousness, and absence of cogitation—which we call calculative thinking—characterize him. As we learned earlier, according to the philosopher Heidegger, there are two modes of thinking: One is called calculative thinking *(das vorstellende Denken);* the second is called inspired thinking *(das andenkende Denken).* Unenlightened man engages in much calculative thinking. What do you think is calculative thinking?

Comment: Cause-and-effect thinking.

Dr. Hora: Cause-and-effect thinking and all the other things connected with the invalid questions, such as scheming, political intrigue, thinking about what others are thinking about what we are thinking. This kind of thinking is serpentine and is very troublesome. It is troublesome to others, and it is troublesome to ourselves if we allow ourselves the luxury of engaging in this error. In our profession, calculative thinking is particularly pernicious; it is called "using psychology" on people, and it is serpentine.

Now the serpent plays a very great role in the Bible. Over and over we come across the symbolism of the serpent. The serpent is a symbol of evil, first with Adam and Eve and later with Moses. When Moses discovered God and engaged in a dialogue with God, the first thing God taught him was how to handle the serpent. God said to Moses: "What is that in thine hand?" Moses answered: "A rod." So God said to him: "Cast it on the ground" (Exodus 4:2, 3). So Moses obeyed and cast it on the ground and, lo and behold, it became a serpent. Moses got scared and wanted to run away. But God said:

"Hold it, come back! Pick it up!" So with great trepidation Moses reached for the serpent and, lo and behold, it became a rod. And suddenly Moses was secure and reassured, he now had a handle on the serpent. Some people may say: "Well, Moses was an Egyptian, and in Egypt it was customary to perform all sorts of magic tricks. God was teaching him a few tricks with which to impress Pharaoh." If you read the Bible from a historical vantage point, you might be inclined to say this describes how Moses was learning tricks to impress Pharaoh. And interestingly enough, the magicians of Egypt were known to perform such feats of magic through hypnotism and sleight of hand. But if we look at this incident in the context of the entire Bible from beginning to end, we discover the fantastic importance of learning the art of dealing with the serpent. The serpent stands for all the evil of calculative thinking and particularly the self-confirmatory aspect of calculative thinking.

You remember, some time ago we said that the meaning of all pathology and all human problems everywhere in the world is the tendency toward self-confirmatory, calculative ideation. We could say then that, in preparing himself for his leadership role, Moses realized that the first thing he had to learn was to deal effectively with calculative, self-confirmatory ideation in himself and others. And, indeed, this lesson enabled him to become a great leader and teacher and liberator of his people.

We encounter another incident with the serpent when the children of Israel were wandering in the desert. Suddenly there arose an epidemic of snake bites by so-called "fiery serpents" which stung the people. Many were dying and panic was spreading among them (Numbers 21:6). They came to Moses to ask him for advice. And Moses turned to God, which means, he went into meditation to receive a creative idea from the divine mind. In our terms, his meditation may have consisted of contemplating our two intelligent questions. He may have started with the question, "I wonder what the meaning is of what seems to be?" He may have then realized that the meaning of what seems to be was that the children of Israel engaged in a deadly form of backbiting as an aspect of vicious calculative thinking. Having understood the meaning of fiery serpents, he may have proceeded to the second question which deals with the issue of reality. Then he may have received the answer: If the problem is calculative thinking, then the answer is forthrightness and love based on the divinely inspired thought. He was then led to recommend to the children of Israel that they raise up an effigy of a serpent for all to see, to remember what the problem was, and to guard themselves against it. The result was healing.

This is a fascinating story, but we could still be skeptical about it if it stood alone. But as we read the Bible a little further, we come across more serpents. For instance, in Psalm 91:13 it says: "Thou shalt tread upon the lion and adder: the young lion and the dragon shalt thou trample under feet" (if you dwell in the secret place of the most High). What does that mean? If you learn inspired thinking, you will have the wisdom and the dominion over calculative poisonous, aggressive thinking. You will have the power to become immune against aggressive and poisonous thoughts within yourself and others.

But there is more reference to the serpent in the Bible. If we read on a little further, we find Jesus saying: "And these signs shall follow them that believe; In my name shall they cast out devils; they shall speak with new tongues; They shall take up serpents; and if they drink any deadly thing, it shall not hurt them" (Mark 16:7, 8). And further on he says: "Behold, I give you power to tread on serpents and scorpions, and over all the power of the enemy: and nothing shall by any means hurt you" (Luke 10:19). How could he say such a thing? We see that good Christians are being bitten by serpents and that they even die, but Jesus said: "I give you power to be immune to serpents and scorpions, and over all the power of the enemy, and nothing shall by any means hurt you." What did he mean? It must be that he was using serpents and scorpions as symbols. What do they symbolize? Who is the enemy?

Comment: Calculative thinking.

Dr. Hora: Yes, our only enemies are the serpent and the scorpion. The serpent is devious and poisonous, and the scorpion has a deadly sting; these are the enemy. Later in the Bible, the serpent is called the whisperer, the adversary, the accuser, the great whore, the red dragon—these are all symbolic representations of the one human problem, namely, calculative, self-confirmatory ideation. We all have to understand God as the mind of man. God, Love-Intelligence, is the only valid basis of thinking. Jesus was teaching the world how to think in an existentially valid way so that we might become completely free from calculative, self-confirmatory ideation with which we are hurting ourselves and our fellow man.

One of the very harmful ways of calculative thinking is the clinical eye. We had here a session where we spoke of the clinical eye. What is the clinical eye? That's when we are looking to see what is wrong with people, finding fault with them. We are trying to figure out, we are calculating what is wrong. When we gain complete dominion over the serpent of self-confirmatory ideation and calculative thinking, we are ready to be enlightened; we become open and receptive to a continuous flow of loving and intelligent ideas coming to us from infinite mind. Calculative thinking is the veil which separates us from God. It is the "cloud of unknowing" as a famous medieval book is entitled. When we are free of calculative thinking, it is impossible for us to be unloving because the serpent isn't there; only God is there. And God is Love-Intelligence.

As you see, this is an entirely different mode of being-in-the-world. It is totally guileless and innocent. Jesus also said something very interesting. He said: "Behold, I send you forth as sheep in the midst of wolves: be ye therefore wiser than serpents, and harmless as doves" (Matthew 10:16). Again we see the serpent. How can sheep survive among wolves if they are harmless as doves? Who are the wolves? It is the world of calculative thinking.

The enlightened man is not susceptible to the three ways of the serpent. The serpent has three modes of operation: seduction, provocation, and intimidation. Have you ever seen the devil's pitchfork? It has three prongs and at the end of each prong there is a little hook. It is interesting that some artist was inspired to portray the devil with a three-pronged pitchfork, with every prong having a little hook, like a fishhook, at the end. Now we could say that the three prongs stand for the three ways the devil approaches us, his three modes of operation. Once the devil gets his hook into us, it is very hard to extricate ourselves. It is, therefore, of great importance to understand the differences between calculative thinking and inspired thought. The universal enemy is nothing else than an erroneous mode of thinking.

Session No. 38

THE PEARL
OF GREAT PRICE

CASE PRESENTATION

Patient is a thirty-three-year-old divorced woman who has a daughter living with her father. At present she is unemployed, dresses in a "hippie" style—blue jeans and leather jackets—appears to be brash and loud, rather outspoken, clearly endeavoring to make an impression. Claims to be despondent and anxious, and complains of insomnia. She spent a year and a half in a drug rehabilitation center due to overindulgence in alcohol and benzedrine pills. She still drinks wine and smokes marijuana. She considers feeling "comfortable" the most important thing in life. She freely admits to sexual promiscuity. Complains of having no confidence in herself and of loneliness. She feels very uncomfortable with decent men. She identifies herself with so-called "street people," admires hustlers and considers them smarter than other people. She is worried about getting older and out of step with her favorite crowd.

Commentary on Case Presentation

Dr. Hora: What would be the official diagnostic category in this case?

Comment: Addictive personality.

Dr. Hora: There are two things which stand out in this case presentation: Here is a young woman who is struggling to be "comfortable" in life, and is aware of a certain lack of self-esteem. That's all she knows, discomfort—physical and psychological—and a lack of self-esteem. And she has found certain ways of alleviating her discomfort through pills, alcohol, relationships with others, and perhaps through sex and by subscribing to certain values which are symbolically expressed through wearing leather jackets and dungarees.

Question: Isn't her main problem rebelliousness?

Dr. Hora: We are used to thinking of rebelliousness in teen-agers who dress in such a manner, but this woman has nothing to rebel against. Nobody is forcing her to be ladylike, she has great freedom to choose her own life-style according to her best understanding of what is desirable. Not everyone who likes to wear a leather jacket is a rebel. What are we dealing with in this case?

Question: Could you please define rebelliousness?

Dr. Hora: Rebellion is acting against certain standards required by authorities.

Comment: I get the feeling of a lack of responsibility in her.

Dr. Hora: Is this a feeling, or is it a thought?

Comment: It is a thought.

Dr. Hora: Yes, it is important to be precise. We must not say that we feel something if we are just thinking it. I wonder what the meaning of this tendency is?

Comment: We are more responsible for our thoughts than for our feelings.

Dr. Hora: Right. It is really a cop-out when we say, "I feel" instead of "I think."

We have here a particular mode of being-in-the-world which is quite widespread nowadays, afflicting many quite innocently. It is also important to keep in mind that the patient is innocent. We cannot speculate why a patient is the way she is, who is to blame for it, and so on. We are all innocent until proven guilty, but in psychotherapy no one is proven guilty. Guilt is assigned to what? To ignorance. And in this particular case we have a special kind of ignorance which, at present, is stylish.

Comment: I have noticed that women in their thirties are reluctant to let go of their youth, and they continue to dress like teen-agers. They seem to want to push away their age.

Dr. Hora: This would be a sort of cause-and-effect reasoning. We are not asking the question "Why?" We only want to understand the meaning. Age has little to do with it. The concept of what constitutes the good life has a lot to do with it. And where do people find information about what constitutes the good life?

Comment: Magazines, television, movies—the sea of mental garbage.

Dr. Hora: Yes. This young woman has found a certain idea about what is good, and she pursues the "good life." Her idea of the "good life" is leather jackets, blue jeans, alcohol, pills, promiscuity, and irresponsibility. What we have here is a simple tragic case of miseducation. There are innumerable ways in which we can be miseducated, just as there are innumerable wrong answers to the question: How much is two and two? But there is only one right answer. Imagine, innumerable possibilities of invalid answers and only one right answer. Similarly, there are innumerable invalid modes of being-in-the-world, and there is only one valid way to be in the world. Who is to tell us what is the right way to be in the world? Who is to tell us what constitutes the good of life? Who is to tell us what values to espouse and to live by? Who can provide us with that kind of education? Where can we find it? Can Freud give us this education? Can Jung give it to us? Can Adler give it to us? Where can we find the pearl of great price?

How can a therapist presume to be helpful to a patient who suffers from miseducatedness unless he himself has received the right education? The saying goes: "Physician, heal thyself." If the therapist is miseducated concerning what constitutes the existentially valid mode of being-in-the-world, he will inevitably transmit his own invalid ideas to the patient. These ideas may be somewhat better than the patient's, but they may have their own pitfalls. Who among you knows the parable of the pearl of great price?

Comment: Jesus was asked about the kingdom of God and he said: "The kingdom of heaven is like unto a merchant man, seeking goodly pearls: Who, when he had found one pearl of great price, went and sold all that he had, and bought it" (Matthew 13:45, 46).

Dr. Hora: Does everyone understand this parable? It is really very simple. When we come to understand what is existentially valid, then everything that is invalid loses its value for us and we lose interest in it, regardless of whether it is fashionable, timely, or offered to us by highly regarded authorities. We can sometimes find this pearl of great price trampled in the mud, or in a sea filled with pollution; but no matter how much it may be spurned, it is the pearl of great price.

Now we often talk here in a certain way which may sound religious and evangelistic. Of course, some people may find it unattractive because this pearl of great price has been sullied for thousands of years by distortions, misrepresentations, and ignorance. Nevertheless, it is the pearl of great price and nothing will ever change that. We must not be afraid to pick it up, wash it clean, and take a good look at it, for it will heal us, it will save us, it will show us the right way, which is compatible with the perfect good. Once we know what this pearl stands for, we will not be easily misled by fashionable trends and fads all around us.

Now this young woman is an example of a misdirected mode of being-in-the-world. You see, all pathology could be summed up under this existential term: the misdirected mode of being-in-the-world, based on an invalid value system. It may be constantly changing but still it remains invalid. *Plus ça change, plus c'est la même chose* (the more things change, the more they remain the same). But the pearl of great price has never changed and never will. Two and two was always four and it always will be four. There will never be a time when it will be otherwise.

Suppose the therapist is one of those blessed fellows who have found the pearl of great price. How would he go about helping this patient? He would start from where the patient is. He would help the patient to see that whatever suffering and unhappiness she is experiencing in life has something to do with her idea of the good. And the more clearly the patient can see the connection between her problems and the invalidity of her concepts of the good, the more receptive she will become to the desirability of other ways of seeking happiness.

So first we have to help the patient to be as miserable as possible, or at least to become more and more conscious of her misery. It is amazing how much suffering people can endure without allowing themselves to realize it. As long as the patient does not have a clear perception of the connection of her various troubles with her particular mode of being-in-the-world, it is hard to help her. So the initial task is to help the patient see the connection between the suffering and the specific mode of being-in-the-world. Once it is clearly seen, there emerges a certain motivation to reexamine the value system, and perchance even a desire to find a better one. No one is interested in the pearl of great price on a purely ideological basis. We are first driven, and then we are drawn. A skillful therapist can discern areas of maximum pain within the patient and focus the attention on that. And he will try to utilize this maximum pain to show the patient that short-term solutions are not really helpful. It is very hard to help a patient who is comfortable, and this patient clearly said that when she takes a drink, or a pill, she is comfortable. Severe discomfort is a very good road to therapy.

Someone said: "We come to you crying and you receive us laughing." There are two ways to attain enlightenment. One is through suffering, the other is through wisdom. Most of us choose the first route.

So here is a patient. We don't ask her what's wrong; we don't ask her how she feels; we don't ask her why she feels the way she feels; we are not trying to find out whom to blame. Neither are we thinking about what we should do or how to do it. When we are sitting with this patient, we are only asking ourselves: What is the meaning of what seems to be? And then we ask: What is what really is? What really is is the perfect life, the perfect good of God which already is. It only needs to be discerned. We don't have to change anyone, or cure anyone, or do anything to anyone. All that is needed is to shed light on that which already *is*.

There is a great deal of talk in the literature about resistance. What is the patient resisting when there seems to be resistance?

Comment: The therapist is trying to do something to the patient.

Dr. Hora: Or *for* the patient. The patient is resisting the intentions of the therapist. Most of the time, resistance is iatrogenic, that is, physician-induced. There can be lack of motivation due to insufficient suffering, but resistance is not necessary. All therapeutic schools claim the absolute inevitability of resistance and transference. But we say that not only is it not inevitable but it is highly undesirable. How can this be accomplished?

Comment: What is called transference is the patient's reaction to the manipulative aspect of the therapist's intentions.

Dr. Hora: That's right. As long as we assume that the therapist is a manipulator and that influencing is inevitable, then transference is inevitable. But if the therapist is a shining light in whose proximity the truth is illuminated, then there is neither influencing nor manipulation; neither transference nor countertransference.

Session No. 39

AS THOU SEEST . . .

CASE PRESENTATION

The patient is a sixty-year-old, twice divorced businessman whose main complaint is sexual impotency. His current life situation comprises three unsatisfactory relationships: one with a business partner whom he considers incompetent, one with a very cooperative lady whom he considers boring, and a third with a highly intellectual lady who holds two doctor's degrees and is in psychoanalytic training, and whom he considers utterly frustrating. He also visits two psychiatrists simultaneously. His attitude toward the psychotherapist is a condescending, competitive, and challenging one.

Commentary on Case Presentation

Dr. Hora: What is the diagnosis? Would you like to know it? The perfect American male. What makes him perfect in terms of our culture? The horizontal perspective on life. What do we mean by that?

Comment: The main focus is on interpersonal relationships.

Dr. Hora: Right. How does this man see life? He sees life in terms of opponents; everyone is an opponent to him, either a challenging or an inconsequential one. If an opponent is a challenging one, he will keep working at him until he succeeds in turning him into an inconsequential one. What is an inconsequential opponent? One who is not a challenge. He now has affairs with two ladies; one is a

consequential lady, the other an inconsequential lady. Neither of
them are satisfying. So perhaps there is something wrong with the
horizontal perspective on life. Can a man be helped to find his
balance in interpersonal relationships? When we have a horizontal
perspective on life, we are always on a seesaw with people, and that
kind of life is not very satisfying. We keep discarding people who are
not a challenge, and we are disturbed by people who are a challenge;
so we are either bored or uptight. Such a patient would be inclined
to render the therapist inconsequential. As soon as he succeeded, he
would—momentarily—have the illusion that he is cured.

Let us now consider the alleged sexual problem. What are sexual
problems? Are they problems located in the genitals? Where are
sexual problems located?

Comment: In the head.

Dr. Hora: Sexual problems are not really sexual problems, they are
problems of modes of being-in-the-world; whatever our mode of
being-in-the-world is will be reflected in our sexual functioning. The
tail does not wag the dog, it is the dog that wags the tail, right? What
would be the therapeutic solution to a mode of being-in-the-world
that is so prevalent in our culture and considered quite normal?
From the standpoint of our culture, this is a normal, successful,
healthy man. He made it. He is financially successful. His business
is successful. He is a lady's man. He is twice divorced. He has two
lady friends, two psychiatrists, two apartments, and two daughters
from two previous marriages.

You see how the consideration of a man's mode of being-in-the-
world is much more revealing and helpful than the standard diagnostic categories. This case reveals that there is something existentially
invalid about the horizontal perspective on life. "As thou seest, so
thou beest." When we understand that the patient's problem lies in
the way he sees life, then, of course, the therapeutic task becomes
immediately clear. What would be the therapeutic task in this case?
It wouldn't help us to waste time on finding out why he sees life
horizontally, and who is to blame and what he should do. What we
need is to help this patient see that he does not see.

Comment: This is very amazing because I know that this man has
very poor eyesight, too. His car is full of dents from colliding with
other cars and objects.

Dr. Hora: Could it be that eyesight is like sex? What do we mean by that?

Comment: That it is in the head and not in the eyes.

Dr. Hora: It occasionally happens that some people discover that their eyesight has improved when their perspective on life has become more existentially valid. What is it that this man would have to come to see in order that his life might become more harmonious and wholesome and satisfying? The Bible says: "I will behold thy face in righteousness: I shall be satisfied, when I awake, with thy likeness" (Psalms 17:15). What does that mean? This man seems to have a visual distortion of reality and he needs to regain a right perspective. To behold means to see; he has to learn to see the face of God in every face he is looking at.

The primary requisite for communicating a new idea to a patient is that the therapist has already had a realization of that idea. Once the therapist has attained the realization of an idea in his own life, then he will be able to communicate it in a meaningful way. If he only knows *about* the idea, it will only be intellectual, theoretical, and will have no therapeutic consequence. A therapist needs to understand that there is more to life than interpersonal relationships and power balances. What else is there in life?

Comment: The spiritual dimension.

Dr. Hora: How do people live in the spiritual dimension? They coexist harmoniously, they do not impinge upon each other, they do not influence each other. They jointly participate in the good of God. They live harmoniously alongside each other, they potentiate the good through closeness but they do not wrestle. There is no wrestling in divine reality. There is no friction. It is a frictionless universe.

How do we acquire a horizontal perspective on life? Through "normal" miseducation. We all grow up more or less miseducated. Let us take for example our popular game of football. What does football teach us about life?

Comment: To be competitive, hostile, aggressive, the importance of winning over others and trampling on others.

Dr. Hora: And conquering one another. There is a Latin saying: *Homo homini lupus,* which loosely translated means, "dog eat dog." We all need to outgrow our faulty education and conditioning.

Enlightened man sees life in the context of omniaction rather than interaction. Omniaction reveals the presence of omniactive divine intelligence in the universe and in the affairs of man. The ability to discern this presence, and be aware of this power gives us a great sense of peace, assurance, gratitude, love, and dominion.

INFLUENCING

CASE PRESENTATION

I am working with three patients who entered treatment within a short time span, and I have recently discovered that they are from the same family, two daughters and their mother. They have sought treatment seemingly on their own, yet they were influenced by one another. In addition, several of their friends have come to the clinic for treatment at the same time. There is an additional interesting quality about their participation in the treatment process, namely, they pretend not to have been affected at all by their previous sessions, so that they seem to start every session as if it were their first session. What could be the meaning of this?

Commentary on Case Presentation

Comment: It might be a form of resistance.

Dr. Hora: Resistance to what? It would seem to indicate a resistance to being influenced. When we have been influenced all our lives, we can either become extremely suggestible, or very inaccessible. Now there are three ways in which we can be influenced: overtly, covertly, and subliminally. Clearly, these patients are manifesting the consequences of lifelong exposure to being influenced. We also see that they all engage in a great deal of influencing. How do we know that? By their referrals of their friends. So there seems to be much influencing going on in their lives. What kind of influencing were these patients subjected to, overt, covert, or subliminal?

Comment: All of them.

Dr. Hora: Right. Influencing is evidently one of the main characteristics of this family. Is this rare? No, not at all. Previously we were talking about the difference between influencing and being influential. We said that influencing is a sin of trespass. And what we can see in this presentation is that influencing is not only a trespass but it is pathogenic (illness-producing) as well. Parents who try to influence their children are producing illness in them.

What happens when we are being influenced? First of all, our thought processes are being disrupted, interfered with, and subjected to tyranny. We are not given a chance to understand anything. We are not given a chance to discover anything. We are not given a chance to evaluate anything. We are being mentally invaded. It can be done in crude fashion or in subtle ways, with the best of intentions. "Mother knows best." So we see that influencing and being influenced is a great tragedy. It pervades our culture in the form of advertising, persuasion, pressuring, insisting. We are constantly being bombarded with disruptive messages. There is not enough reverence for individual freedom of thought and that is very harmful. Interestingly enough, in certain primitive families where people are not sophisticated enough to consciously seek to mold one another, children have a better chance of growing up without being damaged. Intellectual neglect seems to be preferable to insistent solicitude. It is important for parents to know the difference between influencing and being influential. That way the children will perceive the values their parents live by rather than profess, and they would emulate them voluntarily. There is a popular saying, "Don't do as I do, do as I say."

Question: Would you please further clarify for us the three modes of influencing?

Dr. Hora: What overt influencing means, must be clear to everyone. It consists of saying: "You should do what I say." "You should think what I say." "You should believe what I say because I say it." The covert ways of influencing are disguised forms of communication. For instance, talking to a child about another child and thus hoping to influence him indirectly. Subliminal influences are exerted in such a way as to bypass the conscious awareness of an individual.

For instance, in advertising we may see a beautiful woman in a beautiful setting, with a man at her side, smoking a certain brand of cigarette or drinking a certain brand of whiskey. The subliminal implication is that anyone who will consume these products, will automatically become dignified and attractive. The more subliminal these suggestions are, the more devastating they are.

There is a saying: "A little knowledge is a dangerous thing." Many tend to be half educated; they pick up all sorts of information from the radio, television, newspapers, and books, and tend to function on an intellectual level. These are the families of "little knowledge," and havoc is created by a process of intellectual influencing of one another, imparting false values, and creating conflict. There comes a point when people become saturated with influences, and then there arise certain defence mechanisms against being influenced. That may appear, at times, as schizophrenic affectlessness, indicating the thought of being impervious to influences. Whatever comes into one ear goes out through the other. "No matter what anyone says to me, it will have no effect on me." "What you tell me today, I wouldn't remember an hour later." That is one way of trying to survive the process of being influenced.

A common supposition in the public is that a psychotherapist is someone who is an expert in influencing people by "using psychology" on them. If someone has been the victim of lifelong influencing, then, if he comes to a psychotherapist, he may consciously think that he is seeking help, but actually he is protecting himself against being influenced. And that may appear as a form of resistance. It is not really resistance, it is just protection.

I remember a patient who said: "You doctors always put something into my head and then proceed to take it out." Someone else said: "When a patient agrees with his doctor, he is cured." And indeed, at times we see in mental hospitals that patients who are eager to be released from the hospital, carefully study their doctors and learn what the doctors want to hear, they find out how they are expected to behave, and they feed it back to the doctors. The doctors feel flattered and the patients are pronounced cured and are released from the hospitals. It is no different from the situation in jails, where the inmates have to satisfy the parole board by giving right answers to their questions. Knowing how to pretend to agree with the doctors is not synonymous with being healthy. There is a saying: In politics the main thing is to be honest; if you know how to fake that, you are a success.

Of course, the healthy way to live is by being influential. The Bible refers to it as follows: "Let your light so shine before men, that they may see your good works, and glorify your Father which is in heaven" (Matthew 5:16).

READING LIST

Berends, P. B. *Whole Child-Whole Parent*. New York: Harper's Magazine Press, 1975.

Bradley, F. H. *Appearance and Reality*. London: Oxford University Press, 1955.

Capra, F. *The Tao of Physics*. Berkeley, Ca.: Shambhala, 1975.

Chun-Yuan Chang. *Self-Realization and the Inner Process of Peace* (Eranos Jahrbuch XXVII). Zurich: Rein-Verlag, 1959.

Ehrenwald, J. *New Dimensions of Psychoanalysis*. New York: Gruene & Stratton, 1952.

Fromm, E. *The Art of Loving*. New York: Harper, 1956.

Graham, A. D. *The End of Religion*. New York: Harcourt Brace Jovanovich, 1971.

Haas, W. S. *The Destiny of the Mind, East and West*. New York: Macmillan, 1956.

Heidegger, M. *Gelassenheit*. Pfuellinge: Guenther Neske, 1959.

———. *The Question of Being*. New York: Twaine, 1956.

———. *Sein und Zeit*. Tübingen: Max Niemeyer Verlag, 1953.

———. *Was Heisst Denken*. Tübingen: Max Niemeyer Verlag, 1954.

Hora, T. "The Dynamism of Assumptions." *Topical Problems of Psychotherapy*, vol. 4. Basel, Switzerland: Karger, 1963.

———. "The Epistemology of Love." *Journal of Existential Psychiatry* (Winter, 1962), vol. II, no. 7.

———. "Religious Values in Illness and Health." *Journal of Religion and Health* (April, 1963), Vol. II, no. 3.

James, W. *The Varieties of Religious Experience*. New York: Macmillan, 1961.

Jung, C. G. *Modern Man in Search of a Soul.* New York: Harcourt, 1933.

_____. *The Undiscovered Self.* New York: New American Library, 1974.

Kelley, T. *A Testament of Devotion.* New York: Harper and Row, 1941.

Legge, J. *The Texts of Taoism.* New York: Julian Press, 1959.

Merton, T. *Mystics and Zen Masters.* New York: Farrar, Straus & Giroux, 1966.

Suzuki, D. T. *The Essence of Buddhism.* London: Buddhist Society, 1955.

_____. *Manual of Zen Buddhism.* Kyoto, Buddhist Society, 1935.

Tillich, P. *Dynamics of Faith.* New York: Harper and Row, 1957.

Tyrrell, B. J. *Christotherapy.* New York: The Seabury Press, 1975.